Ten Steps to Complex Learning

A systematic approach to four-component instructional design

Jeroen J. G. van Merriënboer

Paul A. Kirschner

LAWRENCE ERLBAUM ASSOCIATES, PUBLISHERS

2007 Mahwah, New Jersey　　　　　　　　　　　London

Editorial Director: Lane Akers
Editorial Assistant: Anthony Messina
Cover Design: Kathryn Houghtaling-Lacey

Lawrence Erlbaum Associates, Inc., Publishers
10 Industrial Avenue
Mahwah, New Jersey 07430
www.erlbaum.com

**CIP information for this volume may be obtained by contacting
the Library of Congress**

ISBN 978–0–8058–5792–4   —   0–8058–5792–3 (case)
ISBN 978–0–8058–5793–1   —   0–8058–5793–1 (paper)
ISBN 978–1–4106–1805–4   —   1–4106–1805–6 (e book)

Books publsihsed by Lawrence Erlbaum Associates are printed
on acid-free paper, and their bindings are chosen for strength
and durability.

Printed in the United States of America

10   9   8   7   6   5   4   3   2   1

To our families

Contents

CONTENTS

PART III APPLICATIONS

PREFACE

In 1997, the first author published his award-winning book *Training Complex Cognitive Skills*. That book presented a comprehensive description of a training design system for the acquisition of complex skills or professional competencies, based on research conducted on the learning and teaching of knowledge needed for complex jobs and tasks. The basic claim was that educational programs for complex learning need to be built from four interrelated components: learning tasks, supportive information, procedural information, and part-task practice. Each component was related to a fundamental category of learning processes and prescribed instructional methods for each component were based on a broad body of empirical research. Whereas the book was very well received in the academic field of learning and instruction, practitioners in the field of instructional design frequently complained that they found it difficult to systematically design educational programs based on the four components. There was a clear need for more guidance on the design process, which this new book aims to provide. *Ten Steps to Complex Learning* is the follow-up, and complement, to the four-component design system described in *Training Complex Cognitive Skills*. It presents in ten steps a path from a training problem to a training solution in a way that students, practitioners (both instructional designers and teachers) and researchers can understand and use.

The structure of this book is straightforward. Chapters 1, 2, and 3 provide an introduction to the Ten Steps to Complex Learning. Chapter 1 presents a holistic approach to the design of instruction for achieving the complex learning required by modern society. Chapter 2 relates complex learning to the four blueprint components of the Four-Component Instructional Design theory. Finally, Chapter 3 describes the use of the Ten Steps to develop detailed training blueprints.

Each of the Ten Steps is discussed in detail in Chapters 4–13. Whereas *Ten Steps to Complex Learning* does not provide specific guidelines for the actual production, implementation, and evaluation of training materials, they do have important implications for each of these activities.

The main implications for the production of multimedia applications and for the development of self-directed learning are discussed in the discussion Chapters 14 and 15, and implementation issues and future developments are dealt with in Chapter 16.

Practitioners in the field of instructional design may use this book as a reference guide to support their design of courses, materials, and/or environments for complex learning. In order to make optimal use of the book, it may be helpful to consider the following points:

- It is probably best for all readers, regardless of their reason for using this book, to study Chapters 1, 2, and 3 first. They introduce the four blueprint components and the Ten Steps.

- Chapters 4 to 13 describe the Ten Steps. You should always start your design project with Step 1, but you only need to consult the other chapters if these steps are required for your specific project. Each chapter starts with general guidelines that may help you to decide if the step is relevant for your project or not.

- Chapters 14–16 are discussion chapters that mark the transition from the design of an educational blueprint to the development of instructional materials. You should only consult these chapters if you will be involved in the production, implementation, and evaluation of training materials.

If you are a student in the field of instructional design and want to broaden your knowledge of the design of training programs for complex learning, you are advised to study all chapters in the order in which they appear. For all readers, whether practitioners or students, we tried to make the book as useful as possible by including the following:

- Two *Appendices* with example materials are included at the end of this book.

- Key concepts are highlighted in the text with an asterisk (*) before and after the first appearance of the concept. This means that the concept can also be found in the *Glossary*. This glossary contains either pure definitions of terms that might not be familiar and in certain cases may be more extensive (in the case of seminal or foundational concepts, theories or models) and contain background information. In this way, the glossary can help you organize the main ideas discussed in this book.

- In a number of chapters, you will find *Text Boxes* in which the psychological foundations for particular design decisions are briefly explained.

- Each chapter ends with a brief *Summary* of its main points and design guidelines.

ACKNOWLEDGMENTS

The foundation for this book was laid when the first author spent his sabbatical leave at the School of Education of the University of New South Wales in Sydney, Australia. We are grateful to John Sweller, who made all necessary arrangements for this stay, and to Paul Ayres, Paul Chandler, and Slava Kalyuga for their great companionship. Our debt to colleagues and graduate students who in some way contributed to the development of the Ten Steps described in this book is enormous. Without them, this book would not exist. In particular, we thank our PhD students Liesbeth Baartman, Pieter Jelle Beers, Gerard van den Boom, Eddy Boot, Jan van Bruggen, Gemma Corbalan, Pascal van Gerven, Tamara van Gog, Judith Gulikers, Liesbeth Kester, Wendy Kicken, Karen Könings, Karel Kreijns, Rob Nadolski, Ron Salden, Ad Schellekens, Dominique Sluijsmans, Angela Stoof, Huib Tabbers, Sandra Wetzels, and Pieter Wouters for conducting research and writing dissertations that contributed to the development of the Ten Steps. We thank Harmen Abma and Jelke van der Pal of the National Aerospace Laboratory in the Netherlands; Henrik Schlanbusch, Mike Spector, and Barbara Wasson of the University of Bergen in Norway; Clas Folin, Per-Inge Hoffman, and Anders Nyberg of the Swedish Air Traffic Control Academy; Adrian Enright of Eurocontrol in Luxembourg, and Luca Gelati, Alessandro Gigli Cervi, and Luca de Rosa of Piaggio Aero in Italy for their cooperation in the EC-funded ADAPT[IT] project, in which many ideas for the Ten Steps were developed and tested. We thank Carlo Lantsheer and Fernand Klein of the European Patent Office in Munich and The Hague, for testing ideas and using many example materials from their organization. We thank Øyvind Meistad of Enovate AS in Norway for putting the Ten Steps to a test by developing the Blueprint Designer software. We thank Ameike Janssen-Noordman for contributing to the Ten Steps when writing the Dutch booklet *Innovatief Onderwijs Ontwerpen* [Innovative Educational Design]. We thank Theo Bastiaens, Marcel de Croock, Jan Daniels, Bert Hoogveld, Liesbeth Kester and Kathleen Schlusmans for carefully reading a draft of this book and giving many suggestions for improving it. We thank our research groups at the Open University of the Netherlands and Utrecht University for an ongoing academic debate and giving us many inspiring ideas. We thank Bart and Jelle van Merriënboer for preparing several illustrations. A special word of thanks must be given to Frank Slangen and Femke Kirschner who got a little crazy doing the layout for this book, but who nevertheless persevered. And last, but not least, we thank all the learners who in some way participated in the research and development projects that offered the basis for writing this book.

Jeroen van Merriënboer and Paul Kirschner

February, 2007

ABOUT THE AUTHORS

Jeroen J. G. van Merriënboer (1959) is professor of Educational Technology and Research Program Director of the Educational Technology Expertise Center at the Open University of the Netherlands. He is also Educational Director of the Interuniversity Center for Educational Research, an alliance of 10 Dutch universities offering Ph.D. programs in educational science. He holds a Master's degree in experimental psychology from the Free University of Amsterdam and a Ph.D. degree in instructional technology from the University of Twente. Van Merriënboer specializes in cognitive architecture and instruction, instructional design for complex learning, holistic approaches to instructional design, and adaptive e-learning applications. He has published over 100 scientific articles in the area of learning and instruction and serves on the board of highly ranked scientific journals, such as Educational Research Review; Educational Technology, Research and Development; Computers in Human Behavior; Technology, Instruction, Cognition and Learning; Journal of Educational Computing Research, and Educational Technology. His prize-winning monograph Training Complex Cognitive Skills (1997) describes his four-component instructional design model for complex skills training and offers a systematic, research-based approach to designing environments for complex learning. He was declared world leader in educational technology by Training Magazine and received the international contributions award from the Association for Educational Communications and Technology.

Paul A. Kirschner (1951) is professor of Educational Sciences at the Department of Pedagogical and Educational Sciences at Utrecht University (as well as head of the Research Center Interaction and Learning and dean of the Research Master programme Educational Sciences: Learning in Interaction) and professor of Educational Technology at the Educational Technology Expertise Center at the Open University of the Netherlands with a chair in Computer Supported Collaborative Learning Environments. He holds a Master's degree in educational psychology from the City University of Amsterdam and a Ph.D. from the Open University of the Netherlands. He is an internationally recognized expert in his field. A few notable examples of this is his election to the CSCL Board (within the International Society for the Learning Sciences), his associate editorship of the highly ranked journal Computers in Human Behavior and his editorship of two recent and very successful books (Visualizing Argumentation and What we know about CSCL). His areas of expertise include computer supported collaborative learning, designing electronic and other innovative learning environments, media-use in education, development of teacher extensive (distance) learning materials, use of practicals for the acquisition of cognitive skills and competencies, design and development of electronic learning and working environments, and innovation and the use of information technology educational systems.

PART I

INTRODUCTION

1
A NEW APPROACH TO INSTRUCTION

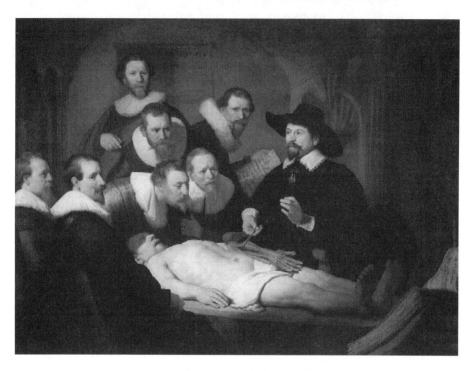

When Rembrandt van Rijn painted the Anatomy Lesson of Dr. Tulp in 1632 there was very little known about human anatomy, physiology, and morphology and the tools of the trade were rudimentary at best. Medicine was dominated by the teachings of the church where the human body was regarded as a creation of God and the ancient Greek view of the four humors (blood, phlegm, black bile, and yellow bile) prevailed. Sickness was due to an imbalance in these humors and treatments, such as bleeding the patient or inducing vomiting, were aimed at restoring the balance of these four humors. Surgical instruments remained basic. A surgeon would perform operations with the most basic set of instruments: a drill, a saw, forceps and pliers for removing teeth. If a trained surgeon was not available, it was usually the local barber who performed operations and removed teeth. The trained surgeon was possibly more an "artist" than a "scientist". For example, because there were no anesthetics surgeons prided themselves in the speed with which they operated; just a few minutes for a leg amputation. As far as progress toward new knowledge of anatomy, physiology, morphology, and medical techniques was concerned, it was very slow if at all. Although the microscope was invented, it was not powerful enough to see bacteria, so there was no progress in understanding the cause of disease, and this meant that there was little improvement in medical treatments.

Compare this to the situation today where hardly a day goes by that we are not confronted with new medical discoveries, new drugs and treatments, and new medical and surgical techniques. Just a generation or two ago medicine, medical knowledge and skills, and even attitudes of medical practitioners toward patients and the way patients approach and think about their doctors were radically different than they are today. It is no longer enough for surgeons to master the tools of the trade during their studies and then apply and perfect them throughout their careers. Competent surgeons today (and tomorrow) need to master complex skills and competencies during their studies and never stop learning throughout their careers. This book is about how to design instruction for this complex learning.

1.1   Complex Learning

Complex learning involves the integration of knowledge, skills and attitudes; the coordination of qualitatively different *constituent skills*, and often the transfer of what is learned in the school or training setting to daily life and work settings. The current interest in complex learning is manifest in popular educational approaches that call themselves inquiry, guided discovery, project-based, case method, problem-based, design-based, and competency-based. Examples of theoretical design models promoting complex learning are 4-Mat (McCarthy, 1996), cognitive apprenticeship (Collins, Brown, & Newman, 1989), collaborative problem solving (Nelson, 1999), constructivism and constructivist learning environments (Jonassen, 1999), instructional episodes (Andre, 1997), learning by doing (Schank, Berman, & MacPerson, 1999), multiple approaches to understanding (Gardner, 1999), star legacy (VanderBilt learning technology group: Schwartz, Lin, Brophy, & Bransford, 1999), and the four-component instructional design model (Van Merriënboer, 1997). Though all of these approaches differ in many ways, what they have in common is their focus on *authentic learning tasks* based on real-life tasks as the driving force for teaching and learning. The basic idea behind this focus is that such tasks help learners to integrate knowledge, skills and attitudes, stimulate them to learn to coordinate constituent skills, and facilitate transfer of what is learned to new problem situations (Merrill, 2002b; van Merriënboer, 2007; van Merriënboer & Kirschner, 2001).

This current interest in complex learning should not be seen as "just a fad", but rather as an inevitable reaction of education and teaching to societal and technological developments as well as students' and employers' uncompromising views about the value of education and training. Due to new technologies, routine tasks have been taken over by machines and the complex cognitive tasks that must be performed by humans are becoming increasingly important. Moreover, both the nature and the skills needed for currently available jobs are rapidly changing while the information relevant to carrying out those jobs quickly becomes obsolete. This poses higher demands on the workforce with employers stressing the importance of problem solving, reasoning, and creativity to ensure that employees can and will flexibly adjust to rapid changes in their environment. Two examples might drive this home. Many aspects of the job of an air traffic controller, for example, have been technically automated over the last decade. But even though this is the case, the complexity of what these controllers have to do is greater than ever before due to the enormous increase in air traffic, the growing number of safety regulations, and the advances in the technical aids themselves (see Figure 1.1).

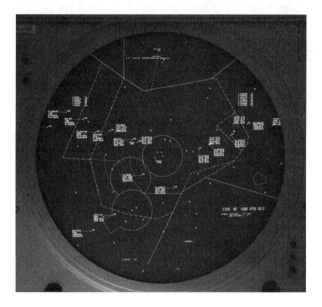

Figure 1.1   Photo of an air traffic control screen.

The same is true for the family doctor, who not only needs to care about physical, psychological, and social aspects of his or her patients - but is also confronted with a much more varied list of clients with different cultural backgrounds, a flood of new medicines and treatments, and issues dealing with registration, liability, insurance, and so forth.

   The field of education and training has become increasingly conscious of these new demands posed by society, business, and industry. In response to these demands, there has been a concomitant increase in the attempts to better prepare graduates for the labor market, which is apparent in the aforementioned educational approaches that stress complex learning and the development of professional *competencies* throughout the curriculum. But educational institutes lack proven design approaches which often results in the implementation of innovations that aim at a better preparation to the labor market, but that do so with varying degrees of success. An often-heard student complaint is that they experience the curriculum as a disconnected set of courses or modules, with only implicit relationships between the courses and an unclear relevance of what they are supposed to learn for their future professions. Often, as a compromise with the instructors who still want to "teach their subjects", curricula implement a separate "stream" in which projects, cases, or other learning tasks are used for the development of complex skills or competencies. However, even in those curricula, students often have difficulties relating what they are required to do in this stream to both the theoretical course-work, which is typically divided in traditional subjects, and what they perceive to be important for their future professions. Not surprisingly, students have difficulties combining all the things they learn into an integrated knowledge base and employ-ing this knowledge base to perform real-life tasks and solve practical work-related problems once they have graduated. In other words, they do not achieve the re-quired *transfer* of learning.

The fundamental problem facing the field of instructional design these days is the inability of education and training to achieve transfer of learning. Design theory must support the development of training programs for students who need to learn and transfer professional competencies or complex cognitive skills to an increas-ingly varied set of real-world contexts and settings. The Ten Steps to Complex Learning (from this point on referred to as the Ten Steps) claim that a holistic ap-proach to instructional design is necessary to reach this goal. In the next section of this chapter, this holistic design approach is discussed along with why it should help improve transfer of learning. This discussion is followed by a positioning of the instructional design model discussed in this book in the field of learning and instruction and a description of the main elements of the model. Finally, an over-view is given of the structure and the contents of the book and some suggestions are provided for how to use it.

1.2   A Holistic Design Approach

A *holistic design* approach is the opposite of an atomistic one. In an atomistic approach, complex contents and tasks are continually reduced to simpler elements. This reduction continues to a level where the elements can be transferred to the learners through presentation and/or practice. Though this approach may work very well if there are few interactions between the elements, it does not work well if the elements are closely interrelated. When this is the case, the whole is more than the sum of its parts. This is the basis of the holistic approach. Holistic design ap-proaches attempt to deal with complexity without loosing sight of the separate ele-ments and the interconnections between those elements. Using a holistic design approach can offer a solution for three persistent problems in the field of education, namely, compartmentalization, fragmentation, and the transfer paradox.

Compartmentalization

Instructional design models usually focus on one particular domain of learning, such as the cognitive, the affective, or the psychomotor domain. A further distinc-tion, for example in the cognitive domain, is the differentiation between models for *declarative learning*, emphasizing instructional methods for the construction of conceptual knowledge, and models for *procedural learning*, emphasizing methods for acquiring procedural skills. This *compartmentalization* - the separation of a whole into distinct parts or categories - has had disastrous effects on the fields of vocational and professional education (see Figure 1.2).

Figure 1.2   Compartmentalization in a store.

Suppose you have to undergo surgery. Would you prefer a surgeon with great technical skills, but with no knowledge of the human body? Or would you prefer a surgeon with great knowledge of the human body, but with two left hands? Or would you want a surgeon with great technical skills, but who has a horrible bedside manner and a hostile attitude toward her patients? Or, finally, a surgeon that has all of the knowledge, skills and attitudes that were learned 35 years ago, but has not kept them up-to-date? These questions clearly indicate that it makes little sense to distinguish domains of learning for professional competencies. Many complex surgical skills simply cannot be performed without in-depth knowledge of the structure and working of the human body, because this allows for the necessary flexibility in behavior. Many skills cannot be performed in an acceptable fashion if they do not exhibit particular attitudes. And so forth. Holistic design models for complex learning therefore aim at the *integration* of declarative learning, procedural learning (including perceptual and psychomotor skills), and affective learning (including the predisposition to keeping all of these aspects up-to-date) and so facilitate the development of an integrated knowledge base that increases the chance that transfer of learning occurs.

Fragmentation

Traditional instructional design models make use of *fragmentation* - the act or process of breaking something into small, incomplete or isolated parts - as their basis technique (see Ragan & Smith, 1996; van Merriënboer & van Dijk, 1998). Typical of fragmented instructional design models is that they first analyze a chosen learning domain, then divide it into distinct learning or performance objectives (e.g., remembering a fact, applying a procedure, understanding a concept, etc.), after which different instructional methods are selected for reaching each of the separate objectives (e.g., rote learning, skills-labs, problem solving, etc.). In the training blueprint or lesson plan for that domain, the objectives are dealt with one-by-one. For complex skills, each objective corresponds with one sub skill or con-stituent skill, and sequencing the objectives naturally results in a part-task se-quence. Thus, the learner is taught only one or a very limited number of constituent skills at the same time. New constituent skills are gradually added, and it is not un-til the end of the instruction - if at all - that the learner has the opportunity to prac-tice the whole complex skill.

In the 1960s, Briggs and Naylor (1962; Naylor & Briggs, 1963) reported that this approach is only suitable if little *coordination* of constituent skills is required and if each of the separate constituent skills is difficult for the learners to acquire. The problem with this fragmented approach is that most complex skills or profes-sional competencies are characterized by numerous interactions between the differ-ent aspects of task performance with very high demands on their coordination. In the intervening period overwhelming evidence has been obtained showing that breaking a complex domain or task down in a set of distinct elements or objectives, and then teaching or training those objectives without taking their interactions and required coordination into account does not work because learners ultimately are not able of integrating and coordinating the separate elements in transfer situations (Clark & Estes, 1999; Perkins & Grotzer, 1997; Spector & Anderson, 2000; Wightman & Lintern, 1985). In order to facilitate transfer of learning, holistic de-sign models focus on reaching highly integrated sets of objectives and, especially, the *coordinated* attainment of those objectives in real-life task performance.

The Transfer Paradox

In addition to the compartmentalization and fragmentation, the use of a non-integrated list of specific learning objectives as the basis for instructional design has a third undesired effect. Logically, the designer will select instructional meth-ods that minimize the number of *practice items* required, the time-on-task spent, and the learners' investment of effort made to reach those objectives. Designing and producing practice items costs time and money, both of which is often scarce. In addition, the learner does not have unlimited time or motivation to study (the learner, as almost all of us, is a *homo economicus*). Take the situation that students must learn to diagnose three different types of errors (e1, e2, e3) in a technical sys-tem. If a minimum of three practice items is required to learn to diagnose each er-ror, one may first train the students to diagnose error 1, then error 2, and finally error 3. This leads to the following training blueprint:

$$e1, e1, e1, e2, e2, e2, e3, e3, e3$$

Although this practice schedule will probably be most efficient for reaching the three objectives, minimizing the required time-on-task and student investment of effort, it also yields *low* transfer of learning. The reason for this is that the chosen instructional method invites students to construct highly specific knowledge for diagnosing each distinct error, which only allows them to perform in the way specified in the objectives, but not to performances that *go beyond* the given objectives. If a designer is aiming at transfer of learning, and the objective is to train students to diagnose as many errors as possible in a technical system, then it is far better to train the students to diagnose the three errors in a random order. This leads, for instance, to the following training blueprint:

e3, e2, e2, e1, e3, e3, e1, e2, e1

This sequence is probably less efficient than the first for reaching the three isolated objectives because it may increase the necessary time-on-task or the investment of effort by the learners. It might even require four instead of three practice items to reach the same level of performance for each separate objective. But in the long run it yields higher transfer of learning! The reason for this increase of transfer is that this instructional method invites students to construct knowledge that is general and abstract rather than entirely bound to the three concrete, specific errors and thus, allows them to better diagnose new, not earlier encountered, errors. This phenomenon - where the methods that work the best for reaching isolated, specific objectives are often not the methods that work best for reaching integrated objectives and increasing transfer of learning - is known as the *transfer paradox* (van Merriënboer & de Croock, 1997). A holistic design approach takes the transfer paradox into account and is always directed toward more general objectives that go beyond a limited list of highly specific objectives. The differentiation between different types of learning processes should ensure that students who are confronted with new problems not only have specific knowledge to perform the familiar aspects of those problems but, above all, have the necessary general or abstract knowledge to deal with the unfamiliar aspects of those problems.

To recapitulate, traditional design models usually follow an atomistic approach and as a result of this are not very successful in preventing compartmentalization and fragmentation or dealing with the transfer paradox. A holistic approach, in contrast, offers alternative ways for dealing with complexity. Most holistic approaches introduce some notion of "modeling" to attack this problem. A powerful two-step approach to modeling first develops simple-to-complex models of reality or real-life tasks, and then "models these models" from a pedagogical perspective to ensure that they are presented in such a way that students can actually learn from them (Achtenhagen, 2001). Thus, in this view, instruction should ideally begin with a simplified but "whole" model of reality, which is then conveyed to the learners according to sound pedagogical principles. The Ten Steps offers a broad range of instructional methods to deal with complexity without loosing sight of whole, real-life tasks.

1.3   Four Components and Ten Steps

The Ten Steps are a practical, modified and - as strange as it may sound simplified version of the four-component instructional design model (*4C/ID-model*: van Merriënboer, 1997; see also Janssen-Noordman & van Merriënboer, 2002; van Merriënboer, Clark, & de Croock, 2002; van Merriënboer & Dijkstra, 1997; van Merriënboer, Jelsma, & Paas, 1992). Previous descriptions of this model had an analytic-descriptive nature, with an emphasis on the cognitive-psychological basis of the model and the relationships between design components and learning processes. The Ten Steps, in contrast, are mainly prescriptive and aim to provide a version of the model that is practicable for teachers, domain experts involved in training-design, and instructional designers. The focus of this book is on design rather than on learning processes, but for interested readers, some of the chapters include text boxes in which the psychological foundations for particular design decisions are briefly explained.

The Ten Steps can be seen as a model of instructional design specifically directed toward programs of vocational and professional education, job-oriented university programs (e.g., medicine, business administration, law), and competency-based training programs in business, industry, government, and military organizations. It will typically be used to develop training programs of substantial duration - ranging from several weeks to several years. In terms of curriculum design, the model will typically be used to design a - substantial - part of a curriculum for the development of one or more professional competencies or complex skills.

The basic assumption that forms the basis of both 4C/ID and the Ten Steps is that blueprints for complex learning (see Chapter 2.1) can always be described by four basic components, namely: (a) learning tasks, (b) supportive information, (c) procedural information, and (d) part-task practice (see the left hand column of Table 1.1).

Table 1.1   Four blueprint components of 4C/ID and the Ten Steps.

Blueprint Components of 4C/ID	Ten Steps to Complex Learning
Learning Tasks	1. Design Learning Tasks
	2. Sequence Task Classes
	3. Set Performance Objectives
Supportive Information	4. Design Supportive Information
	5. Analyze Cognitive Strategies
	6. Analyze Mental Models
Procedural Information	7. Design Procedural Information
	8. Analyze Cognitive Rules
	9. Analyze Prerequisite Knowledge
Part-task Practice	10. Design Part-task Practice

The term *learning task* is used in a generic sense: It may refer to a case study that must be studied by the learners, a project that must be carried out, a problem that must be solved, and so forth. The *supportive information* helps students learn to perform non-routine aspects of learning tasks that often involve problem solving and reasoning (e.g., what could be the reason for the short circuit in the wiring). The *procedural information* enables students learn to perform routine aspects of learning tasks, that is, those aspects of the learning task that are always performed in the same way (e.g., an ammeter is always connected in series and a voltmeter in parallel). Finally, *part-task practice* pertains to additional practice of routine aspects that learners need to develop to a very high level of *automaticity*.

As indicated in the right hand column of Table 1.1, the four blueprint components directly correspond with four design steps: The design of learning tasks (Step 1), the design of supportive information (Step 4), the design of procedural information (Step 7), and the design of part-task practice (Step 10). The other six steps are auxiliary to these design steps and are only performed when necessary. Step 2, in which task classes are sequenced, organizes learning tasks in easy-to-difficult categories ensuring that students work on tasks that begin simply, and smoothly increase in difficulty. Step 3, where the performance objectives are identified, specifies the *standards* for acceptable performance. It is needed to assess student performance and to provide them with useful feedback. Steps 5 and 6 may be necessary for in-depth analysis of the supportive information that would be helpful for learning to carry out the non-routine aspects of learning tasks. Steps 8 and 9 may be necessary for in-depth analysis of the procedural information needed for performing routine aspects of learning tasks.

It should be noted that real-life design projects are never a straightforward progression from Step 1 to Step 10. New findings and decisions will often require the designer to reconsider previous steps, causing iterations in the design process. One may design a few learning tasks, in a process of *rapid prototyping,* before designing the complete educational program. In addition, particular steps may be superfluous for particular design projects. As a result, "zigzagging" between the ten steps is quite common. Then, it is the trick of the trade to keep a good overview of all - intermediate - design and analysis products as well as their relations to the ultimate training blueprint. Computer-based tools will be very helpful to carry out larger design projects, because they facilitate the systematic development of an educational blueprint and help designers to keep the required overview of the whole project – even when they zigzag between different design steps. The Norwegian company eNovate[AS], for example, produces and sells computer-based instructional design tools that are fully consistent with the Ten Steps (www.enovateas.com).

2
FOUR BLUEPRINT COMPONENTS

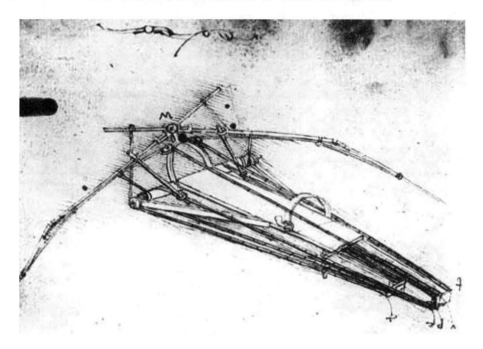

When an architect designs a house or an industrial designer designs a product or artifact, he or she - after consulting with the client and determining the program of requirements - makes a blueprint for the ultimate product. The blueprint for a 'flying machine' by Leonardo da Vinci above is an example of such a blueprint. Such a blueprint is not just a schematic drawing of the final product, but is rather a detailed plan of action, scheme, program, or method worked out beforehand for the accomplishment of an objective. This is also the case for the instructional designer.

Having globally discussed a holistic approach to design and the Ten Steps to Complex Learning in Chapter 1, this chapter proceeds to describe the four main components of a training blueprint, namely (a) learning tasks, (b) supportive information, (c) procedural information, and (d) part-task practice. It also explains how well-designed blueprints deal with the three problems discussed in the previous chapter. To prevent compartmentalization, the blueprint assures that the instruction integrates skills, knowledge, and attitudes into one interconnected knowledge base. To avoid fragmentation, it focuses on learning to coordinate those parts in real-life performance and not on learning separate parts. Finally, to deal with the transfer paradox, it acknowledges that complex learning involves qualitatively different learning processes with different requirements for the use of instructional methods. The first section of this chapter gives a schematic overview of the four components. The next three sections discuss the need for integration, coordination, and differentiation as well as implications for training design. The fifth section explains why the four components result in transfer of learning. The chapter concludes with a brief summary.

It should be noted that most of the things discussed in this chapter are further elaborated on in Chapters 4–13. This chapter provides you with basic knowledge and an overview to help you to better understand and integrate that which follows.

2.1 Training Blueprints

The central message of this chapter and, indeed of this whole book, is that environments for complex learning can always be described by four interrelated blueprint components (see Figure 2.1), namely:

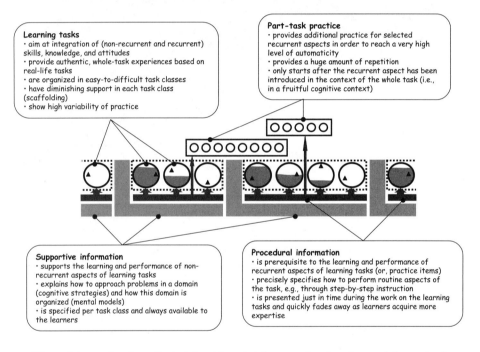

Figure 2.1   A schematic training blueprint for complex learning and the main features of each of the four components.

1   *Learning tasks*: authentic whole-task experiences based on real-life tasks that aim at the integration of skills, knowledge, and attitudes. The whole set of learning tasks exhibits a high variability, is organized in easy-to-difficult task classes, and has diminishing learner support throughout each task class.

2   *Supportive information*: information helpful for learning and performing the problem-solving and reasoning aspects of learning tasks. It explains how a domain is organized and how problems in that domain are (or should be) approached. It is specified per *task class* and is always available to learners.

This information provides a bridge between what learners already know and what they need to know to fruitfully work on the learning tasks.

3 *Procedural information*: information prerequisite for learning and performing routine aspects of learning tasks. It specifies exactly how to perform the routine aspects of the task and is best presented just in time; precisely when learners need it. It is quickly faded as learners gain more expertise.

4 *Part-task practice*: practice items provided to learners to help them reach a very high level of automaticity for selected routine aspects of a task. Part-task practice typically provides huge amounts of repetition. It only starts after the routine aspect has been introduced in the context of a whole, meaningful learning task.

The next sections explain how these four components can help to solve the problems of the compartmentalization of skills, knowledge, and attitudes, the fragmentation of what is learned in small parts, and the transfer paradox.

2.2   Integration rather than compartmentalization

Complex learning is always involved with a learner acquiring integrated sets of learning goals. Its ultimate aim is the integration of knowledge, skills, and attitudes in one rich, interconnected knowledge base. If people encounter a new and thus unfamiliar situation, such an interconnected knowledge base allows them to activate many different kinds of knowledge that may possibly help them to solve the problem. Figure 2.2 provides a schematic representation of the constituent skills and associated knowledge and attitudes that make up the moderately complex skill "searching for relevant research literature".

A well-designed training program for librarians will not teach each of these constituent skills separately, but will teach them in an integrated fashion; for example, by having the learners perform increasingly more difficult real-life literature searches for their clients.

As can be seen from Figure 2.2, a hierarchy of constituent skills is used as an organizing framework for the whole knowledge base. Knowledge and attitudes are fully integrated in this framework, subordinate to the constituent skills. Constituent skills adjacent to each other horizontally can be performed *sequentially* (e.g., you first "select an appropriate database" and then "formulate the search query" for the selected database) or *simultaneously* (e.g., you simultaneously "formulate a search query" and "perform the search" until you have a relevant and manageable list of results). Constituent skills at a lower level, on the vertical dimension, *enable* the learning and performance of skills higher in the hierarchy (e.g., you must be able to "operate a search program" in order to be able to "perform a search").

Furthermore, many constituent skills can only be performed if the learner has the necessary knowledge about the domain itself (e.g., you can only "select an appropriate database" if you have the necessary knowledge about the databases available as well as their characteristics) or require particular attitudes and the behaviors that follow from those attitudes to be performed in an acceptable fashion (e.g., "translating your client's research question into relevant search terms" requires a client-centered attitude to ensure that the research question becomes fully clear in a discussion with the client). Chapter 6 discusses the construction of a *skill hierarchy* in more detail.

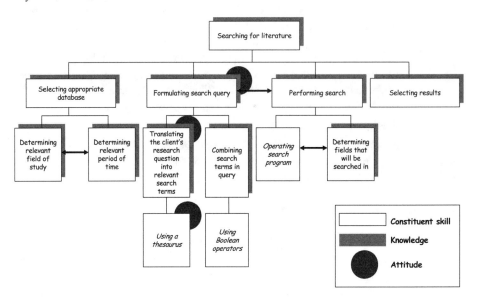

Figure 2.2   A hierarchy of constituent skills with an indication of associated knowledge and attitudes for the moderately complex skill "searching for relevant research literature".

Learning Tasks

Learners work on tasks that help them develop an integrated knowledge base through a process of *inductive learning*, in which they induce knowledge from concrete experiences (see Box 2 in Chapter 4). Therefore, each learning task should offer whole-task practice. This means that the learning task confronts the learner with all or almost all of the constituent skills important for real-life task performance, together with their associated knowledge and attitudes. In the example, the first learning task would ideally confront learners with the selection of appropriate databases, the formulation of a search query, the execution of the search, and the selection of results. All learning tasks are meaningful, authentic, and representative for the tasks that a professional might encounter in the real world. In this whole-task approach, learners quickly develop a holistic vision of the task that is gradually embellished during the training. A sequence of learning tasks provides the *backbone* of a training program for complex learning. Schematically, it simply looks like this:

Variability

The first "requirement", thus, is that each learning task is a whole task to encourage the development of an integrated knowledge base. In addition to this, it is important that all learning tasks differ from each other on all dimensions that also differ in the real world, such as the context or situation in which the task is performed, the way in which the task is presented, the saliency of the defining characteristics, and so forth. This allows the learners to abstract more general information from the details of each single task. For example, learning tasks for the literature-search example may differ with regard to the field of study in which the search is performed, the bibliographical databases that need to be searched, and the way the client gives the assignment to the librarian (by phone, letter, email, or face-to-face). There is strong evidence that such *variability of practice* is important for achieving transfer of learning - both for relatively simple tasks (e.g., Paas & van Merriënboer, 1994b; Quilici & Mayer, 1996) and highly complex real-life tasks (e.g., Schilling, Vidal, Ployhart, & Marangoni, 2003; van Merriënboer, Kester, & Paas, 2006). A sequence of *different* learning tasks, thus, always provides the backbone of a training program for complex learning. Schematically, it looks like this:

2.3   Coordination rather than Fragmentation

Complex learning is, to a large degree, learning to coordinate the - often many - constituent skills that make up real-life performance. Note that the whole complex skill is clearly more than the sum of its parts; playing a musical piece on the piano with two hands is more than playing it with the left and right hand separately. Constituent skills often need to be controlled by higher-level strategies because they make little sense without taking their related constituent skills and associated knowledge and attitudes into account. For this reason, constituent skills are seen as *aspects* rather than *parts* of a complex skill (this is also the reason that the term "constituent skill" is used and not the term "sub skill"). In a whole-task approach, learners are directly confronted with many different constituent skills from the start of the training, although they cannot be expected to independently coordinate all those aspects at that moment. Thus, it is necessary to simplify the tasks and to give learners *support* and *guidance*.

Task Classes

It is clearly not possible to use very difficult learning tasks, with high demands on coordination, right from the start of a training program. The common solution is to let learners start work on relatively easy whole learning tasks and progress toward more difficult whole tasks. Categories of learning tasks, each representing a version of the task with a particular difficulty, are called *task classes*. For example, the easiest task class in the literature-search example can be defined as a category of learning tasks that confronts learners with situations where the search is performed in a field of study with clearly defined concepts, on titles and keywords in one particular bibliographical database, with very few search terms, and yielding a limited number of relevant articles. The most difficult task class can be defined as a category of learning tasks that confronts learners with situations where concept definitions within or between fields of study are very unclear or even differ, in which full-text searches have to be performed in several relevant databases, with many search terms interconnected by Boolean operators in order to limit the otherwise large amount of relevant articles. Additional task classes of an intermediate difficulty level can be added in between these two extremes.

Learning tasks within a particular task class are always equivalent in the sense that the tasks can be performed based on the same body of (general) knowledge. However, as indicated in the previous section, the tasks differ from each other on dimensions that also vary in the real world. A more difficult task class requires more knowledge or more embellished knowledge for effective performance than the preceding, easier task classes. In the blueprint discussed later, the learning tasks are organized in an ordered sequence of task classes (i.e., the dotted boxes) that represent easy-to-difficult versions of the whole task.

Support and Guidance

When learners start to work on a new, more difficult task class, it is essential that they receive support and guidance for coordinating the different aspects of their performance. *Support* - actually task support - focuses on providing learners with assistance with the products involved in the training, namely the givens, the goals, and the solutions that get them from the givens to the goals (i.e., it is product oriented). *Guidance* - actually solution-process guidance - focuses on providing learners with assistance with the processes inherent to successfully solving the learning tasks (i.e., it is process oriented). These two topics will be discussed in more depth in a number of different chapters such as Chapters 4, 5, and 7.

This support and guidance diminishes in a process of *scaffolding* as learners acquire more expertise. The continuum of learning tasks with high support to learning tasks without support is exemplified by the continuum of support techniques ranging from case studies to *conventional tasks*. The highest level of support is provided by a case study where learners receive a description of an interesting literature search and are asked questions about the effectiveness of the approach taken, possible alternative approaches, the quality of the final list of selected articles, and so on. Intermediate support might be provided by an incomplete case study where the learners receive a research question, a set of search queries and a list of potential articles, from which they have to make a final selection of relevant articles by further specifying the search queries (i.e., they have to *complete* a given, partial solution). This type of scaffolding known as the *completion strategy* (van Merriënboer, 1990; van Merriënboer & de Croock, 1992) has been shown to be highly effective. Finally, no support is given by a conventional task, for which learners have to perform all actions by themselves. In the schematic training blue-print discussed later, each task class starts with one or more learning tasks with a high level of support and guidance (indicated by the grey in the circles), continues with learning tasks with a lower level of support and guidance, and ends with conventional tasks without any support and guidance.

2.4 Differentiation and the Transfer Paradox

Figure 2.2 illustrates another typical characteristic of complex learning outcomes, namely that for expert task-performers, there are qualitative differences between constituent skills involved (Schneider & Shiffrin, 1977; Shiffrin & Schneider, 1977). Some constituent skills are controlled, schema-based processes that are performed in a variable way from problem situation to problem situation. For example, "formulating a search query" involves problem solving and reasoning to cope with the specific requirements of each new search. Experienced librarians can perform such skills effectively because they possess knowledge in the form of cognitive schemas or concrete memories that can be interpreted so as to be able to reason about the task domain (i.e., in the form of *mental models*) and to guide their problem solving in this domain (i.e., in the form of *cognitive strategies*). These constituent skills, thus, involve the *different use of the same knowledge* in a new problem situation. Sometimes, generalized cognitive schemas are interpreted by the task performer so as to generate new behavior, and sometimes concrete cases that are retrieved from memory serve as an analogy.

Other constituent skills, lower in the skill hierarchy, may be *rule-based processes* that are performed in a highly consistent way from problem situation to problem situation. For example, "operating the search program" is a constituent skill that does not require any reasoning or problem solving from an experienced librarian. He or she "just does it". Experts can effectively perform such constituent skills because they have formed cognitive and psychomotor rules (Anderson, 1993; Anderson & Lebiere, 1998) that directly drive particular actions under particular circumstances, such as when the finger movements of a touch-typist are directly driven by reading a text. These constituent skills, thus, involve the *same use of the same knowledge* in a new problem situation. It might even be argued that these skills do not rely on "knowledge" at all because this knowledge is fully embedded in the rules. Indeed, the rules are often difficult to articulate and are not open to conscious inspection. Experts may reach a level of performance where they operate the search program fully "automatically", without paying attention to it. Conscious control is not required because the rules have become fully automated. The result is - in our example - that trained experts are able to focus their attention on other things while operating the search program.

Although they simultaneously occur in complex learning situations, schema-based and rule-based processes develop in fundamentally different ways (van Merriën-boer & Paas, 1989). As already indicated in Section 2.2, the key to the development of schema-based processes is variability. In a process of *schema construction*, learners construct general schemas that abstract information away from the details and provide models and approaches that can be used in a wide variety of situations. In contrast, the key to the development of rule-based processes is repetition. In a process of *rule* or *schema automation*, learners develop highly specific cognitive and psychomotor rules that evoke particular—mental or physical—actions under particular conditions.

Constituent skills are classified as *non-recurrent skills* if they will be performed as schema-based processes after the training, which refer to the problem-solving and reasoning aspects of behavior. Constituent skills are classified as *recurrent skills* if they will be performed as rule-based processes after the training, which refer to the routine aspects of behavior. For instance, constituent skills that may be classified as recurrent in the literature-search example are "using thesauri", "using Boolean operators", and "operating the search program", because the performance of these skills is highly consistent from problem situation to problem situation (in Figure 2.2, these skills are indicated in *italics* and do not have knowledge associated with them). The classification of skills as non-recurrent or recurrent is important in the Ten Steps because instructional methods for the effective and efficient acquisition of them are very different.

Supportive versus Procedural Information

Supportive information is important for those constituent skills classified as *non-recurrent*. It explains to the learners how a learning domain is organized and how to approach problems in that domain. It is made available to the learner to work on the problem solving and reasoning aspects of learning tasks within the same task class (i.e., equivalent learning tasks that can be performed based on the same body of knowledge). In the literature-search example, supportive information would explain how bibliographic databases are organized (i.e., to help the learner to build a mental model of databases) and could present heuristics for translating a research question into relevant search terms (i.e., to help the learner build a cognitive strategy). Instructional methods for the presentation of supportive information should facilitate schema construction such that learners are encouraged to deeply process the new information, in particular by connecting it to already existing schemas in memory in a sub process of schema construction called *elaboration* (see Box 3 in Chapter 7). Because supportive information is relevant to all learning tasks within the same task class, it is typically presented before learners start to work on a new task class and kept available for them during their work on this task class. This is indicated in the L-shaped shaded areas in the schematic training blueprint:

Procedural information is primarily important for those constituent skills that have been classified as *recurrent*. It specifies for the learners how to perform the routine aspects of learning tasks and preferably takes the form of direct, step-by-step instruction. In the literature-search example, procedural information could be presented in a quick reference guide or learning aid with operating instructions for the search program or in the case of an electronic learning program it could be presented with the aid of clickable hot-words linked to the information or windows which become visible when the cursor is moved to a certain area of the screen. Instructional methods for the presentation of procedural information should facilitate rule automation and should make the information available during task performance so that it can be easily embedded in *cognitive rules* in a sub process of rule automation called *knowledge compilation* (see Box 4 in Chapter 10). Because procedural information is relevant to the routine aspects of learning tasks, it is best presented to learners exactly when they first need it to perform a task (i.e., "just in time") after which it is quickly faded for subsequent learning tasks. In the schematic training blueprint, the procedural information (black beam) is linked to the separate learning tasks:

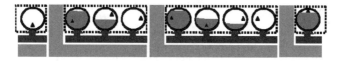

Part-task Practice

Learning tasks, as described in the previous sections, only provide whole-task practice. This shift from part-task to whole-task paradigm, designed to prevent compartmentalization and fragmentation may, however, not always be sufficient. There are situations where it may be necessary to include additional part-task practice in a training program. This is usually the case when a very high level of automaticity is desired for particular recurrent aspects of a task. In this case, the series of learning tasks may not provide enough repetition to reach that level. For those aspects classified as *to-be-automated recurrent constituent skills*, additional part-task practice may be provided - such as when children drill the multiplication tables or when musicians practice specific musical scales.

In the literature-search example, part-task practice could be provided for learning to use Boolean operators (cf. Carlson, Sullivan, & Schneider, 1989). The instructional methods used for part-task practice facilitate rule automation and, in particular, facilitate a sub process called *strengthening*. Strengthening is a process where cognitive rules accumulate strength each time they are successfully applied by the learner (see Box 5 in Chapter 13). Part-task practice for a particular recurrent aspect of a task can begin only after it has been introduced in a meaningful whole learning task. In this way, the learners start their practice in a fruitful cognitive context. For literature-search, learners would only start to practice constructing and using Boolean operators after they had studied them in the context of a whole learning task. As for recurrent aspects of learning tasks, procedural information might also be relevant for part-task practice because this always concerns a recurrent constituent skill (according to the Ten Steps, no part-task practice for non-recurrent constituents skills is provided). In the schematic training blueprint, part-task practice is indicated by series of small circles (i.e., practice items).

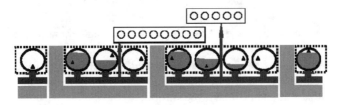

This concludes the construction of our training blueprint and completes the schematic outline originally introduced in Figure 2.1. A well-designed training blueprint ensures that learners are not overwhelmed with the complexity of a task, because tasks are ordered from easy to difficult, support and guidance are given when needed, and different types of information are presented precisely at the right time (see Box 1). Learners should not invest all their cognitive resources in performing the task, but should also invest sufficient mental effort in genuine *learning*, that is, schema construction and rule automation. Only then can transfer of learning to daily or professional life be expected.

Box 1 - Cognitive Load Theory and the Four Components

Recent instructional theories such as those discussed in this book stress the use of authentic, whole-tasks as the driving force for learning. A severe risk of the use of such tasks, however, is that learners have difficulty learning because they are overwhelmed by task complexity. *Cognitive Load Theory* offers guidelines to deal with the very limited processing capacity of the human mind.

Cognitive Load Theory (CLT)

Central to CLT is the notion that human cognitive architecture should be a major consideration when designing instruction. According to CLT, this cognitive architecture consists of a severely limited working memory with partly independent processing units for visual/spatial and auditory/verbal information, which interacts with a comparatively unlimited long-term memory. The theory distinguishes between three types of cognitive load, dependent on the type of processing causing it, namely:

1. *Intrinsic load* is a direct function of performing the task, in particular, of the number of elements that must be simultaneously processed in working memory ('element interactivity'). For instance, a task with many constituent skills that must be coordinated (e.g., playing a Bach sonata) yields a higher intrinsic load than a task with less constituent skills that need to be coordinated (e.g., playing a major musical scale).
2. *Extraneous load* is the extra load beyond the intrinsic cognitive load mainly resulting from poorly designed instruction. For instance, if learners must search in their instructional materials for the information they need to perform a learning task (e.g., searching for the proper placement of the fingers for a similar sonata which is not explicated in the musical lesson), this search process itself does not directly contribute to learning and thus causes extraneous cognitive load.

3. *Germane load* is related to processes that directly contribute to learning, in particular to schema construction and rule automation. For instance, consciously connecting new information with what is already known, rather than focusing on task details (e.g., making explicit that the playing of this sonata is very much like a different one already learned, but varies on a specific part), is a process that yields *germane cognitive load*.

A basic assumption of CLT is that an instructional design that results in unused working memory capacity due to low extraneous cognitive load because of appropriate instructional procedures may be further improved by encouraging learners to engage in conscious cognitive processing directly relevant to learning. Intrinsic, extraneous, and germane cognitive load are additive in that, if learning is to occur, the total load of the three together cannot exceed the working memory resources available. Consequently, the greater the proportion of germane cognitive load created by the instructional design, the greater the potential for learning.

Four Components and Cognitive Load

1. The cognitive load associated with performing *learning tasks* is controlled in two ways. First, intrinsic cognitive load is managed by organizing the learning tasks in easy-to-difficult task classes. For learning tasks within an easier task class, less elements and interactions between elements need to be processed simultaneously in working memory; as the task classes become more complex, the number of elements and interactions between the elements increases. Second, extraneous cognitive load is managed by providing a large amount of support and guidance for the first learning task(s) in a task class, thus preventing weak-method problem solving and its associated high extraneous load. This support and guidance decreases as learners gain more expertise ("scaffolding").
2. Because *supportive information* typically has high element interactivity, it is preferable not to present it to learners while working on the learning tasks. Simultaneously performing a task and studying the information would almost certainly cause cognitive overload. Instead, supportive information is best presented before learners start working on a learning task. In this way, a cognitive schema can be constructed in long-term memory that can subsequently be activated in working memory during task performance. Retrieving the already constructed cognitive schema is expected to be less cognitively demanding than activating the externally presented complex information in working memory during task performance.
3. *Procedural information* consists of cognitive rules and typically has much lower element interactivity than supportive information. Furthermore, the development of cognitive rules requires that relevant information is active in working memory during task performance so that it can be embedded in those rules. Studying this information beforehand has no added value whatsoever; therefore, procedural information is preferably presented precisely when learners need it. This is, for example, the case when teachers give step-by-step instructions to learners during practice, acting as an "assistant looking over the learners' shoulders".
4. Finally, *part-task practice* automates particular recurrent aspects of a complex skill. In general, an over-reliance on part-task practice is not helpful for complex learning. But the automated recurrent constituent skills may decrease the cognitive load associated with performing the whole learning tasks, making performance of the whole skill more fluid, and decreasing the chance of making errors due to cognitive overload.

Limitations of CLT

CLT is fully consistent with the four components, but this is not to say that CLT alone is sufficient to develop a useful instructional design model for complex learning. Application of CLT prevents cognitive overload and (equally important) frees up processing resources that can be devoted to learning. To ensure that the freed-up resources are actually devoted to learning, the Ten Steps relies on several specific learning theories to prescribe instructional methods for each of its four components: models of induction for learning tasks (see Box 2 in Chapter 4); models of elaboration for supportive information (see Box 3 in Chapter 7); models of knowledge compilation for procedural information (see Box 4 in Chapter 10), and models of strengthening for part-task practice (see Box 5 in Chapter 13).

Further Reading

Kirschner, P. A. (Ed.) (2002). Cognitive load theory [Special Issue]. *Learning and Instruction, 12.*

Paas, F., Renkl, A., & Sweller, J. (Eds.) (2003). Cognitive load theory and instructional design: Recent developments [Special Issue]. *Educational Psychologist, 38*(1).

Paas, F., Renkl, A., & Sweller, J. (Eds.) (2004). Advances in cognitive load theory, development, and instructional design [Special Issue]. *Instructional Science, 32.*

Paas, F., van Merriënboer, J. J. G., & Adam, J. J. (1994). Measurement of cognitive load in instructional research. *Perceptual and Motor Skills, 79,* 419–430.

Sweller, J., van Merriënboer, J. J. G., & Paas, F. (1998). Cognitive architecture and instructional design. *Educational Psychology Review, 10,* 251–296.

Van Merriënboer, J. J. G., & Ayres, P. (Eds.) (2005). Research on cognitive load theory and its design implications for e-learning [Special issue]. *Educational Technology, Research and Development, 53*(3).

Van Merriënboer, J. J. G., & Sweller, J. (2005). Cognitive load theory and complex learning: Recent developments and future directions. *Educational Psychology Review, 17,* 147–177.

2.5   Realizing Transfer of Learning

There are three reasons why well-designed training blueprints result in transfer of learning. First, whole learning tasks explicitly aim at developing one integrated knowledge base that increases the chance of finding some useful knowledge in new problem situations. Second, easy-to-difficult task classes combined with learner support and guidance help students learn to coordinate constituent skills with their associated knowledge and attitudes, so that after the training they can strategically recombine those aspects for solving new problems. Finally, differentiating schema-construction from rule-automation yields automated rules as well as cognitive schemas - both of which are necessary for transfer to occur. Rules may directly drive the performance of familiar aspects of new problems, while schemas may be interpreted to perform the unfamiliar aspects of the same problems.

Figure 2.3 shows the relationship between the application of specific rules and the interpretation of schemas in the *transfer cycle*. After rules have been fully automated, they not only perform familiar aspects of a new problem, but also free up processing resources that may be devoted to handling unfamiliar aspects of the problem. This process of rule-based transfer is in accordance with the *component fluency hypothesis* (Carlson, Khoo, & Elliott, 1990) stating that the automaticity of recurrent constituent skills makes cognitive resources available that may subsequently be devoted to the performance of non-recurrent constituent skills, including the coordination of all aspects involved in whole-task performance. Thus, drilling multiplication tables helps children solve real-world mathematical problems in two ways, namely (a) they can effortlessly carry out the necessary multiplication and

(b) they can use their cognitive resources to better work on the unfamiliar aspects of the real-world problems. In the same way, practicing musical scales helps musicians effortlessly carry out the necessary finger work and better use their cognitive resources to coordinate their actions and artistically interpret musical pieces.

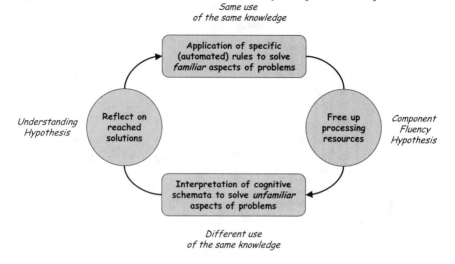

Figure 2.3   The transfer cycle.

Learners interpret cognitive schemas to deal with unfamiliar aspects of new problems either by applying specific principles to reason about the problem in question or by applying heuristics to guide their problem-solving process. The use of *analogies*, for example, is an important interpretation method for drawing comparisons between a current problem situation and possible relevant cognitive schemas or memories acquired in other - more or less - similar problem situations. If analogy operates on useful, well-organized, and rich schemas, then it is a very effective process to easily retrieve schemas and then map them on the new problem situation in order to reach a solution. This process of analogical or schema-based transfer is in accordance with the *understanding hypothesis* (Ohlsson & Rees, 1991), which reflects the common belief that understanding a subject-matter domain through the availability of schemas that may be used to interpret a problem situation in general terms, enables a person to monitor and evaluate her or his own performance, detect and correct any errors made, and reflect on the quality of solutions reached - including solutions reached by the application of rules.

Reflective experts show evidence of both transfer mechanisms (Frederiksen, 1984; Gick & Holyoak, 1987). They possess both automated rules for performing routine aspects of tasks and freeing up processing resources and rich schemas for performing genuine problem-solving activities and continuously evaluating the quality of their performance and generated solutions. In contrast to beginners, reflective experts are often "opportunistic" - if known approaches do not work they can easily generate alternative approaches. Well-designed training blueprints should help develop such reflective experts.

2.6   Summary

- A high-variability sequence of whole, authentic learning tasks provides the backbone of a training program for complex learning because it ensures the integration of what is learned into one interconnected knowledge base.
- Easy-to-difficult sequencing of learning tasks in task classes and supporting learners' performance through scaffolding are necessary to help them learn to coordinate all aspects of real-life task performance.
- To facilitate the construction of cognitive schemas, supportive information explains how a domain is organized and how to approach problems in this domain so that learners can fruitfully work on the non-recurrent aspects of learning tasks within the same task class.
- To facilitate rule automation, (a) procedural information specifies exactly how to perform the recurrent aspects of learning tasks and (b) part-task practice provides additional repetition for those recurrent, routine aspects that need to be developed up to a very high level of automaticity.
- Training blueprints built from the four components are fully consistent with Cognitive Load Theory because they reduce unnecessary cognitive load and free up cognitive resources that can be devoted to learning, namely schema-construction and rule-automation.
- Training blueprints built from the four components help achieve transfer of learning, because they simultaneously aim at (a) the development of auto-mated rules to perform routine aspects of tasks and to free up processing resources, and (b) the construction of rich schemas to carry out genuine problem-solving activities and to evaluate the quality of performance and generated solutions.

3
TEN STEPS

When painting a room (a fairly simple task), a fixed procedure can be easily used. First, the room is emptied and all of the panel work, wall sockets and fixtures, floor coverings, hanging lamps, et cetera are removed and stored. After removing old wallpaper and/or paint from the walls, the walls and ceilings can be repaired (e.g., plastered, sanded, spackled). After this, the room and the window and/or door frames are painted (often with different paints and paint colors) and the panel work, wall sockets, and fixtures are returned to their places. Finally, lamps are re-hung, floors are carpeted, and the furniture is returned to the room. When painting a whole house which is a much more complex task, these same steps could again be followed in a linear order and the job could be carried out in the same way. However, it is more often if not always the case that it is done quite differently because doing it in this linear manner would mean first removing and storing all of the furniture from the whole house, removing all of the panel work, fixtures and wall hangings, covering all of the floors, steaming off all of the wall paper and so forth, and so forth until in the reverse order all of the furniture can be finally moved back in to the completed house. Unfortunately, is this not only impracticable, it will also often not lead to very satisfying results. It is not practicable because those who live in the house would have nowhere to eat, sleep, and live for the whole period that the house is being repainted. It would also probably not lead to the most satisfying results because those involved could not profit from lessons learned and new ideas generated along the way. Instead of following the fixed procedure, a zigzag strategy through the house would probably be followed, doing certain - parts of - different rooms in a certain order until the whole house was completed.

This third and last introductory chapter describes the instructional design process in Ten Steps. But to do this, it must first begin with a description of ten design activities rather than steps. The reason for this is very simple. Though there are - theoretically - ten steps which could be followed in a specific order, in real-life instructional design projects switches between those activities are common, yielding zigzag design behaviors. Be that as it may, a linear description of the activities is necessary to present a workable - and understandable - model description that is needed for a systematic approach to the design process. To this end, David Merrill's *pebble-in-the-pond* principle (2002b) is used to order the activities. Merrill's approach takes a practical and content-oriented view of design, starting with the key activity that is at the heart of our model, namely, the design of learning tasks. The learning task serves as the pebble that is cast in the pond and as the first of the Ten Steps. This one pebble starts all of other activities rolling. The nine remaining steps are then discussed in the order in which they are called up by the design of learning tasks.

The chapter begins with a description of the ten activities that make up the design process, followed by a discussion of the role of system dynamics in instructional design where each activity affects, and is affected by, all other activities. After this, Merrill's pebble-in-the-pond principle is presented and is used as a framework for ordering the activities into the Ten Steps. At this point, the Ten Steps are positioned within the *Instructional Systems Design* (ISD) process and the *ADDIE model* (i.e., Analysis, Design, Development, Implementation, and Evaluation). The chapter concludes with a brief summary. The reader should not be daunted by the pace of this chapter, because most of the activities discussed are further elaborated on in Chapters 4–13. This chapter merely provides an overview.

3.1 Ten Activities

Figure 3.1 presents, in one glance, the whole design process for complex learning. The grey boxes in the figure show ten activities that are carried out when properly designing training blueprints for complex learning. These activities are typically employed by a designer to produce effective, efficient, and appealing educational programs. This section explains the different elements in the figure from the bottom up.

The lower part of the figure is identical to the schematic training blueprint and contains the four activities that correspond with the four blueprint components. The *design of learning tasks* is the heart of the training blueprint. For each task class, learning tasks are designed that provide learners with variable whole-task practice at a particular difficulty level until they reach the pre-specified standards for this level, whereupon they continue to the next, more complex or difficult task class. The *design of supportive information* pertains to all information that may help learners to carry out the problem solving and reasoning (i.e., non-recurrent) aspects of the learning tasks within a particular task class. The *design of procedural information* pertains to all information that exactly specifies how to carry out the routine (i.e., recurrent) aspects of the learning tasks. And finally, the *design of part-task practice* may be necessary for selected recurrent aspects that need to be developed to a very high level of automaticity.

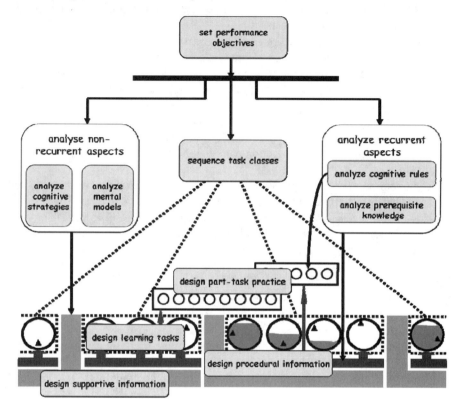

Figure 3.1   A schematic overview of the ten activities (grey boxes) in the design process for complex learning.

The middle part of the figure contains five activities. The central activity - *sequence task classes* - describes an easy-to-difficult progression of categories of tasks that learners may work on. It organizes the tasks in such a way that learning is optimized. The least difficult task class is linked to the entry level of the learners (i.e., what they already know when they enter the training program) and the final, most complex or difficult task class is linked to the final attainment level as defined by the performance objectives for the whole training program.

The analyses of cognitive strategies and mental models (left in the middle part of the figure) are necessary for helping learners achieve the non-recurrent aspects of carrying out the task. The *analysis of cognitive strategies* answers the question: How do proficient task performers systematically approach problems in the task domain? The *analysis of mental models* answers the question: How is the domain organized? The resulting systematic approaches to problem solving and domain models are used as a basis for the design of supportive information for a particular task class (see Chapter 7.1). There is a clear reciprocity between the specification of task classes and the analysis of non-recurrent task aspects: More difficult task classes require more detailed and/or more embellished cognitive strategies and mental models than easier task classes.

The analyses of cognitive rules and *prerequisite knowledge* (right in the middle of the figure) are necessary for helping learners achieve the recurrent aspects of carrying out the task. The *analysis of cognitive rules* identifies the condition-action pairs that enable experts to perform routine aspects of tasks without effort (IF *condition* THEN *action*). The *analysis of prerequisite knowledge* identifies what they need to know in order to correctly apply those condition-action pairs. Together, the results of these analyses provide the basis for the design of procedural information. In addition, identified condition-action pairs help to specify practice items for part-task practice.

The upper part of the figure contains only one activity, *setting performance objectives*. Because complex learning deals with highly integrated sets of learning objectives, the focus is on the decomposition of a complex skill into a hierarchy describing all aspects or constituent skills relevant to performing real-life tasks. In other words, we are interested in the specification of performance objectives and standards for acceptable performance for each of the constituent skills, and a classification of the skills within these objectives as either non-recurrent or recurrent. Performance objectives provide a starting point for the analyses of non-recurrent and recurrent aspects of skills and set the level of performance that must be attained by the learners.

As indicated by the arrows, some activities provide preliminary input for other activities. This may suggest that the best order for performing the activities would be to start with setting performance objectives, then to continue with *sequencing* task classes and analyzing non-recurrent and recurrent aspects, and to end with designing the four blueprint components. Indeed, the ten activities have previously been described in this analytical order (e.g., van Merriënboer & de Croock, 2002). But in real-life design projects, each activity affects, and is affected by, all other activities. This leaves it an open question as to which order for using the ten activities is most fruitful.

3.2 System Dynamics

The model presented in this book takes a *sytem dynamics* view of instruction, which it shares with many other instructional design models (Banathy, 1987). This view emphasizes the interdependence of the elements constituting an instructional system and recognizes the dynamic nature of this interdependence which makes the system an irreducible whole. Such a systems approach is both systematic and systemic. It is systematic because the input-process-output paradigm is inherent to it. According to this paradigm, the outputs of particular elements of the system serve as inputs to other elements, and the outputs of particular design activities serve as inputs for other activities. For example, the output of an analysis is the input for the design of supportive information in the blueprint. At the same time, it is actually also a *systemic* approach because it is accepted that the performance or function of each element directly or indirectly has an impact on, or is impacted by, one or more of the other elements - thereby making the design process highly dynamic and non-linear. For example, this same analysis of non-recurrent aspects of a skill can also affect the choice and sequencing of task-classes. This will be further explained in the next sections.

Iteration

The preliminary input-process-output relations depicted in Figure 3.1 indicate the systematic nature of the Ten Steps. Setting performance objectives yields input for sequencing task classes as well as for analyzing non-recurrent and recurrent aspects of the complex skill; sequencing task classes yields input for designing learning tasks; analyzing non-recurrent aspects yields input for designing supportive information, and, finally, analyzing recurrent aspects yields input for designing procedural information as well as designing part-task practice. This process, however, is not singular but occurs in *iterations* where the results of activities in a lower part of the figure provide input for activities in a higher part of the figure. In other words, iteration is a procedure in which a cycle of operations is repeated to more closely approximate a required result. These iterations are very important and are a sign of the systemic nature of the process. The analyses of non-recurrent and recurrent aspects of a skill, for example, often provide new insights in the structure of a complex skill, yielding input for the revision of - the hierarchically ordered structure of - performance objectives. The design of the four components often reveals weaknesses in the analysis results, providing input for more detailed or alternative analyses. And even "final" media choices, such as the decision to use e-learning for implementing the training program, may call for additional task and knowledge analyses to reach the required level of specificity and detail.

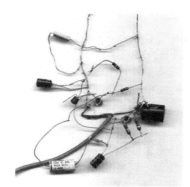

Figure 3.2   Original functional proto-prototype of the Zener noise airboard
http://www.ciphersbyritter.com/noise/airboard.htm.

Iteration will always occur in real-life design processes, so that it may be worthwhile to plan the major iterations beforehand in a form of *rapid prototyping* (e.g.,

Nixon & Lee, 2001; Tripp & Bichelmeyer, 1990). In rapid prototyping, the designer quickly develops one or more learning tasks (prototypes; see Figure 3.2), which fit one particular task class, and then tests them with real users. The results of these user tests are not only used to refine the prototype, but they also impact on the whole design process including the setting of performance objectives, the specification of new task classes, and the analysis of different aspects of the complex skill.

Layers of Necessity

In real-life design projects, designers will often not perform all design activities, or at least not perform them at the same level of detail. Based upon the development time and resources available, they choose activities that will be incorporated into the project as well as the level of detail necessary for those activities. In other words they flexibly adapt their professional knowledge. Wedman and Tessmer (1991) describe this process in terms of *layers of necessity*. In this process, goal analysis (i.e., setting performance objectives) is considered fundamental, whereas a thorough *needs assessment* could be considered a second-layer activity, to be accomplished when conditions permit. The instructional design model is then described as a nested structure of sub models, ranging from a minimalist model for situations with severe time and resource limitations, to a highly sophisticated model for ideal situations with ample time and resources. A minimalist version of the Ten Steps (i.e., the first layer of necessity) might, for example, only contain the development of a series of learning tasks - because this is at the heart of the training blueprint. The most sophisticated version of the model might contain the development of a highly detailed training blueprint, where the descriptions of supportive information, procedural information, and part-task practice are actually based on comprehensive task and content analyses. Obviously, the key to using layers of necessity is a realistic assessment of the time and resource constraints associated with a particular design project.

A related issue is the *reuse* of instructional materials. Many instructional design projects do not design training programs from scratch, but *re*design existing training programs. This would clearly reduce the need to perform certain analysis and design activities, and will almost certainly reduce the need to perform them at a very high level of detail. The redesign of an existing training program according to the Ten Steps, for example, will always start with the specification of a series of learning tasks which are then organized into task classes. With respect to designing the information that learners will need to productively work on those tasks, it might be sufficient to only reorganize already available instructional materials such that they are connected to the relevant task classes and learning tasks. Obviously, there is no need for an in-depth task and content analysis. Furthermore, reuse of materials is also increasingly popular for the design of new courses. The concept of *reusable learning objects* (RLOs; see van Merriënboer & Boot, 2005; Wiley, 2001) refers to the employment of repositories of digital instructional materials which are developed in such a way that they can be easily re-used in new courses. Again, the analysis necessary to determine which RLOs are useful for a particular training program is probably much less detailed than the analysis necessary to develop those materials from scratch.

Zigzag Design

As indicated in the previous sections, designers frequently switch between activities (iterations) and often neglect some of the activities, or at least do not perform all activities at the same high level of detail (layers of necessity). In addition, for some of the activities there is no preferred order whatsoever. For instance, in Figure 3.1, there is no preferred order for analyzing the non-recurrent and the recurrent aspects of the skill, there is no preferred order for the design of supportive information, procedural information, and part-task practice, and, finally, there is no necessity of completing one step before beginning on another. Taken together, iterations, layers of necessity, and switches between independent activities result in highly dynamic, non-linear forms of *zigzag design*. Nevertheless, it is important to prescribe the execution of the ten activities in an order that gives optimal guidance to designers. This is discussed in the next section.

3.3 The Pebble-in-the-Pond: From Activities to Steps

M. David Merrill (2002a) proposed a pebble-in-the-pond approach for instructional design that is fully consistent with the Ten Steps. It is a content-centered modification of traditional instructional design in which the contents-to-be-learned and not the abstract learning objectives are specified first. The approach consists of a series of expanding activities initiated by first casting in a pebble in the pond, that is, designing one or more learning tasks of the type that learners will be taught to accomplish by the instruction. This simple little pebble initiates further ripples in the design pond. Thus, whereas the Ten Steps acknowledges that designers do not design in a linear fashion and allow for zigzag design behaviors, the steps are ordered according to the pebble-in-the-pond approach. This prescriptive model is believed to be workable and useful for teachers and other practitioners in the field of instructional design.

A Backbone of Learning Tasks: Steps 1, 2, and 3

The first three steps aim at the development of a series of learning tasks that serve as the backbone for the educational blueprint:

> Step 1: Design Learning Tasks
> Step 2: Sequence Task Classes
> Step 3: Set Performance Objectives

The *first step*, the pebble, is to specify one or more typical learning tasks that represent the whole complex skill that the learner will be able to perform following the instruction. Such a task has, in the past, been referred to as an epitome; the most overarching, fundamental task that represents the skill (Reigeluth, 1987b; Reigeluth & Rodgers, 1980; Reigeluth & Stein, 1983). In this way, it becomes clear from the beginning, and at a very concrete level, what the training program aims to achieve.

Normally, providing only a few learning tasks to learners will not be enough to help them develop the complex skills necessary to perform the whole task. Therefore, another unique characteristic of the pebble-in-the-pond approach is - after casting the first whole learning task pebble into the pond - to specify a progression of such tasks of increasing difficulty such that if learners were able to do all of the tasks identified, they would have mastered the knowledge, skills, and attitudes that are to be taught. This ripple in the design pond, or Step, involves the assignment and sequencing of learning tasks to task classes with different levels of difficulty. Tasks in the easiest class are at the learners' entry level, whereas tasks in the most difficult task class are at the training program's exit level. In order to be able to give learners the necessary feedback on the quality of their performance, and to decide when they may proceed from one task class to the next, it is necessary to state the standards that need to be achieved for acceptable performance. This next ripple in the design pond, or Step, consists of the specification of performance objectives that, among other things, articulate the standards that learners must reach to carry out the tasks in an acceptable fashion. In this way, the pebble-in-the-pond approach avoids the common design problem that the objectives that are determined early in the process are abandoned or revised later in the process to correspond more closely to the content that has finally been developed.

Component Knowledge, Skills, and Attitudes: Steps 4 to 10

Further ripples in the design pond identify the knowledge, skills, and attitudes necessary to perform each learning task in the progression of tasks. This results in the remaining blueprint components, which are subsequently connected to the backbone of learning tasks. We make a distinction here between supportive information, procedural information, and part-task practice. The steps followed for designing and developing supportive information are:

> Step 4: Design Supportive Information
> Step 5: Analyze Cognitive Strategies
> Step 6: Analyze Mental Models

Supportive information is that information that helps the learner for performing the non-recurrent aspects of the learning tasks related to problem solving and reasoning. Units of supportive information are connected to task classes, and more complex task classes typically require more detailed or more embellished supportive information than easier task classes. If useful instructional materials are already available, Step 4 may be limited to re-organizing existing instructional materials and assigning them to task classes. Steps 5 and 6 may then be neglected. But if instructional materials need to be designed and developed from scratch, it may be helpful to perform Step 5 where the cognitive strategies that proficient task-performers use to solve problems in the domain are analyzed, and/or Step 6, where the mental models that describe how the domain is organized are analyzed. The results of the analyses in Steps 5 and 6 provide the basis for designing supportive information. Analogous to the design and development of supportive information, the steps for designing and developing procedural information are:

Step 7: Design Procedural Information
Step 8: Analyze Cognitive Rules
Step 9: Analyze Prerequisite Knowledge

Procedural information is that information necessary for performing the recurrent aspects of the learning tasks. It specifies exactly how to perform these aspects (and is thus procedural) and is preferably presented just in time, in other words precisely when learners need it during their work on the learning tasks. For subsequent learning tasks, this procedural information quickly fades away, often replaced by new specific information for carrying out new procedures. If useful instructional materials such as job aids, quick reference guides, or even Electronic Performance Support Systems (EPSSs) are available, Step 7 may be limited to updating those materials and linking them to the appropriate learning tasks. Steps 8 and 9 may then be neglected. But if the procedural information needs to be designed from scratch, it may be helpful to perform Step 8, where the cognitive rules specifying the condition-action pairs that drive routine behaviors are analyzed, and Step 9, where the knowledge that is prerequisite to a correct use of cognitive rules is analyzed. The results of the analyses in Steps 8 and 9 then provide the basis for the design of procedural information. Finally, depending on the nature of the task and the knowledge and skills needed to carry it out, it may be necessary to perform the tenth and final step:

Step 10: Design Part-task Practice

Under particular circumstances, additional practice is necessary for selected recurrent aspects of a complex skill in order to develop a very high level of automaticity. This, for example, may be the case for recurrent constituent skills that are critical because their incorrect performance can cause danger to life and limb, loss of expensive or hard to replace materials, or damage to equipment. If part-task practice needs to be designed, the analysis results of step 8 (i.e., the condition-action pairs) provide useful input. The remaining chapters of this book will discuss the Ten Steps in detail.

3.4 Ten Steps within an ISD Context

The Ten Steps will often be applied in the context of Instructional Systems Design (ISD). ISD-models have a broad scope and typically divide the instructional design proess into five phases: (a) analysis, (b) design, (c) development, (d) implementation and (e) summative evaluation. In this so-called ADDIE-model, formative evaluation is conducted during all of the phases. The Ten Steps is narrower in scope and focus on the first two phases of the instructional design process, namely, task and content analysis and design. In particular, the Ten Steps concentrates on the analysis of a to-be-trained complex skill or professional competency in an integrated process of task and content analysis and the conversion of the results of this analysis into a training blueprint that is ready for development and implementation. The Ten Steps is best applied in combination with an ISD-model in order to support activities not treated in the Ten Steps, such as needs assessment and needs analysis, development of instructional materials, implementation and delivery of materials, and summative evaluation of the implemented training program.

At the front end, the Ten Steps assume that there is a performance problem that can be solved through training, and that there is an overall instructional goal, namely, to teach the complex skill or professional competency involved. If this assumption cannot be fully justified, it is desirable to conduct a *needs assessment* prior to the Ten Steps to find answers to questions such as "What should the learners be able to do after the instruction?" "Can they already do this, or is there a performance problem?" "What might be the possible causes for a signaled performance problem?" "Can the performance problem be solved with training?" and so forth (Gupta, 1999; Kaufman & English, 1979; Rossett, 1987). After carrying out such a needs assessment, a detailed task analysis should then be conducted. The analysis techniques discussed in this book (in Chapters 5-6, 8–9, & 11–12) are fully integrated in the Ten Steps, but share many features with other comprehensive task-analytical models such as Integrated Task Analysis (ITA) from Ryder and Redding (1993; Redding, 1995).

At the rear end, the Ten Steps results in a highly detailed training blueprint which forms the basis for developing a learning environment and producing instructional materials. In the terminology of ISD, it marks the transition from the design phase to the development or production phase. Although the Ten Steps do *not* provide detailed guidelines for these later phases, they have some important implications that must be taken into account. The focus on performing whole learning tasks, for example, requires availability of a real or simulated task environment, with clear implications for selecting suitable media. It also has implications for assessment and the development of self-directed learning because knowledge-oriented testing, for example, is not in agreement with the Ten Steps and should be replaced, or at least be supplemented, by the testing of complex performances (i.e., constructive alignment; Biggs, 1996). These issues are discussed in Chapters 14 and 15.

3.5 Summary

- The instructional design process consists of ten activities: The design of learning tasks, the design of supportive information, the design of procedural information, the design of part-task practice, the sequencing of task classes, the analysis of cognitive strategies, the analysis of mental models, the analysis of cognitive rules, the analysis of prerequisite knowledge, and the setting of performance objectives.
- System dynamics indicate that the output of each activity affects all other activities. In real-life design projects, iterations, skipping activities (layers of necessity), and switches between independent activities are very common, resulting in zigzag design behaviors.
- The pebble-in-the-pond approach is a content-centered modification of traditional instructional design in which one or more learning tasks are first specified rather than the specification of abstract learning objectives. The process

is thus initiated by first casting in a pebble, that is, one or more whole learning tasks, in the instructional design pond. The process unrolls as a series of expanding activities or ripples initiated by this pebble.

- The Ten Steps, ordered according to the pebble-in-the-pond approach, are: (1) design learning tasks, (2) sequence task classes, (3) set performance objectives, (4) design supportive information, (5) analyze cognitive strategies, (6) analyze mental models, (7) design procedural information, (8) analyze cognitive rules, (9) analyze prerequisite knowledge, and (10) design part-task practice.
- The Ten Steps is best used in combination with a broader ISD model that provides guidelines for needs assessment, production, implementation, and evaluation.

PART II

THE TEN STEPS TO COMPLEX LEARNING

4
STEP 1: DESIGN LEARNING TASKS

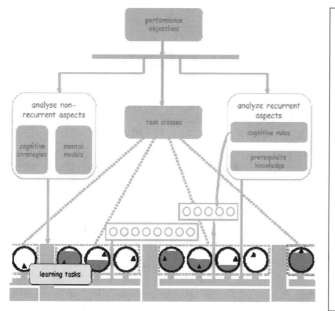

Traditional school tasks are highly constructed, well-structured, well-defined, short, oriented toward the individual, and designed to best fit the content to be taught instead of reality. An archetypical problem of this type is: "Two trains traveling toward each other at a speed of … leave their stations at … How long will it take …?" Such tasks, though often seen as highly suitable for acquiring individual skills, are neither representative for the type of problems that are perceived of as being relevant by the student nor proven to be especially effective for achieving transfer or for acquiring complex skills and competencies.

This chapter presents guidelines for the design of learning tasks, the first design component of the Ten Steps and basic to it. It is the pebble that is cast in the pond. Learning tasks immediately clarify what the learners will be required to *do* during the training. Traditional instructional design models typically use the presentation of subject matter as the skeleton of the training and then add learning tasks, often called "practice items", as meat on these bones. In contrast, the Ten Steps start from the design of meaningful whole-task practice tasks, which are subsequently used as the backbone for connecting the other design components.

The structure of this chapter is as follows. First, the use of real-life tasks as the basis for designing learning tasks is discussed. Second, different types of learning tasks are described, including conventional tasks, imitation tasks, and cases among others, each of which provides different levels of support.

Several methods to provide support and guidance to learners working on the learning tasks are subsequently described. Then, the principle that support and guidance should be diminished in a process of "scaffolding" as learners acquire more expertise is explained. Finally, the importance of the use of a set of varied learning tasks is emphasized. This variability of practice is probably the most powerful instructional method for achieving transfer of learning. The chapter concludes with a brief summary.

4.1   Real-Life Tasks

Real-life tasks, as seen in this book, can be characterized along three major dimensions which influence their design and use, namely the structure of the problem, the equivocality of the solution, and the solver of the problem. The first two dimensions deal with the clarity of the problems and the equivocality of their solutions. In school or training, traditional problems are well-structured, while in the real world problems are often ill-defined or *ill-structured*. Structured problems are problems that are characterized by being limited to a specific domain, as having a set number of possible solutions and as having solutions that are either 100% right or 100% wrong; that is to say, the solutions are unequivocal. Ill-structured problems are fundamentally different. Simon (1973) characterized ill-structured problems as prob-

lems that go further than one specific area, often including important social, political, economic, and scientific problems. Voss (1988) adds that in order to resemble situations in the real world, ill-structured problems have both unclear goals and incomplete information. Finally, ill-structured problems often have no "correct" answer, but rather a number of possible answers that are more adequate or less adequate than others; that is to say, the solutions are not unequivocal.

In other words, real-life problems are problems that cannot usually be described completely, cannot be resolved with a high degree of certainty, and about which experts will often disagree on what the best solution is. The final dimension is often a consequence of the complexity of real-life problems, namely that real-life problems are often so complicated that they need to be solved by a team or group of people - often with expertise in different domains - rather than by an individual. Such a real-life problem encountered every day is a traffic jam.

Real-life tasks that can be used as a basis for the design of learning tasks are best identified by interviewing both professionals working in the task domain and trainers with experience in teaching in that domain. Preparatory activities typically include the study of documentation materials such as technical handbooks, on-the-job documentation, and function descriptions, as well as existing training programs so as to avoid duplicate work. The document study should provide an instructional designer with enough background knowledge to effectively and efficiently interview professionals.

Using real-life tasks as the basis for learning tasks ensures whole-task practice, confronting learners with all or most of the constituent skills that make up complex task-performance. This provides the best opportunities for integration of knowledge, skills, and attitudes and to reach the coordination of constituent skills. It ensures that the learning tasks engage the learners in activities that directly involve them with the constituent skills involved - as opposed to activities in which they have to study general information about or related to the skills. Such a careful design should also guarantee that learning tasks put learning before performance, that is, stimulate learners to focus their attention on cognitive processes for learning rather than solely executing the tasks. This may be reached by making changes to the *environment* in which the tasks are performed and, especially, by providing *support and guidance* to the learners performing the tasks.

Real and Simulated Task Environments

Learning tasks can be performed in a "real" task environment. Computer programming, for example, can be taught in a regular programming environment, repairing cars in an actual garage, and troubleshooting electronic circuits by having learners diagnose and repair actual faulty electronic circuits. However, real task environments sometimes make it difficult or even impossible to provide the necessary support or guidance to learners (e.g., when training fighter pilots in a single-person aircraft or if there are no qualified people available at the time and/or place needed to provide this support and guidance); make it difficult to present the needed tasks (e.g., when training how to deal with situations such as calamities that rarely occur or with technical problems that occur either sporadically or intermittently, and thus cannot be assured to happen); lead to dangerous, life-threatening situations or loss

of materials (e.g., if novice medical students were to practice surgery on real patients), or lead to inefficient training situations that take more time than necessary (e.g., when carrying out a chemical titration where the chemical reaction takes a long time to occur). Furthermore, real task environments may confront learners with a level of detail and work stress that interferes with learning. Thus, it is often worthwhile to use *simulated* task environments that offer a safe and controlled environment where learners may develop and improve skills through well-designed practice.

Simulated task-environments must allow the performance of realistic, authentic tasks right from the beginning of the training program. These simulations, however, often differ in *fidelity*: the degree of correspondence - either physical (i.e., looks like) or psychological (i.e., feels or seems like) - of a given quality of the simulated environment with the real world. Though students of medicine, for example, need to learn to diagnose and treat diseases right from the start, it is not the case that they should immediately begin with real patients. It may be better to start with low-fidelity simulations (e.g., textual problems or case descriptions of prospective patients), then continue with medium-fidelity simulations (e.g., computer-simulated patients, models, or simulated patients played by peer students), continue with high-fidelity simulation (e.g., simulated patients played by actors), and end with the real environment (e.g., real patients during an internship in hospital; see Maran & Glavin, 2003).

Although, in some - impersonal, non-social - domains the added value of practicing in the real environment rather than a high-fidelity simulation of it is questionable because they are almost indistinguishable from each other. This guideline is in agreement with the finding that high-fidelity task environments may be detrimental to novice learners because they provide too many "seductive details", but that they become increasingly important for more experienced learners (e.g., Gulikers, Bastiaens, & Martens, 2005). Above all, it is consistent with the finding that the *psychological* or *functional* fidelity, that is, the degree to which the skills in the real task are captured in the simulated task, is much more important than the physical fidelity of the environment (Patrick, 1992).

Learner Support and Guidance

Learning tasks often provide support and guidance to learners. To design support and guidance, it is of the utmost importance not to merely describe the real-life tasks on which the learning tasks are based in terms of a given situation that professionals might encounter in their domain, but as a full *case study* including an acceptable solution for the problem and, if possible, the problem-solving process that can or has been used for generating this solution. In other words, both a fully *worked out example* of a solution (i.e., task support) and the process-related information used to reach the solution (i.e., guidance) are necessary for the design of suitable learning tasks and the associated support and guidance structures. A general framework of human problem solving (Newell & Simon, 1972) helps distinguish between task support and guidance. According to this framework, four elements are needed to fully describe the learner's work on a learning task or problem: (a) the given state a learner is confronted with; (b) the criteria for an acceptable goal state; (c) a solution, that is, a sequence of *operators* that enables the transformation from the given state to the goal state, and (d) a problem-solving process, which may be seen as the tentative application of mental operations, or, the learner's attempts to reach a solution (see Figure 4.1).

For complex learning, the non-recurrent aspects of learning tasks are often ill-structured; there is not one optimal solution, but rather many acceptable solutions. Furthermore, there may be several intermediate solutions in addition to the final solution. There may also be a number of acceptable solution paths to arrive at similar or different solutions. And finally, the goal states and given states may also be ill-defined, requiring problem analysis on part of the learner (which is then one of the constituent skills involved). Taken together, these characteristics often make it difficult to analyze a real-life task in its given state, goal state, acceptable solution, and problem-solving process for generating a solution. Table 4.1 provides some examples.

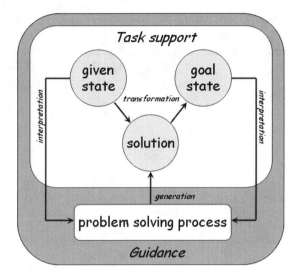

Figure 4.1   A model to distinguish task support provided by different types of learning tasks, and guidance provided by measures that guide learners through the problem-solving process.

The distinction between the solution and the problem-solving process is characteristic for complex learning. This type of learning primarily deals with non-recurrent skills; both the whole skill and often a number of its constituent skills are non-recurrent. To perform such skills, operators are tentatively applied to problem states in order to find a sequence of operators that transforms the initial state into a new state, which must satisfy the criteria for an acceptable goal state. It is like playing chess or checkers, where the sequence of moves made represents the solution and all the provisional moves that are only made in the player's head represent the problem-solving process. In the worst case, random selection of operators or "trial-and-error" behavior occurs where the behavior looks like aimless floundering to an outside observer (Ohlsson & Rees, 1991).

Normally, the search process is guided by cognitive schemas or instructional measures that allow the learner to approach the problem systematically (cognitive strategies) and reason about the domain (mental models). Here, the framework is used to distinguish between task support and guidance. Task support does not pay attention to the problem-solving process itself, only involving given states, goal states, and solutions (e.g., if you are going to go on a vacation trip this would be where the trip begins, where the trip ends, and the routes that can be followed). Guidance, on the other hand, also takes the problem-solving process itself into account and typically provides useful approaches and heuristics to the learners to guide their problem-solving process and help them to reach a solution (e.g., for that same vacation this would be descriptions of different routes for different reasons (shortest, historical, most picturesque), things to see along the way, et cetera).

Table 4.1   Short description of given(s), goal(s), acceptable solution, and problem solving process for four real-life tasks.

Real-life Task	Given(s)	Goal(s)	Acceptable Solution	Problem-Solving Process
Performing literature searches	Client's research question	List with relevant research articles	One ore more search queries that can be run on selected database(s) to produce a list of relevant articles	Applying rules-of-thumb to interview clients and to construct search queries
Trouble-shooting electrical circuits	Electrical circuit with unknown status	Tested electrical circuit with known status	Actions (e.g., traversing a fault tree, diagnostic testing) necessary to reach the goal state	Reasoning about the (mal) functioning of the system to come up with a solution
Controlling air traffic	Radar and voice information reflecting a potentially dangerous situation	Radar and voice information reflecting a safe situation	Actions (e.g., ascertaining aircraft speeds and directions, giving flight directions to pilots) necessary to preserve or reach a safe situation	Continuously devising strategies that may help to maintain or reach a safe situation
Designing buildings	List of requirements	Blueprint and detailed building plan	Actions taken (e.g., requirement specification, drafting blueprint) to design a building plan	Creating alternative and aesthetic solutions within the constraints of given requirements

4.2   Learning Tasks and Support

Different types of learning tasks provide different amounts of support by providing differing amounts of information on the given state, the goal state, and/or the solution. At one end of the continuum are real-life tasks or conventional problems which confront the learner with only a given state and a set of criteria for an acceptable goal state (e.g., starting with a certain mixture distill alcohol with a purity of 98%). These real-life tasks or conventional problems provide the learner with no support and the learner must independently generate the proper solution. At the other end of the continuum where the highest level of support is provided is the case study, which confronts the learner with a given state, a goal state, and a full solution to be studied or evaluated.

A well-designed case study presents learners with descriptions of actual or hypothetical problem situations situated in the real world and requires them to participate actively in the solution (Brown, Collins, & Duguid, 1989; Ertmer & Russell, 1995). For the literature-search example presented in Chapter 2, a case study would confront learners with a research question that a prospective client has (the "given state"), a list of research articles that is not too long and that are directly relevant for the research question (criteria for the "goal state"), and worked-out examples of the search queries for particular databases needed to produce this list of articles (the "solution"; see the top row of Table 4.2). In order to arouse the learners' interest, it may be desirable to use a case study that describes a spectacular event, such as an accident, a success story, or a disputed decision. For example, the case study in question may present a literature-search that uses the keyword "lexicon" to find studies of how children acquire their vocabulary, but that unexpectedly yields a list of dictionaries. In a well-designed case study, learners would be required to answer questions that provoke deep processing of the problem state and of the associated operators (i.e., solution steps) so that they can compare that case with other cases in order to induce generalized solutions. By studying the - intermediate - solutions, learners can get a clear idea of how a particular domain is organized. In this case, they get a good idea about how databases are structured and how search queries are constructed.

As indicated by the columns labeled "Given", "Goal", and "Solution", different types of learning tasks can be constructed by manipulating the information given, the goal state, and/or the solution.

A *reverse task**, for example, presents both a goal state and an acceptable solution (indicated by a plus-sign), but the learners have to trace the implications for different situations. In other words, they have to predict the given. In the context of troubleshooting, Halff (1993) describes "reverse troubleshooting" tasks as tasks for which learners are simply told that a particular component is faulted or has failed. They are then required to predict the behavior of the system based on this information (i.e., what they should have observed in order to reach a correct diagnosis themselves; usually the "given" in a traditional troubleshooting task). Like case studies, reverse tasks focus learners' attention on useful solutions and require them to relate solution steps to given situations.

An *imitation task** presents a conventional task in combination with a case study of an analogous task. The solution presented in the case study provides a blueprint for approaching the new task, focusing attention on possibly useful solution steps. The required imitation is a sophisticated cognitive process where learners must identify the analogy between the case study and the given task, and use the case study to map a new solution (Gick & Holyoak, 1980; Vosniadou & Ortony, 1989). Imitation tasks are quite authentic, because experts often rely on their knowledge of specific cases to guide their problem solving behavior on new problems - a process known in the field of cognitive science as case-based reasoning.

Table 4.2   Examples of different types of learning tasks for the complex skill "searching for relevant research literature" ordered from high task-support (case study) to no task-support (conventional task).

Learning Task	Given	Goal	Solution	Task Description
Case study	+	+	+	Learners receive a research question, a list with articles, and a search query used to produce the list of articles. They must evaluate the quality of the search query and the list of articles.
Reverse	Predict	+	+	Learners receive a list with articles and a search query used to produce the list of articles. They must predict possible research questions for which the list of articles and search query are relevant.
Imitation	+Analog +	+Analog +	+Analog Find	Learners have a worked-out example of a research question available, a list with articles, and a search query used to produce the list of articles. They receive another research question and the goal to produce a list with a limited number of relevant articles. By imitating the given example, they must formulate the search query, perform the search, and select articles for the new research question.
Non-specific goal	+	Define	Find	Learners receive a research question and a highly a-specific goal, for instance to come up with as many search queries as possible that might be relevant to the research question. They must formulate those queries.
Comple-tion	+	+	Complete	Learners receive a research question, the goal to produce a list with a limited amount of relevant articles, and an incomplete search query. They must complete the search query, perform the search and make a selection of articles.
Conven-tional	+	–	Find	Learners receive a research question and the goal to produce a list with a limited amount of relevant articles. They must formulate the search query, perform the search and make a selection of articles.

Tasks with a *non-specific goal* stimulate learners to explore relationships between solutions and the goals that can be reached by those solutions. Usually, learners are confronted with goal-specific problems, such as "A car with a mass of 950 kg accelerating in a straight line from rest for 10 seconds travels 100 meters. What is the final velocity of the car?" This problem could be easily made goal nonspecific by replacing the last line with "Calculate the value of as many of the variables involved here as you can". Here the learner would not only calculate the final velocity, but would also calculate the acceleration and the force exerted by the car at top acceleration. Non-specific goal problems invite learners to move forward from the givens and to explore the problem space, which may help them construct cognitive schemas. This is in contrast to traditional, goal-specific problems that force learners to work backward from the goal. For novice learners, working backward is a cumbersome process that may hinder schema construction (Ayres, 1993; Paas, Camp, & Rikers, 2001; Sweller, 1988; Sweller & Levine, 1982).

Completion tasks provide learners with a given state, criteria for an acceptable goal state, and a partial solution. The learners must then complete the partial solution by determining and adding the missing steps, either at the end of the solution or at one or more places in the middle of the solution. A particularly strong point of completion tasks is that learners must carefully study the partial solution provided to them, because they will otherwise not be able to come up with the complete solution. Completion tasks seem to be especially useful in design-oriented task domains and were originally developed in the domain of software engineering (van Merriënboer, 1990; van Merriënboer & de Croock, 1992), where learners had to fill in missing command-lines in partial computer programs. Well-designed completion tasks ensure that learners can understand the partial solution and still have to perform a non-trivial completion.

The common element of all of the learning tasks discussed is that they direct the learners' attention to problem states, acceptable solutions, and useful solution steps. This helps them mindfully abstract information from good solutions or use inductive processes to construct cognitive schemas that reflect generalized solutions for particular types of tasks. Research on learning tasks other than conventional tasks has provided strong evidence that they facilitate schema construction and transfer of learning for novice learners (for an overview, see Sweller, van Merriënboer, & Paas, 1998; van Merriënboer & Sweller, 2005). The bottom line is that having students solve many problems on their own is often not the best thing for *teaching* them problem solving! For novice learners, studying useful solutions together with the relationships between the characteristics of a given situation and the solution steps applied is much more important for developing problem solving and reasoning skills than solving equivalent problems. Only more experienced learners, who have already developed most of the cognitive schemas necessary to guide their problem solving, should use conventional tasks without support and guidance. Needless to say, eventually providing conventional tasks is important because they provide the most authentic learning tasks, as well as an opportunity for the *summative assessment* of learner performance. In this way, they are similar to real-life tasks (Gulikers, Bastiaens, & Kirschner, 2006a, 2006b).

4.3 Problem Solving and Guidance

Though different types of learning tasks provide different amounts of support, depending on the information presented in the givens, goals, and/or solutions, they do not deal with the problem-solving process that needs to take place to generate an acceptable solution (see the bottom square in Figure 4.1). Another way to provide support to learners is to *guide* them through the problem-solving process. To provide such guidance, one could specify the phases an expert typically goes through while performing the task or solving the problem, as well as the rules-of-thumb that may be helpful to successfully complete each of the phases. Such a *Systematic Approach to Problem solving* (SAP) may result from an analysis of cognitive strategies (see Chapter 8). Problem-solving guidance may be provided in the form of modeling examples, process worksheets, and performance constraints.

Modeling Examples

Maximum guidance is provided by *modeling examples* because they confront learners with professionals performing the complex task, simultaneously explaining why the task is being performed the way it is. A modeling example is, thus, similar to a case study that needs to be studied and evaluated by the learner, but which also pays explicit attention to the processes needed to reach an acceptable solution. According to the theory of *cognitive apprenticeship* (Collins, Brown, & Newman, 1989), where modeling is one of the main features, it is essential to present a credible, appropriate role model. Thinking-aloud during the solution process, for example, may be a very helpful technique for bringing the hidden mental problem-solving processes of the professional out into the open (Van Gog, Paas, van Merriënboer, & Witte, 2005). The thinking-aloud protocol yields the information that is necessary to specify the process information in a modeling example or the transcript may be directly presented to the learners. As for case studies, learners who study modeling examples often can either be confronted with the "thinking" involved in the narrative of the case description or they can be asked to answer questions that provoke deep processing and abstraction of cognitive strategies supplemental to the narrative. By studying the modeling example, learners can get a clear impression of the problem-solving phases that professionals go through and the rules-of-thumb that they use to complete each phase successfully.

For the literature-search example presented in Chapter 2, a modeling example might take the form of a one- or two-day internship that allows the learner to accompany and observe an experienced librarian. Observations would yield a complete picture of the whole task and include conversations that the librarian has with clients to determine the relevant field of study and select appropriate databases for the research question; formulating search queries including the use of thesauri and the application of Boolean operators; performing the search with relevant search programs and different databases; and evaluating and selecting useful search results. The librarian should explain what is being done and why it is being done in a particular way. The modeling example should also allow the learner to see how systematic approaches to problem solving and rules-of-thumb are used to reason through difficult situations and overcome impasses. Of course, such modeling can also be "canned" using video or multimedia materials in which the model solves a problem while simultaneously explaining what she or he is doing.

Process Worksheets

A *process worksheet* (van Merriënboer, 1997; van Gog, Paas, & van Merriënboer, 2004) provides learners with the steps that they need to take to solve a problem and guides them through the problem solving process. In other words it provides them with a systematic approach to problem solving (SAP) for the learning task. A process worksheet may be as simple as a sheet of paper with an indication of the problem-solving phases (and, if applicable, sub phases) that might be helpful for carrying out the learning task. The learner literally uses it as a guide for solving the problem. For each phase, rules-of-thumb are provided that may be helpful for successfully completing the phase. These rules-of-thumb may take the form of statements (e.g., When preparing a presentation, take the prior knowledge of your audience into account) or be posed in the form of guiding questions (e.g., which aspect(s) of your audience should be taken into account when preparing a presentation, and why?). An advantage of using the interrogatory form is that learners are provoked to *think* about the rules-of-thumb. Furthermore, if they write their answers to these questions down on the process worksheet, it allows the teacher to observe their work and provide feedback on the applied problem-solving strategy. It should be clear that both the phases and the rules-of-thumb have a heuristic nature: They may help the learner to solve the problem, but they do *not* necessarily do so. This distinguishes them from procedures which are algorithmic in nature. Table 4.3 provides an example of phases in problem-solving and rules-of-thumb used in a course for Law students who were trained to carry out a plea in court.

On the other hand, process worksheets can be complex and highly sophisticated. Computer supported applications, for example, can add new functionalities to traditional process worksheets. Some SAPs, for example, might be branched such that certain phases may be different for different types of problems.

Table 4.3   Phases and rules-of-thumb for the complex skill "preparing a plea" (adapted from Nadolski, Kirschner, van Merriënboer, & Hummel, 2001).

Phase in Problem-solving Process	Rules-of-thumb / Guiding Questions
1. Order the documents in the file	Try to order the documents chronologically, categorically (e.g., legal documents, letters, notes), or by relevance.
2. Get acquainted with the file	Answer questions such as "Which sub domain of law is relevant here"? or "How do I estimate my client's chances"?
3. Study the file thoroughly	Answers questions such as "What is the specific legal question here"? "What sections of the law are relevant in this case"? or "What legal consequence is most convenient for my client"?
4. Analyze the situation for preparing and conducting the plea	Answer questions such as "Which judge will try the case"? "Where will the trial take place"? or "At what time of day"?
5. Determine a useful strategy for preparing and conducting the plea	Weigh the importance of the results of phases 3 and 4 and take your own capabilities (e.g., your style of pleading) into account when deciding about aspects to include in your plea.
6. Determine the way to proceed from the strategy to pleading	Write a draft plea note in spoken language using the results of phases 3 and 5. Always keep your goal in mind and use a well-argumented style to express yourself.
7. Determine the way to proceed from the plea note to conducting the plea	Transform the plea note into index cards containing the basic outline of your plea and practice the plea with the index cards paying attention to verbal and non-verbal aspects of behavior.
8. Make the plea and practice it	Ask friends to give you feedback on your plea, and record your practice pleas on videotape for self-evaluation.
9. Plead in court	Pay attention to the reactions of the various listeners and adapt your style to them.

With the aid of the computer, it is currently possible to change or adapt an electronic process worksheet according to the decisions the learners make, their progress through the solution of the problem, and the outcomes of the previous phases which have been completed (i.e., learner adaptation). In addition, to providing a process worksheet to learners, one may also offer them *cognitive tools* (Lajoie, 2000) or mindtools (Jonassen, 1999, 2000) that help them to perform the problem solving activities for a particular phase. Mindtools are not pieces of specialized software that "teach" a subject, but computer programs and applications that facilitate meaningful professional thinking and working (Kirschner & Wopereis, 2003). Such tools invite and help learners to approach the problem at hand as an expert would. For example, a mindtool could offer an electronic form for performing a situational analysis (phase 4 in Table 4.3); another, more advanced tool could offer facilities for evaluating video recordings of pleas on their strong and weak points (phase 8).

At this point, a distinction needs to be made between learning *with* something (e.g., a tool, a computer program, ICT) and learning *from* something. In learning with something, short-term goals are achieved where the thing that has been used is the enabler. Using project-planning software in project-centered learning will help learners plan their projects properly in the short-term, and hand them in on time. In learning from something, long-term goals are achieved where the thing that has been used causes a change in the way the learner thinks and works. Using the same example, in the long run if the project planning software has taught learners to organize their thoughts, take critical paths and products into account, and plan their work efficiently (long) after having completed the project, then this is a case of learning from the mindtool (Kirschner & Davis, 2003).

Performance Constraints

Process worksheets are designed to guide learners through the problem-solving process, but learners are free as to whether they use them and if they do use them, skip phases, ignore rules-of-thumb, and so forth. A more directive approach to giving guidance uses *performance constraints*, also known as the *training wheels approach* (Carroll, 1998; Carroll & Carrithers, 1984), because there is a clear resemblance to using training wheels on children's bicycles. The basic idea is to make particular actions that are not relevant in a particular phase of the problem-solving process unavailable to the learners in that phase (Dufresne, Gerace, Thibodeau-Hardiman, & Mestre, 1992). Those actions can only be taken after the learners have successfully completed the previous phase(s) and start to work on the phase for which the actions *are* relevant. For instance, Law students learning to prepare a plea that is to be made in court would not be allowed to start reading documents (phase 2) before they have acceptably ordered all documents (phase 1); or they would not be allowed to use the electronic form for performing a situational analysis (a tool for phase 4) before thoroughly studying the whole file (phase 3; Nadolski, Kirschner, & van Merriënboer, 2005). Well-designed performance constraints might also reduce the number of phases, or increase the complexity of each phase, if learners acquire more expertise (Nadolski, Kirschner, van Merriënboer, & Wöretshofer, 2005). Because performance constraints are more directive than process worksheets, they may be particularly useful for early phases in the learning process.

4.4   Scaffolding Support and Guidance

Scaffolds, in their original meaning within educational psychology (Bruner, 1975; Wood, Bruner, & Ross, 1976) was defined as an "adult controlling those elements of the task that are essentially beyond the learner's capacity, thus permitting him to concentrate upon and complete only those elements that are within his range of competence" (Wood et al., p. 90). According to Rosenshine and Meister (1992) scaffolds include those devices or strategies that sustain a student's learning. Finally, according to Greenfield (1984, 1999) analogous to scaffolds as used in construction a scaffold for learning has "five characteristics: it provides a support; it functions as a tool; it extends the range of the worker; it allows the worker to accomplish a task not otherwise possible; and it is used selectively to aid the worker where needed" (p. 118). Scaffolding is currently seen to be a combination of learner support and the fading of that support, as in a scaffold that supports the construction of a new building and that is slowly taken apart as the building nears completion. Initially, support and guidance enable a learner to achieve a goal or carry out an action that is not achievable without that support and guidance.

When the learner becomes capable of achieving the desired goal or of carrying out the required action, the support and guidance is gradually diminished until it is no longer needed. Because irrelevant, ineffective, excessive, or insufficient support and guidance can hamper the learning process (by adding extraneous cognitive load to the learner), it is critical to determine the right type and amount of learner support and guidance needed and to fade it at the appropriate time and rate.

Scaffolding complex performance does not "direct" learners, as is the case when teaching an algorithm, but rather guides them during their work on rich learning tasks. Modeling the use of cognitive strategies by thinking aloud; providing process worksheets, guiding questions and checklists; applying performance constraints, and giving parts of the solution as is done in several types of learning tasks are all examples of such problem-solving support and guidance (see Table 4.4).

Table 4.4   Scaffolding techniques and type of fading.

Technique	Fading
Modeling cognitive strategies by thinking aloud	First explicate all decision-making, problem-solving, and reasoning processes in detail but reduce the level of detail as learners acquire more expertise.
Providing process worksheets, guiding questions, or checklists	Slowly reduce the amount of (sub) phases, questions, and rules-of thumb that are given to the learner.
Applying performance constraints	First block all learner actions not necessary to reach a solution and continuously make more and more actions available to the learner.
Examples or parts of the solution	Work from case studies or fully worked examples, via completion assignments, toward conventional tasks. This fading guidance is also known as the 'completion strategy'.

There is a strict necessity for scaffolding due to the *expertise reversal effect*. Research on expertise reversal indicates that that highly effective instructional methods for novice learners can lose their effectiveness and even have negative effects when used with more experienced learners (for examples, see Kalyuga, Ayres, Chandler, & Sweller, 2003; Rikers & Paas, 2005; Van Gog, Ericsson, Rikers, &

Paas, 2005). There is overwhelming evidence that conventional tasks force novice learners to use weak problem-solving methods that bear little relation to schema-construction processes concerned with learning to recognize problem states and their associated solution steps. Thus, for novice learners, learning to carry out conventional tasks is different from and incompatible with the way they are "supposed to be" carried out; that is, the way that experts carry them out. Giving novices proper support and guidance is necessary to allow learning to occur (van Merriënboer, Kirschner, & Kester, 2003). For more experienced learners, on the other hand, support and guidance may not be necessary or may even be detrimental to learning because more experienced learners have already acquired the cognitive schemas that may guide their problem-solving and reasoning processes. These cognitive schemas may interfere with the examples, process worksheets, or other means of support and guidance provided to them. Rather than risking conflict between the experienced learners' available cognitive schemas and the support and guidance provided by the instruction, it is preferable to eliminate the support and guidance. This means that large amounts of support and guidance should be given for learning tasks early in the training program (when the learners are novices), whereas no support and guidance should be given for the final learning tasks in a training program (when these same learners have become experienced). Thus, "external guidance" by instructional materials is gradually replaced by "self guidance".

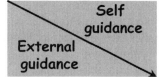

One especially powerful approach to scaffolding is known as the "completion strategy" (van Merriënboer, 1990; van Merriënboer & de Croock, 1992). In this strategy, learners first study cases, then work on completion tasks, and finally perform conventional tasks (Appendix 2 presents an example of this sequence). Such completion tasks offer a bridge between case studies and conventional tasks, because case studies can be seen as completion tasks with a *full* solution, while conventional tasks can be seen as completion tasks with *no* solution. This completion strategy was implemented in an e-learning program for introductory computer programming by van Merriënboer, Krammer, and Maaswinkel (1994; see also van Merriënboer & Luursema, 1995; van Merriënboer, Luursema, Kingma, Houweling, & de Vries, 1995). The learners studied, evaluated, and tested existing computer programs at the beginning of their training so that they could develop cognitive schemas of the templates (i.e., stereotyped patterns of code) used in computer programs. In the course of the training, learners had to complete larger and larger parts of given computer programs. The completion tasks were (dynamically) constructed in such a way that learners received a partial program consisting of templates for which they had *not* yet constructed cognitive schemas, and had to complete this partial program with templates for which they already *did* have useful schemas in memory. Finally, the learners had to independently design and write full computer programs from scratch. This completion strategy has been applied in several other domains and experimental studies carried out there have consistently shown positive effects on learning (e.g., Renkl & Atkinson, 2003; Renkl, Atkinson, Maier, & Staley, 2002; van Merriënboer, Kirschner, & Kester, 2003).

4.5 Variability of Practice

Well-designed learning tasks should always facilitate a process known as *inductive learning*: Students construct general cognitive schemas of how to approach problems in the domain, and of how the domain is organized, based on their concrete experiences offered by the tasks (see Box 2). This process may be further stimulated by the use of a varied set of learning tasks differing on those dimensions in the same way that they also differ in the real world. The use of a varied set of tasks is probably the most commonly recommended method for enhancing transfer of learning and, indeed, has been shown most consistently to have beneficial effects on transfer (Cormier & Hagman, 1987; Detterman & Sternberg, 1993). One may ensure that learning tasks differ from each other on dimensions such as the conditions under which the task is performed (e.g., a literature-search task that is time constrained as is the case when a research proposal is nearing deadline or not as is the case when there is no deadline), the way of presenting the task (e.g., a literature-search task based upon a written request or a personal visit of the client), the saliency of defining characteristics (e.g., a literature-search task that must deliver specific outcomes or an open task), and the familiarity of the task (e.g., a literature-search task in a familiar domain as opposed to a domain foreign to the learner), and/or one may require learners to perform different versions of a task over different problem situations (e.g., diagnosing a car problem or repairing a car in a clean, warm, and fully equipped garage is quite different than diagnosing or repairing that same car problem on a cold, dark, rainy street with a limited set of tools). It may also be helpful to tell the learners *that* variability is applied, and explain to them in some detail *why* it is applied to increase their awareness and their willingness to invest effort in *mindful abstraction* (Annett & Sparrow, 1985).

Box 2 - Induction and Learning Tasks

Well-designed learning tasks offer learners concrete experiences for constructing new cognitive schemas and modifying existing ones in memory. *Induction* is at the heart of complex learning and refers both to generalization and discrimination:

Generalization

When learners *generalize* or abstract from concrete experiences, they construct schemas that leave out the details so that they apply to a wider range of events or to less tangible events. A more general or abstract schema may be constructed if a set of successful solutions is available for a class of related problems. Then, the schema describes the common features of successful solutions. For instance, a child may find out that 2 + 3 and 3 + 2 both add up to 5. One simple schema or principle that might be induced here is "if you add two digits, the sequence in which you add them is not important for the outcome"; the law of commutativity. Another, even more general schema that might be induced is 'if you add a *list* of digits, the sequence in which you add the digits is of no importance for the outcome.'

Discrimination

In a sense, *discrimination* is the opposite of generalization. Suppose the child makes the *over-*

---

generalization "if you perform a computational operation on two digits, the performance sequence is not important for the outcome". In this case, discrimination is necessary fto arrive at a more effective schema. Such a schema may be constructed if a set of failed solutions is available for a class of related problems. Then, particular conditions may be added to the schema and restrict its range of use. For instance, if the child finds out that 9-4 = 5 but 4-9 = -5 (*minus* 5), the more specific schema or principle induced is "if you perform a computational operation on two digits, *and this operation is not subtraction (added condition)*, the sequence in which you perform it is not important for the outcomes". While this schema is still an overgeneralization, discrimination has made it more effective than the original schema.

Mindful Abstraction

Induction is typically a strategic and controlled cognitive process, requiring conscious processing from the learners to generate plausible alternative conceptualizations and/or solution paths when faced with novel or unfamiliar tasks or task situations. While mindful abstraction may be based on one single learning task, it is greatly facilitated by the use of a number of learning tasks differing from each other on those dimensions that also differ in the real world. Such *variability of practice* is expected to encourage inductive processing because it increases the chances that similar features can be identified and that relevant features can be distinguished from irrelevant ones. Mindful abstraction can be learned, and includes processes as comparing and contrasting information, searching for analogical knowledge, analyzing new information in its parts or kinds, and so on. These higher-order skills are the key for effective schema-construction, and for some target groups it may be necessary to explicitly teach self-study skills and learning strategies.

Implicit Learning

Some tasks lacking clear decision algorithms involve integrating large amounts of information. In this case, *implicit learning* is sometimes more effective than mindful abstraction to induce cognitive schemas. Implicit learning is more-or-less unconscious and occurs when learners work on learning tasks that confront them with a wide range of positive and negative examples. For example, if air traffic controllers must learn to recognize dangerous air traffic situations from a radar screen, one may confront them with thousands of examples of dangerous and safe situations. They are in this way trained to distinguish between these situations in a split second - without the need to articulate the schema that allows them to make the distinction.

Further Reading

Gick, M. L., & Holyoak, K. J., (1983). Schema induction and analogical transfer. *Cognitive Psychology, 15,* 1–38.

Holland, J. H., Holyoak, K. J., Nisbett, R. E., & Thagard, P. R. (Eds.) (1989). *Induction: Processes of inference, learning, and discovery.* Cambridge, MA: MIT Press.

Lewis, M. W., & Anderson, J. R. (1985). Discrimination of operator schemata in problem solving: Learning from examples. *Cognitive Psychology, 17,* 26–65.

Reber, A. S., (1989). Implicit learning and tacit knowledge. *Journal of Experimental Psychology: General, 118,* 219–135.

Reber, A. S., (1996). *Implicit learning and tacit knowledge: An essay on the cognitive unconscious.* Oxford: Oxford University Press.

A special kind of variability deals with the issue of how to sequence learning tasks. If adjacent learning tasks cause learners to practice exactly the same constituent skills, then so-called *contextual interference* (Shea, Kohl, & Indermill, 1990) is low. If, on the other hand, adjacent learning tasks cause learners to practice different - versions of - constituent skills, interference is high and will help learners develop a more integrated knowledge base. Take, for example, the situation when a troubleshooting task where three types of malfunctions (m1, m2, m3) can occur in four different components of a technical system (c1, c2, c3, c4) is trained. Low contextual interference would imply a sequence of learning tasks where the skills for troubleshooting one particular type of malfunction are fully practiced in each of the components before the skills for troubleshooting other types of malfunctions, yielding a 'blocked' practice schedule like this:

m1c1, m1c2, m1c3, m1c4 m2c1, m2c2, m2c3, m2c4 m3c1, m3c2, m3c3, m3c4	A blocked sequence of learning tasks

In contrast, a high contextual interference condition would sequence the learning tasks in such a way that they each require different solutions, using a 'random' practice schedule like this:

m3c1, m2c2, m3c4, m1c1 m1c3, m2c1, m2c3, m2c4 m1c4, m1c2, m3c3, m3c2	A randomized sequence of learning tasks

Studies on contextual interference show that it is not only the variability per se, but also the way in which this variability is structured across learning tasks that determines the extent of transfer of learning. Learners who practiced under high contextual interference were better able to solve new problems than students who practiced under low contextual interference (de Croock, van Merriënboer, & Paas, 1998). Thus, it is advised to use a varied set of learning tasks and to sequence those tasks in a randomized order. Although variability and random sequencing may lead to a somewhat longer training time and/or to a higher number of learning tasks needed to reach a pre-specified level of performance, every bit of it pays itself back in a higher transfer or learning. This is an example of what has been called the *transfer paradox* in Chapter 1 (see Sweller, van Merriënboer, & Paas, 1998; van Merriënboer, de Croock, & Jelsma, 1997). If you want to reach transfer of learning, you need to work harder and longer. As the saying goes: "No pain, no gain".

At the conclusion of this chapter a warning is needed. We have seen that, for novice learners, conventional tasks without support and guidance are not the best way to facilitate learning. But a varied set of such conventional tasks, sequenced in a randomized order, is even more likely to be disastrous for novice learners because they can be overwhelmed with the complexity and variation. For novice learners, there is an important interaction between variability and type of learning tasks that is explicitly taken into account in the Ten Steps: If variability or high interference is combined with learning tasks with ample support and guidance (e.g., case studies, reverse tasks, tasks with process worksheets), it typically has a positive effect on transfer of learning (see Figure 4.2).

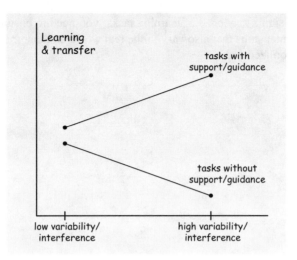

Figure 4.2   Effect of guidance and support on learning and transfer with tasks of Differing variability and interference.

Consequently, this is what should be done at the beginning of a training program. But if variability or high interference is combined with learning tasks without any support and guidance, it has either no effect or even detrimental effects on learning and transfer (Paas & van Merriënboer, 1994a; van Merriënboer, Schuurman, de Croock, & Paas, 2002; Wulf & Shea, 2002). Thus variability and high interference can only be safely combined with conventional tasks for experienced learners.

4.6   Summary of Guidelines

- If you design learning tasks, you need to take real-life tasks as a starting point for design.
- If you design task environments, you need to consider starting with safe, simulated, low-fidelity task environments, and work via increasingly higher-fidelity task environments toward the real task environment.
- If you design learner support for learning tasks, you need to distinguish between built-in task support and guidance for problem solving.
- If you design task support, you need to consider the use of case studies, reverse tasks, imitation tasks, tasks with a-specific goals, and completion tasks.
- If you design guidance for problem solving, you need to consider the use of modeling examples, process worksheets, and performance constraints or training wheels.
- If you design a sequence of learning tasks, you need to ensure that learners start with learning tasks with a high level of support and guidance, but end with tasks without support and guidance ("scaffolding").

STEP 1

- If you design a sequence of learning tasks, you need to ensure that they vary on the dimensions that also vary in the real world and that they are sequenced in a randomized order.

5
STEP 2: SEQUENCE TASK CLASSES

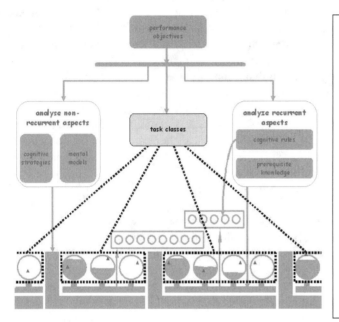

Necessity

Task classes organize learning tasks in easy-to-difficult categories. In highly exceptional cases as short training programs, you might skip this step and treat all learning tasks as belonging to one-and-the-same task class.

Although the Ten Steps makes use of authentic whole tasks, it is definitely not the case that the learner is "thrown into the deep end of the swimming pool to either swim or drown". When learning to swim - in the Netherlands in any event - children begin in very shallow water with very simple techniques and with the aid of different types of flotation devices. They progress through a series of eight stages until they are capable of doing all of the things necessary for getting their first swimming diploma such as treading water for 15 seconds fully clothed, swimming two different strokes (crawl and backstroke) for 25 meters each, and swimming under water for 3 meters. After getting this diploma they can go on to their next diplomas in the same way. The techniques they have to learn and the steps that they have to carry out are, for the most part, organized from simple to difficult through the stages.

This chapter discusses methods for the sequencing of task classes that define easy-to-difficult categories of learning tasks. Task classes have also been called *equivalence classes* (Scandura, 1983), *problem sets* (White & Frederiksen, 1990), and *case types* (van Merriënboer, 1997). For each task class, the characteristics or features of the learning tasks that belong to it need to be specified. This allows both already developed learning tasks to be assigned to their appropriate task classes as well as additional tasks to be selected and developed. The progression of task classes, filled with learning tasks, provides a global outline of the training program.

The structure of this chapter is as follows. First, *whole-task sequencing*, including simplifying conditions, emphasis manipulation, and knowledge progression methods for defining task classes, is discussed. These methods all start the training program with a task class immediately containing *whole* tasks, representative for tasks encountered in the real world. Then, the issue of learner support for tasks within the same task class is considered. Whereas learning tasks within the same task class are equivalent in terms of difficulty, a high level of support is typically available for the first learning task; this is gradually and systematically decreased through the following tasks until no support is available for the final learning task(s) within the same task class. Third, *part-task sequencing* is discussed. In exceptional cases where it proves to be impossible to find a task class easy enough to start the training, it may be necessary to break the complex skill down into meaningfully interrelated clusters of constituent skills (the "parts") that are subsequently dealt with in the training program. The chapter concludes with a brief summary.

5.1   Whole-Task Sequencing of Learning Tasks

Whole-task sequencing ensures that learners work on whole tasks in each task class: Task classes only differ in difficulty. This is in contrast to part-task sequencing, where learners sometimes work on parts of the whole task and task classes may differ in the parts practiced (see Section 5.3). The Ten Steps strongly advocate a whole-task approach to sequencing. This is based on the premise that learners should quickly acquire a complete view of the whole skill that is gradually embellished during training. Ideally, even the first task class refers to the easiest version of whole tasks that professionals encounter in the real world. Each new task class contains learning tasks in the learner's *zone of proximal development* (Vygotsky, 1934/1987, 1978); "…the distance between the actual development level as determined by independent problem solving and the level of potential development as determined through problem solving under adult guidance or in collaboration with more capable peers" (1978, p. 86). This provides learners the best opportunities to pay attention to the integration of all skills, knowledge, and attitudes involved and to the necessary coordination of constituent skills. It is akin to the "global before local skills" principle in *Cognitive Apprenticeship Learning* (Collins, Brown, & Newman, 1989) and the "zoom lens metaphor" in Reigeluth's *Elaboration Theory* (1987b; Reigeluth & Rodgers, 1980; Reigeluth & Stein, 1983; see Figure 5.1). If you study a picture through the zoom lens of a camera, you will usually start with a wide-angle view. This provides the whole picture with its main parts and the relationships between them, but without any detail. Zooming in on different parts of the picture allows you to see more detail of the subparts and the relationships between those subparts. A continuing process of zooming in and out of the whole picture allows the learner to gradually progress to the level of detail and breadth desired. This technique is often used in learning programs. For example, for learning the structural and functional elements of a car and the relationships between them one would present an overview of the major parts (i.e., chassis, engine, drive train, steering, et cetera) at a first hierarchical level and then continually zoom in and out to teach about the specific parts (e.g., crank shaft, gear box) as well as the relationships between the parts.

Figure 5.1   The zoom lens metaphor.

The next sections discuss three whole-task methods for sequencing easy-to-difficult task classes. The *simplifying conditions* method identifies conditions that simplify task performance and describes each task class in terms of whether those conditions are present or not. The *emphasis manipulation* method identifies sets of constituent skills that may be emphasized or de-emphasized during training and includes more and more sets of emphasized skills for later task classes. Finally, *knowledge progression* methods base a sequence of task classes on the results of an in-depth task analysis and knowledge analysis.

Simplifying Conditions

In the simplifying conditions approach, the learner is taught all constituent skills at the same time, but the conditions under which the whole skill is trained change, and gradually increase in difficulty during the training. The first task class is representative of the easiest version of whole tasks that professionals might encounter in the real world; the final task class represents all real-life tasks that the learners must be able to perform after the training. This approach was illustrated in Chapter 2 for "searching for literature". Examples of simplifying conditions that can be identified for this skill are varying the:

- *clarity of concept definitions* within or between research domains for the search (ranging from clear to unclear)
- *number of articles* written about the topic of interest (ranging from few to many)
- *number of research domains* in which relevant articles have been published and hence, the number of databases that need to be searched (ranging from one familiar database to many, sometimes unfamiliar, databases)
- *type of search needed* (ranging from a search on unrelated words that might be used to a search based on domain specific phrases or combinations of words)
- *number of search terms* and Boolean operators that need to be used (ranging from few search terms to many search terms interconnected with Boolean operators)

These simplifying conditions indicate the lower and upper limits for the progression of easy-to-difficult task classes. The easiest task class contains learning tasks that confront learners with situations where the search is performed in a neatly arranged research domain with clearly defined concepts; resulting in only a few relevant articles; in one bibliographical database; on simple keywords; and with few search terms. The most complex task class includes learning tasks that confront learners with situations where the search is performed in research domains with vaguely defined or ambiguous concepts; resulting in many and varied relevant articles; in several bibliographical databases; on domain-specific word or letter combinations; and with many search terms that need to be combined with Boolean operators. Within these limits, a limited number of task classes can be defined by varying one or more of the simplifying conditions. For an example of task classes, see the preliminary training blueprint in Table 5.2 later in this chapter.

Another example can be given for the highly complex skill of patent examination. Patent examiners follow a two-year training program before they are able to deal with all common types of patent applications. For new patent applications, they first have to prepare a "search report". They carefully analyze the application, perform searches in vast databases for already granted related patents, and enter the results of this examination in the search report. If the report indicates that similar patents have already been issued, the client is advised to end the application procedure. Otherwise, a "substantive examination" is conducted. Necessary changes to the patent application are discussed with the client in a process that eventually leads to either the granting or rejecting the application. Amongst others, the following simplifying conditions influence the complexity of patent examination:

- The *clarity* of the patent application (clear or unclear)
- The *conciseness of the claims made* in the application (one single independent claim or a number of related and dependent claims)
- The *need to analyze replies* from the applicant (absent or present)
- The *necessity for interlocutory revision* during the examination process (absent or present)

Given these simplifying conditions, the first task class may be defined as a category of learning tasks that confronts learners with a clear application in which a single claim is made, there is one clear and complete reply by the applicant, and there is no need for interlocutory revision during the examination process. The final task class may be defined as a category of learning tasks that confronts learners with an unclear application where many claims are made with multiple dependencies, with many unclear and incomplete replies from the applicant, and with a need for interlocutory revisions during the examination process. As shown in Table 5.1, additional task classes with an intermediate difficulty level may be added between these two extremes by varying one or more of the simplifying conditions (see also Figure 5.3).

Emphasis Manipulation

In *emphasis manipulation*, learners perform the whole task from the beginning, but different sets of constituent skills are emphasized in different task classes (Gopher, Weil, & Siegel, 1989) allowing learners to focus on the emphasized aspects of the task without losing sight of the whole task. Learners also experience/learn the costs of carrying out the de-emphasized aspects of the task. For example, when teaching medical students to examine patients, specific diagnostic skills may be emphasized in a particular phase of the training program. This will not only help medical students to further develop their diagnostic skills, but will also allow them to experience the costs of developing other skills; their interpersonal and social skills, for example, may suffer from the chosen emphasis on diagnostic skills. Emphasizing and de-emphasizing different - sets of - constituent skills during training, thus requires learners to monitor their priorities and change the focus of their attention to comply with the changes of emphasis. In this way, the emphasis manipulation approach is expected to lead to the development of cognitive schemas that enable learners to better coordinate the constituent skills involved. In contrast to the simplifying conditions method, the learners are exposed to the whole task in its full complexity throughout the training period. This often makes the emphasis manipulation approach less useful for defining early task classes for highly complex tasks.

Table 5.1   Example of task classes for training the highly complex skill of patent examination.

Task Class 1

Learning tasks that confront learners with a clear application in which one single independent claim is made, there is one clear and complete reply of the applicant, and there is no need for interlocutory revision during the examination process. Learners have to prepare the search report and perform the substantive examination.

Task Class 2

Learning tasks that confront learners with a clear application in which one single independent claim is made, there are many unclear and incomplete replies from the applicant, and there is a need for interlocutory revisions during the examination process. Learners have to prepare the search report and perform the substantive examination.

Task Class 3

Learning tasks that confront learners with an unclear application in which a number of claims is made with multiple dependencies, there are many unclear and incomplete replies from the applicant, but there is no need for interlocutory revisions during the examination process. Learners have to prepare the search report and perform the substantive examination.

More task classes may be inserted

Task Class n

Learning tasks that confront learners with an unclear application where a number of claims are made with multiple dependencies, with many unclear and incomplete replies from the applicant, and with a need for interlocutory revisions during the examination process. Learners have to prepare the search report and perform the substantive examination.

A well-chosen sequence of task classes in which different sets of constituent skills are emphasized and de-emphasized is critical to the success of the emphasis manipulation method. Gopher, Weil, and Siegel (1989) propose emphasizing - sets of - constituent skills that (a) are in themselves difficult and demanding for the learners,

(b) when applied, lead to marked changes in the style of performance for the whole task, and (c) are sufficiently different from each other. An example can be found in teacher-training programs where trainees learn to give lessons (i.e., the whole task). Relevant constituent skills deal with presenting subject matter, questioning students, leading group discussions, and so forth. Four possible task classes in agreement with the emphasis manipulation approach would be to:

1 Teach lessons, focusing on the presentation of subject matter
2 Teach lessons, focusing on questioning students
3 Teach lessons, focusing on initiating, maintaining, and leading group discussions
4 Teach lessons

Note that the emphasis manipulation approach typically assumes that the next task class is inclusive. In other words, once the learner has learned to teach a lesson with a subject matter focus, she will continue to do this in the next task class where the focus is on questioning. In the example mentioned earlier, there is also a logical order because it is hard to focus on questioning if there is no subject matter being taught.

Another example, but this time without such a logical order is the replacement of jet engines. This is a complex, but straightforward process with very few simplifying conditions. One can hardly ask a maintenance person to fix a jet engine, but not take care of the fuel system! In this case, emphasis manipulation may be a good

alternative. The main phases in the process are removing the old engines, testing electrical, fuel, and mechanical connections to ensure that they can properly supply the new engine, installing the new engines, and running a test program. A training program for aircraft maintenance could use the following task classes:

1 Replace engines, focusing on safety issues
2 Replace engines, focusing on tool use
3 Replace engines, focusing on accuracy and speed
4 Replace engines

Knowledge Progression

The learning tasks within one task class are always equivalent to each other because they can be performed on the basis of the same body of knowledge. More difficult task classes require more detailed or more embellished knowledge than easier ones. Thus, each task class can be characterized by its underlying body of knowledge or, the other way round, a progression of "bodies of knowledge" can be used to define or refine task classes. This, however, requires an in-depth process of task and knowledge analysis. A first approach is to analyze a *progression of cognitive strategies*. Such strategies specify how to effectively approach problems in the task domain . The progression starts with relatively simple, straightforward strategies and ends with complicated, elaborate strategies. Each cognitive strategy in the progression is then used to define a task class, containing learning tasks that can be performed by applying the cognitive strategy at the given level of specification. This will be further discussed in Chapter 8. Another approach is to analyze a *progression of mental models* that specify how the learning domain is organized. Again, the progression starts with relatively simple models and proceeds toward highly detailed ones. Each mental model is used to define a task class containing learning tasks that can be solved by reasoning on the basis of the associated mental model. This will be further discussed in Chapter 9.

Concluding, it should be noted that the different methods for whole-task sequencing could easily be combined with each other. The simplifying conditions method is typically tried out first. If it is difficult to find enough simplifying conditions, either the emphasis-manipulation approach or a combination of simplifying conditions with emphasis manipulation may be applicable. For instance, the first task class for training patent examination (see the top row in Table 5.1) may be further divided into easier task classes using emphasis manipulation by emphasizing the analysis of applications, the performance of searches, the writing of pre-examination results, the performance of substantive examinations, and finally all those aspects at the same time (in that order). Knowledge progression methods are only applicable if an in-depth task and knowledge analysis is conducted. If these analysis results are available, they are particularly useful for refining an already existing global description of task classes.

5.2   Task Classes and Learner Support

Task support and guidance should decrease as learners acquire more expertise (see Chapter 4). This pattern of diminishing support and guidance (i.e., scaffolding) is repeated *in each task class*. Once the task classes are defined, already developed learning tasks can be classified accordingly and/or additional learning tasks can be developed. Such a clear specification of task classes is very helpful for finding real-life tasks that serve as the basis for learning tasks. A sufficient number of learning tasks is needed for each task class to ensure that learners can practice until mastery before they continue on to a next task class with more difficult learning tasks. The description of the task classes may guide the process of finding useful real-life tasks and developing - additional - learning tasks. For example, one could specifically ask an experienced librarian to come up with concrete examples of tasks in which a successful search has been performed in a clearly defined research field, on keywords that can be used in several databases, with many search terms that had to be connected with Boolean operators, and which yielded a large number of articles (i.e., tasks that fit the second task class in Table 5.2, noted later). In general, a clear specification of task classes is very helpful for finding appropriate real-life tasks that serve as the basis for learning tasks.

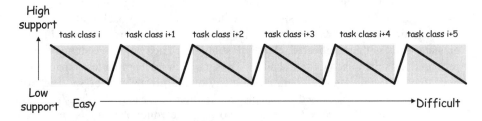

Figure 5.2   A training program with a typical saw-tooth pattern of support.

Whereas the learning tasks within one task class are equivalent to each other and do *not* differ in difficulty, they should exhibit a high level of variability and initially give support and guidance to learners. Above all, support and guidance should be high for the first learning task within a task class and diminish in a process of scaffolding for subsequent tasks, yielding a saw-tooth pattern of support (see Figure 5.2). These principles from Step 1, variability and decreasing support (see Chapter 4), yield a training blueprint consisting of (a) task classes, (b) a varied set of learning tasks within each task class, and (c) learning tasks with high support and guidance in the beginning of the task class and without support in the end of the task class. This basic structure is illustrated for the searching-for-literature example in Table 5.2.

Table 5.2   A preliminary training blueprint: Task classes and learning tasks with decreasing support in each task class for the moderately complex skill "searching for relevant research literature".

Task Class 1
Learners are confronted with situations where the concepts in the to-be-searched domain are clearly defined. Only a small number of articles have been written about the subject and articles have only been written in one field of research. Therefore, the search needs only to be performed on very specific keywords in one database from the particular field of research. There are only a few search terms needed to perform the search and the search will yield a limited number of articles.

Learning Task 1.1: *Case study*
Learners receive three worked-out (good) examples of literature searches. Each example describes a different research question in the same subject matter domain, the search query and the produced list of articles. The learners have to study the examples and explain why the different search queries produced the desired results

Learning Task 1.2: *Completion*
Learners receive a research question and an incomplete search query that produces a list also containing many irrelevant items. They must refine the search query using additional search terms, perform the search, and select the relevant articles.

Learning Task 1.3: *Conventional*
Learners receive a research question. They must perform a literature search for the 10 most relevant articles.

Task Class 2

Learners are confronted with situations where the concepts in the to-be-searched domain are clearly defined. A large number of articles have been written about the subject, but only in one field of research. Therefore, the search needs only to be performed on titles of articles in one database from the particular field of research. However, many search terms need to be interconnected with Boolean operators to limit the otherwise large number of articles the search can yield.

Learning Task 2.1: *Imitation + Constraints*

Learners receive a worked-out example of a research question, a list of articles, and an elaborate Boolean search query to produce the list of articles. They receive a similar research question, and a goal to produce a list with a limited amount of relevant articles. By imitating the example, they formulate the search query, perform the search, and select relevant articles. They can only perform the search after the search query is approved.

Learning Task 2.2: *Completion*

Learners receive a research question and a list of search terms. They have to formulate a search query by combining the given search terms using Boolean operators

Learning Task 2.3: *Conventional*

Learners receive a research question. They have to perform a literature search for the 10 most relevant articles.

Task Class 3

Learners are confronted with situations where the concepts in the to-be-searched domain are *not* clearly defined. Identical terms are used for different concepts, and identical concepts are described by different terms. A large number of articles have been written about the subject and articles have been written in several fields of research. Therefore, along with searching titles of articles, the search also needs to be performed on abstracts and texts using specific phrases/word combinations. Also, databases from different fields of research have to be searched. Many search terms need to be interconnected with Boolean operators to make sure that all relevant articles (using different terminology) are found and that irrelevant articles (using the same terminology as relevant ones) are excluded.

Learning Task 3.1: *Completion + Reverse*

Learners receive a research question and an elaborate search query. They have to predict which databases should be used and then perform the query. They then have to refine the query and select relevant articles.

Learning Task 3.2: *Conventional*

Learners receive a research question. They have to perform a literature search for the 10 most relevant articles.

5.3   Part-Task Sequencing of Learning Tasks

For almost all training programs, whole-task sequencing works and results in a preliminary training blueprint such as the ones presented in Tables 5.1 and 5.2. In exceptional cases, however, it might not be possible to find a task class easy enough to start the training with, that is, it would take more than a few days of preparation before learners can even start to work on the first learning task. Examples of such training situations are complete educational programs for doctors, pilots, or lawyers. *Only* in these cases, is part-task sequencing of learning tasks used to supplement whole-task sequencing (if you are not dealing with such an exceptional case, you may skip this section). Part-task sequencing concerns the determination of the order in which - clusters of - constituent skills (i.e., parts) will be treated in the instruction. Part-task sequencing is very effective in reducing task difficulty, but hinders integration of knowledge, skills, and attitudes and limits the opportunities to learn to coordinate the constituent skills. Therefore, it should be used sparingly and with great care.

Skill Clusters as Parts

Suppose that subject matter experts in the field of patent examination indicate that it will take many weeks to prepare new trainees for even the first task class indicated in Table 5.1 (i.e., clear applications with a single claim, a clear and complete reply of the applicant, with no need for interlocutory revision). Under these circumstances, part-task sequencing may be necessary. A small number of *skill clusters* (usually between 2-5) is identified first. These skill clusters are sets of meaningfully interrelated constituent skills. The smaller the number of skill clusters or "parts" the better it is because this provides better opportunities to reach integration and coordination of knowledge, skills, and attitudes. The chosen clusters must allow learners to start within a reasonable period of time (e.g., in the order of hours or days) with actual practice and each cluster must, in itself, reflect an authentic, real-life task. For example, three meaningfully interrelated parts of the whole-skill "examining patent applications" (see Figure 5.3) are the branches "preparing search reports" (called, for the purpose of generalization part A instead of branch A), "issuing communications or votes" (part B), and "re-examining applications" (part C).

Forward and Backward Chaining with and without Snowballing

Essentially, there are two basic approaches to part-task sequencing, namely forward chaining and backward chaining. *Forward chaining* deals with parts in the same natural process order in which they occur during normal task performance. From knowledge management, it starts with the data available and uses inference rules to include more data until a desired goal is reached. It may take two different forms, namely, with and without *snowballing*. Simple forward chaining (A-B-C) deals with the parts one-by-one. In our example, one would start with teaching "preparing search reports" (part A), then continue with teaching "issuing communications or votes" (part B), and end with teaching "re-examining applications" (part C). Note that learners never practice the whole task. When they practice "issuing communications or votes" they will typically do so on the basis of the reports they prepared in the previous phase, and when they practice "re-examining applications" they will typically do so on the basis of the reports and communications or votes that they prepared in the two previous phases. Forward chaining with *snowballing* (A-AB-ABC) thus includes the previous part(s) in each new part, like a snowball that grows as it rolls down the mountain because new snow continually sticks to it. In our example, one would start with teaching "preparing search reports" (part A), then continue with teaching "preparing search reports" plus "issuing communications or votes" (part AB), and would end with "preparing search reports" plus "issuing communications or votes" plus "re-examining applications" (ABC, which is the whole task). Snowballing generally increases the amount of time necessary for training, but this investment is usually more than worthwhile because it provides better opportunities for integration and learning to coordinate the different skill-clusters that serve as parts.

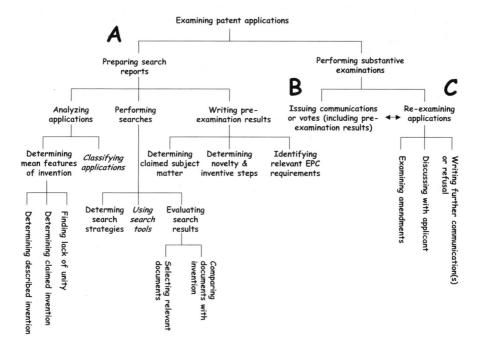

Figure 5.3   Three skill clusters for the highly complex skill "examining patent applications". *Branch A* consists of "preparing search reports" and lower-level skills; *Branch B* consists of "issuing communications or votes", and *Branch C* consists of "re-examining applications" and lower-level skills.

The opposite of forward chaining, *backward chaining*, deals with parts of a whole task in the reverse order or one that is counter-to-performance. In knowledge management, it starts with a list of goals and works backwards to see if there is data which will allow it to conclude any of these goals. Like forward chaining, it may take two different forms. Simple backward chaining (C_{AB} - B_A - A) deals with the parts one-by-one. In our example, one would start with teaching "re-examining applications" (part C_{AB}), then continue with teaching "issuing communications or votes" (part B_A), and end with teaching "preparing search reports" (part A). As in simple forward chaining, learners never practice the whole task, but when they start with part C, they can only do so if they receive ready-made search reports and communications/votes, because they have not yet prepared them - that is to say carried out those parts - themselves. This is indicated by the subscripts: C_{AB} indicates that the learners "re-examine applications" based on search reports plus communications/votes given by the instructor or training program, and B_A indicates that they "issue communications/votes" based upon search reports given by the instructor or training program. Backward chaining with snowballing (C_{AB} - BC_A - ABC) includes the previous part(s) in each new part. In our example, the training would start with "re-examining applications" on the basis of ready-made search reports plus communication/votes (part C_{AB}), continue with "issuing communications/votes" plus "re-examining applications" on the basis of ready-made search reports (part BC_A), and end with "preparing search reports" plus "issuing communications/votes' plus "re-examining applications" (ABC, which is the whole task). Table 5.3 summarizes the four part-task sequencing techniques and presents guidelines for their use.

The guidelines in Table 5.3 are based on two principles. First, sequencing with snowballing is considered to be more effective than sequencing without snowballing because it gives learners the opportunity to practice the whole task (i.e., ABC) and helps them integrate and learn to coordinate the different task-parts. Thus, snowballing should be used if the available instructional time allows for it. Second, backward chaining is considered more effective than forward chaining because it confronts learners with useful examples and models right from the beginning of the training program. This is true for sequencing learning tasks but not for sequencing practice items in part-task practice (see Chapter 13). For instance, if learners first practice the re-examination of patent applications based on given search reports and communications/votes, they get to see and study many useful examples of search reports and communications/votes by the time they start to practice the preparation of those documents themselves.

Table 5.3   Part-task sequencing techniques with guidelines for usage[a].

Simple forward chaining	A-B-C	Do *not* use this for sequencing learning tasks. Use it only for sequencing practice items in part-task practice and if instructional time is severely limited (see Chapter 13)
Forward chaining with snowballing	A-AB-ABC	Do *not* use this for sequencing learning tasks. Use it only for sequencing practice items in part-task practice (see Chapter 13).
Simple backward chaining	C_{AB}-B_A-A	Use this only for sequencing learning tasks if instructional time is severely limited, and if it is impossible to find whole tasks that are easy enough to start the training with.
Backward chaining with snowballing	C_{AB}-BC_A-ABC	*Default* strategy for sequencing learning tasks if it is impossible to find whole tasks that are easy enough to start the training with.

[a]   These techniques should only be used in the exceptional situation that it proves to be impossible to find whole tasks that are easy enough to start the training with.

Several studies have shown that backward chaining with snowballing can be a very effective sequencing strategy. In an old study, Gropper (1973) used it to teach instructional systems design. Initially, learners learn to try out and revise instructional materials (traditionally the *last* part of the instructional design process). They are given model outputs for design tasks - from task descriptions to materials development. In subsequent stages, students learn to design and develop instructional materials. The strategy proved to be very effective because learners had the opportunity to inspect several model-products before being required to perform tasks such as strategy formulation, sequencing, or task analysis themselves. Along the same lines, van Merriënboer and Krammer (1987) described a backward chaining approach for teaching computer programming. Initially, learners evaluated existing software designs and computer programs through testing, reading, and hand tracing (traditionally the *last* part of the development process). In the second phase, they modify, complete, and scale-up existing software designs and computer programs. Only in the third phase did they design and develop new software and computer programs from scratch. The strategy was more effective than a traditional forward-chaining strategy, probably because learners were better able to base their performance on the many models and example programs they had encountered in the early phases.

Whole-Part versus Part-Whole Sequencing

Whole-task sequencing and part-task sequencing may be combined in two ways, namely whole-part sequencing and part-whole sequencing (see Figure 5.4).

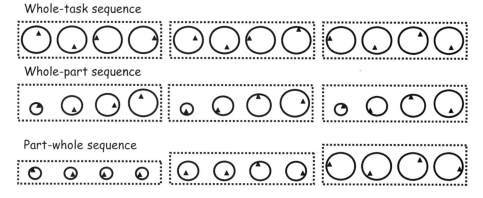

Figure 5.4   A schematic representation of a regular whole-task sequence, a whole-part sequence, and a part-whole sequence. Smaller circles indicate "parts" of the whole task.

In *whole-part sequencing*, a sequence of easy-to-difficult task classes with whole tasks is first developed, using simplifying conditions, emphasis manipulation, and/or knowledge progression. If it turns out that the first task class is still too difficult to start the training, part-task sequencing techniques may be used to divide this first task class and, if desired, subsequent task classes in easy-to-difficult skill clusters or parts. The basic idea is to start with an easy-to-difficult sequence of whole tasks and only then to divide them into parts. *Part-whole sequencing*, in contrast, develops a sequence of easy-to-difficult parts or skill clusters first. If the first part or skill cluster is too difficult to start the training, whole-task sequencing techniques may be used to sequence the parts in easy-to-difficult task classes further. Please note that the term whole-task sequencing is somewhat confusing here, because it pertains to one part or skill cluster that is treated as if it was a whole task. Table 5.4 compares whole-part sequencing with part-whole sequencing. There are three easy-to-difficult task classes (ABC: wholes); three easy-to-difficult skill clusters based on backward chaining with snowballing (C_{AB}, BC_A, ABC: parts), and three learning tasks with high, low, or no support for each task class - skill cluster combination. A clear advantage of whole-part sequencing (left column) over part-whole sequencing (right column) is that learners in a whole-part sequence relatively quickly get the opportunity to practice the whole task (indicated by the shaded cells). This is expected to facilitate integration and coordination. Furthermore, a whole-part sequence makes it possible to easily switch from a whole-part approach to a genuine whole-task approach later in the training program. For example, one might use a whole-part approach in the first task class, but then switch to a whole-task approach by deleting the cells C_{AB}^{me} and BC_A^{mm} from the second task class, and C_{AB}^{de} and BC_A^{dm} from the third task class. Such a switch is not possible in a part-whole sequence.

To recapitulate, whole-part sequencing techniques provide better opportunities to teach coordination and reach integration than part-whole sequencing techniques, and are thus the preferred approach to sequencing complex learning tasks. Part-whole sequencing techniques should only be considered for use if little coordination of constituent skills is required, which may be true for highly complex *recurrent* constituent skills (see Chapter 13 for examples of this).

Table 5.4   A comparison of whole-part sequencing, from task classes to skill clusters, and part-whole sequencing, from skill clusters to task classes. Skill clusters are based on backward chaining with snowballing.

	Whole-Part Sequencing		Part-Whole Sequencing		
Task Class (whole)	Skill Cluster (part)	Learning Task	Skill Cluster (part)	Task Class (whole)	Learning Task
ABC^e	C_{AB}^{ee}	High support	C_{AB}^{e}	C_{AB}^{ee}	High support
	C_{AB}^{ee}	Low support		C_{AB}^{ee}	Low support
	C_{AB}^{ee}	No support		C_{AB}^{ee}	No support
	BC_{A}^{em}	High support		C_{AB}^{em}	High support
	BC_{A}^{em}	Low support		C_{AB}^{em}	Low support
	BC_{A}^{em}	No support		C_{AB}^{em}	No support
	ABC^{ed}	High support		C_{AB}^{ed}	High support
	ABC^{ed}	Low support		C_{AB}^{ed}	Low support
	ABC^{ed}	No support		C_{AB}^{ed}	No support
ABC^m	C_{AB}^{me}	High support	BC_{A}^{m}	BC_{A}^{me}	High support
	C_{AB}^{me}	Low support		BC_{A}^{me}	Low support
	C_{AB}^{me}	No support		BC_{A}^{me}	No support
	BC_{A}^{mm}	High support		BC_{A}^{mm}	High support
	BC_{A}^{mm}	Low support		BC_{A}^{mm}	Low support
	BC_{A}^{mm}	No support		BC_{A}^{mm}	No support
	ABC^{md}	High support		BC_{A}^{md}	High support
	ABC^{md}	Low support		BC_{A}^{md}	Low support
	ABC^{md}	No support		BC_{A}^{md}	No support
ABC^d	C_{AB}^{de}	High support	BC^{d}	ABC^{de}	High support
	C_{AB}^{de}	Low support		ABC^{de}	Low support
	C_{AB}^{de}	No support		ABC^{de}	No support
	BC_{A}^{dm}	High support		ABC^{dm}	High support
	BC_{A}^{dm}	Low support		ABC^{dm}	Low support
	BC_{A}^{dm}	No support		ABC^{dm}	No support
	ABC^{dd}	High support		ABC^{dd}	High support
	ABC^{dd}	Low support		ABC^{dd}	Low support
	ABC^{dd}	No support		ABC^{dd}	No support

Superscripts refer to the difficulty of task classes or learning tasks: ee = easy task class, easy skill cluster; em = easy task class, medium skill cluster or vice versa, md = medium task class, difficult skill cluster or vice versa, and so forth.

Subscripts refer to the output of previous skills given to the learner: C_{AB} = perform C based on given output from A and B; BC_{A} = perform B and C based on given output from A.

Table 5.5 provides an example of a whole-part approach for teaching patent examination. It starts with two task classes that are identical to the task classes presented in Table 5.1 (left column).

Table 5.5   Two Task Classes (Wholes) with Three Skill Clusters (Parts) each for the examination of patents, based on a whole-part sequence and backward chaining with snowballing for the parts.

Task Class 1 Learning tasks that confront learners with a clear application in which one single independent claim is made; there is one clear and complete reply of the applicant, and there is no need for inter-locutory revision during the examination process	Skill Cluster C_{AB} - Task Class 1.1 Learners have to re-examine applications on the basis of given search reports and communications or votes
	Skill Cluster BC_A - Task Class 1.2 Learners have to issue communications or votes and re-examine applications on the basis of given search reports
	Skill Cluster ABC - Task Class 1.3 Learner have to prepare search reports, issue communications or votes, and re-examine applications
Task Class 2 Learning tasks that confront learners with a clear application in which one single independent claim is made; there are many unclear and incomplete replies from the applicant and a need for interlocutory revisions during the examination process.	Skill Cluster C_{AB} - Task Class 2.1 Learners have to re-examine applications on the basis of given search reports and communications or votes
	Skill Cluster BC_A - Task Class 2.2 Learners have to issue communications or votes and re-examine applications on the basis of given search reports
	Skill Cluster ABC - Task Class 2.3 Learners have to prepare search reports, issue communications or votes, and re-examine applications

Add additional task classes / skill clusters

In the first task class, learners deal with clear applications, single independent claims, clear and complete replies, and no need for interlocutory revisions. In the second task class, they still deal with clear applications and single independent claims, but now there are unclear and incomplete replies from the applicant as well as a need for inter-locutory revisions during the examination process. Each task class is further divided into three sub classes representing parts of the task which are carried out in the following order: Learners (a) re-examine applications on the basis of given search reports and communications/votes; (b) issue communications/votes and re-examine applications on the basis of given search reports, and (c) prepare search reports, issue communications/votes, and re-examine applications. Thus, each task class ends with the whole task at an increasingly higher level of difficulty.

5.4   Summary of Guidelines

- If you sequence classes of learning tasks, then you need to start with "whole" tasks that are representative for the easiest tasks a professional might encounter in the real world.
- If you sequence task classes for tasks that occur in easy and more difficult versions, then you need to identify all conditions that simplify task performance and specify the task classes using those simplifying conditions.
- If you sequence task classes for tasks that not occur in easy and more difficult versions, then you need to consider the use of emphasis manipulation where the first task class emphasizes relatively simple aspects and later task classes emphasize increasingly more complex aspects of the task.
- If you want to refine an existing sequence of task classes, then you need to try to identify a progression of cognitive strategies or a progression of mental models enabling the learner to perform the tasks within increasingly more complex task classes.
- If you fill a task class with learning tasks, then you need to apply variability of practice as well as scaffolding, which results in a saw-tooth pattern of support throughout the training program.
- If you are sequencing task classes and it proves to be impossible to find a class of whole tasks that is easy enough to start the training with, then you need to identify a small number of skill clusters or meaningfully interrelated sets of constituent skills (i.e., parts).
- If you sequence skill clusters, then you need to consider the use of a backward-chaining strategy with snowballing first.
- If you combine whole-task sequencing with part-task sequencing for learning tasks that require much coordination, then you need to apply whole-part sequencing rather than part-whole sequencing.

6
STEP 3: SET PERFORMANCE OBJECTIVES

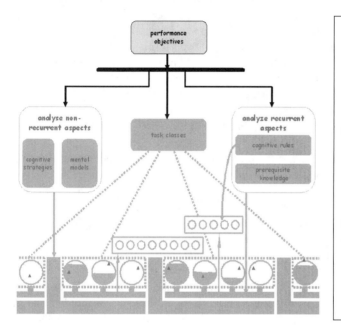

Necessity

An integrated set of performance objectives provides standards for acceptable performance. Standards are used for performance assessment. It is strongly recommended that this step be performed.

As stated in the previous chapter, for children to get their first swimming diploma in the Netherlands, they have to tread water for 15 seconds fully clothed, swim two different strokes (crawl and backstroke) for 25 meters each, and swim under water for 3 meters. These are the performance objectives that have been defined and upon which the swimming lessons are based. Each of these "performances" is further defined, for example, with respect to things such as what constitutes "fully clothed" (i.e., pants, shirt, & shoes), that they have to swim under water through a hoop, how deep they have to be under water, that they have to make a turn along the axis of their body from crawl to backstroke, that there is a specific time minimum for treading water and a maximum for completing the two strokes, et cetera. Children get their first diploma only when they have met these standards for acceptable performance.

This chapter discusses the identification, formulation, and classification of performance objectives. Learning tasks and task classes already give a good impression of what learners will do during and after the training, but performance objectives give more detailed descriptions of the desired "exit behaviors", including the conditions under which the complex skills need to be performed (e.g., fully clothed), the tools and objects that can or should be used during performance (e.g., through a hoop), and, last but not least, the standards for acceptable performance (e.g., 25 meters, turning along their body axis). In the instructional design method proposed, students learn from and practice almost exclusively on whole tasks that are intended to help them acquire an integrated set of performance objectives representing many different aspects of the complex skill. What performance objectives do is help designers to differentiate the many different aspects of whole-task performance and to connect the front end of training design (i.e., What do students need to learn?) to its back end (i.e., Did students learn what they were required to learn?). The standards also provide the basis for performance assessment.

The structure of this chapter is as follows. First, skill decomposition is described as a process for identifying relevant constituent skills and their interrelationships. The result of this skill decomposition is a skill hierarchy. This is followed by a discussion of the formulation of a performance objective for each constituent skill. The whole set of objectives provides a concise description of the contents of the training program, input for subsequent Steps, and feedback to help learners achieve the skills, test them as to this achievement, and evaluate the training program. Third, performance objectives for particular constituent skills are classified as being either non-recurrent or recurrent. Non-recurrent constituent skills always involve problem solving or reasoning and require presenting supportive information while recurrent constituent skills involve the application of rules and require presenting procedural information. Further classifications concern to-be-automated recurrent constituent skills (which may require part-task practice), double-classified constituent skills, and constituent skills that will *not* be taught. The performance objectives of the skills that will be taught provide the basis for discussing the content of the training program with different stakeholders and give input to further analysis and design activities. The final section discusses the use of standards for acceptable performance for the development of a scoring rubric, which is used for performance assessment. The chapter concludes with a brief summary.

6.1 Skill Decomposition

Skill decomposition, splitting a skill into all of its components or basic elements, aims at the description of all constituent skills and the interrelationships between them, which together make up the complex cognitive skill. The result of this decomposition process is a skill hierarchy. As was discussed in Chapter 3.4, the Ten Steps assume that a needs-assessment has been or will be conducted, leading to the conclusion that there actually is a performance problem that can be solved by training, and that there is a preliminary *overall learning goal* for teaching the complex skill involved. This overall learning goal is a statement of what the learners will be able to do after they have completed the training program. In an iterative design process, the overall goal helps decompose the complex skill while the decomposition helps specify the overall goal. The real-life tasks and learning tasks that have been identified in Step 1 will be particularly helpful in facilitating both brainstorming about a good decomposition of the complex skill into its constituent skills and further specification of the overall learning goal. For instance, the preliminary learning goal for a one-and-a-half year training program for patent examiners might be:

> After having followed the training program, the learners will be able to decide upon the granting of patent applications by analyzing the application; searching for relevant prior documents; conducting a substantive examination; delivering a search report where the relevant documents that have been found are cited and their relevancy is acknowledged on the basis of the substantive examination; and communicating the result of the substantive examination to either (a) the examining division so that a patent can be granted immediately, or (b) the applicant so that, at a later stage, a reply can be filed by the applicant and a patent granted, or the application is refused.

Skill Hierarchy

A hierarchy is a system of ranking and organizing things such that lower ranked things are 'contained' or 'subsumed' in the higher level things. Developing a skill hierarchy starts with the primary learning goal (i.e., the top-level skill), which provides the basis for the identification of the more specific constituent skills that enable the performance of the whole skill. The idea behind this is that constituent skills lower in the hierarchy enable the learning and performance of skills that are higher in the hierarchy. This vertical, enabling, relationship is also called a *prerequisite* relationship (Gagné, 1968, 1985). Figure 5.3 in the previous chapter already presented a skill hierarchy for patent examination (another example was provided in Figure 2.2). The hierarchy in Figure 5.3 indicates that in order to be able to examine patent applications, the examiner must be able to prepare search reports; that in order to be able to prepare search reports, the examiner must be able to analyze patent applications; that in order to be able to analyze patent applications, the examiner must be able to determine the main features of a claimed invention; and so forth. Thus, the basic question to reach the next, lower, level in a skill hierarchy is: "Which more specific skills are necessary in order *to be able* to perform the more general skill under consideration?" Levels may be added to the hierarchy until "simple" skills have been identified; skills that can be further analyzed with regular task-analytical techniques (see Chapters 8–9 and 11–12).

The basic question when expanding one particular level of a skill hierarchy is: "Are there any *other* skills necessary to be able to perform the skill under consideration?" This horizontal relationship is indicated from left to right. Figure 5.3 indicates that in order to be able to examine patent applications, one must be able to both prepare search reports *and* perform substantive examinations. This horizontal relationship may be specified in a:

- *Temporal relationship*. This - default - relationship indicates that the skill on the left-hand side is performed *before* the skill on the right-hand side. For instance, when you drive a car you start the engine before you drive away. In Figure 5.3, "preparing search reports" is done before "performing substantive examinations".

- *Simultaneous relationship*. This relationship indicates that the skills are performed at the same time. For example, when you drive a car you will usually be using the gas pedal and the steering wheel simultaneously. In Figure 5.3, "issuing communications or votes" is done simultaneously with "re-examining applications". A double-headed arrow between the skills indicates the simultaneous relationship.
- *Transposable relationship*. This relationship indicates that the skills can be performed in any desired order. For instance, when you drive a car you may first switch off the engine and then set the hand brake or you could just as well do this in the reverse order. In Figure 2.2 "determining the relevant field of study" and "determining the relevant period of time" can be done in any order (or even simultaneously). A double-headed *dotted* arrow between the skills indicates the transposable relationship.

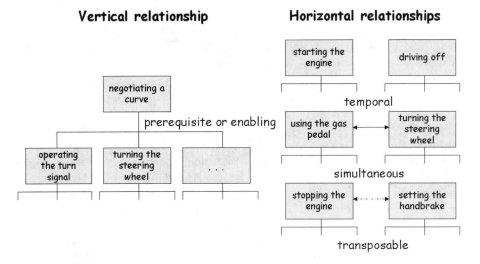

Figure 6.1   Common relationships in a skill hierarchy.

Figure 6.1 summarizes the main relationships distinguished in a skill hierarchy. If desired, relationships other than the horizontal and vertical relation may be used in the skill hierarchy, yielding a so-called *intertwined* hierarchy. In a *heterarchical organization*, the other relationships are limited to the same "horizontal" position level in the hierarchy; thus, a network of constituent skills characterizes each level. In a *reitiary organization*, a complex mapping of relationships may be defined between any two elements to reach a destination; thus, the hierarchy actually becomes a complex network in which constituent skills may have non-arbitrary relationships with any other constituent skills (this is also called a "competence map"; Stoof, Martens, van Merriënboer, & Bastiaens, 2002). For instance, you may specify a *similarity* relationship between two constituent skills indicating that they can be easily mixed up, or you may specify an *input-output* relationship indicating that the performance of one skill provides input for performing another skill. The identification of such relationships may be helpful for further training design.

Data Gathering

The process of building a skill hierarchy is typically conducted by professionals or subject matter experts in the task domain, or by a designer in close cooperation with professionals or subject matter experts. To this end, domain experts are best confronted with real-life tasks or related learning tasks (from Step 1) so that they can explain how those tasks are performed. Alternatively, they can actually perform - parts of - the tasks while thinking aloud allowing close observation or they can be recorded while performing - parts of - the tasks and then questioned about what they did and why they did it afterwards (i.e., cued recall). Professionals are not only necessary for identifying the constituent skills, but are also needed to verify the skill hierarchy in a number of *validation cycles*. In these validation cycles, the designer checks whether the hierarchy contains all of the constituent skills necessary to learn and perform the complex cognitive skill and whether lower-level skills indeed facilitate the learning and performance of those skills higher in the hierarchy. If this is not the case, then the hierarchy needs to be refined or re-organized. Skill decomposition is a difficult and time-consuming process, which needs a number of validation cycles and which is also frequently updated after working on other Steps.

Three helpful guidelines for building a skill hierarchy are *not* to focus (a) directly on a highly complex task, but on simpler versions of the task, (b) only on performance per se, but also on objects and tools used by the task performer, and (c) only on desired task performance, but also on deficiencies in learner performance.

With regard to *task complexity* - a combination of the number of elements in a task and the interactivity between those elements - it will often be the case that real-life tasks and related learning tasks have already been ordered in task classes (Step 2) that distinguish simple and complex versions of the whole task. In order to identify constituent skills, it is best to first confront professional task performers with relatively simple real-life tasks, and only confront them with more difficult (i.e., complex) tasks after all constituent skills for the simpler tasks have been identified.

Objects refer to those things that are changed or attended to while successfully performing a task. As a task performer switches his or her attention from one object to another, this is often an indication of different constituent skills involved. For example, if a patent examiner analyzing an application switches his attention from the application itself to a booklet with classification codes, this may indicate that there are two constituent skills involved, namely: "determining the main features of the invention" and "classifying applications". If a surgeon switches her attention from the patient to a donor organ waiting to be transplanted, it may indicate the constituent skills "preparing the patient" and "getting the donor organ ready".

Tools refer to those things that are used to change objects. As was the case for objects, switches in tools used often indicate that different constituent skills are involved (see also Figure 6.2). For example, if a patent examiner preparing a search report switches between using a marker pen, a search engine, and a word processor, this may indicate that there are three constituent skills involved, namely: "analyzing applications" (where the marker pen is used), "performing searches" (where the search engine is used), and "writing pre-examination results" (where the word processor is used; see Figure 5.3). And if a surgeon switches from using a scalpel to using a forceps, it may indicate the constituent skills "making an incision" and "removing an organ".

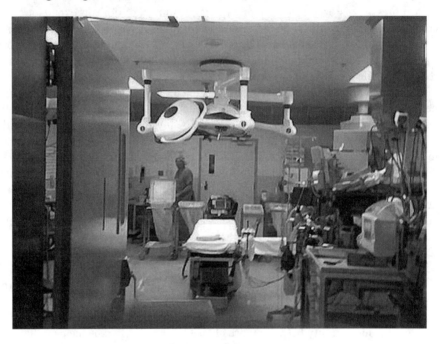

Figure 6.2   Observing the use of objects and tools by proficient task performers may be helpful to identify relevant constituent skills.

Finally, it may be worthwhile not only to focus on the process of gathering data on the desired performance, but also to focus on the *performance deficiencies* of the target group. This change of focus is particularly useful if the target group consists of persons already involved in performing the task or parts of it (e.g., employees that will be trained). This is usually the case when performance problems are observed on the work floor or when such problems are used as the justification for the development of a training program. Performance deficiencies indicate discrepancies between the actual performance of a task and the expected or desired performance of a task. The most common method used to assess such deficiencies is interviewing the trainers themselves (i.e., asking trainers what the typical problems are that their learners encounter), the target learners (i.e., asking employees what problems they encounter), and their managers or supervisors (i.e., asking bosses which undesired effects of the observed problems are most important for them or are most deleterious to the organization). The to-be-developed training program will obviously focus on constituent skills where performance deficiencies are exhibited.

6.2   Formulating Performance Objectives

Many instructional design models use *performance objectives* - the desired result of a learning experience - as the main input for the design decisions to be made. In such models, instructional methods are selected for each performance objective and each objective has its corresponding test item(s) that follow the training program. This is certainly *not* true for the Ten Steps. In complex learning, it is precisely the integration and coordination of constituent skills described by the performance objectives that must be supported by the training program. Thus, instructional methods cannot be linked to one specific objective, but must always be linked to interrelated sets of objectives that can be hierarchical, heterarchical or reitiary and can have a temporal, simultaneous, or transposable relationship. This means that design decisions in the Ten Steps are directly based on the characteristics of learning tasks and task analysis results, *not* on the separate objectives. Nonetheless, a performance objective is specified for each constituent skill identified in the skill hierarchy because in performance of the whole skill, these aspects will also become visible - often in the form of identified problems or deficiencies - and will give the designer or trainer a foothold for solving the learning problems or filling the deficiencies. The integrated set of objectives describes the different aspects of effective whole-task performance. Well-formulated performance objectives contain an *action verb* that clearly reflects the desired performance after the training, the *conditions* under which the skill is performed, the *tools and objects* required, and - last but not least - the *standards* for acceptable performance, including criteria, values, and attitudes (see Figure 6.3).

Figure 6.3   The four main elements of a performance objective.

Action Verbs

An action verb clearly states what learners will be able to do after having completed the training. It should indicate observable, attainable, and measurable behaviors. The most common mistake is to use verbs like 'comprehend,' 'understand,' 'be aware of,' 'be familiar with,' or 'know'. These verbs should be avoided in performance objectives because they do not describe what learners will be able to do after the training, but what they need to know in order to do this. This is another type of analyses that is only performed in Steps 5-6 and 8-9. For an example of the types of action verbs that you can use for Bloom's Taxonomy's two highest levels see Figure 6.4.

Evaluation – Assessing the value of ideas and things. Involves acts of decision-making, judging, or selecting based on criteria and rationale. Requires synthesis in order to evaluate.

Appraise	Discriminate	Rank/Rate
Assess	Estimate	Research
Check	Evaluate	Review
Choose	Grade	Revise
Compare	Inspect	Score
Critique	Judge	Select
Decide on/to	Measure	Value
Determine value of	Monitor	

Synthesis – Assembling a whole into parts. Combines elements to form new entity from original one, the creative process. Requires analysis in order to synthesize.

Arrange	Design	Manage
Assemble	Determine	Organize
Collect	Relationship of parts	Plan
Combine	Diagnose	Prepare
Compose	Differentiate	Propose
Conclude	Dissect	Refute
Construct	Examine	Set up
Create	Formulate	

Figure 6.4   Action verbs in the cognitive domain. (U.S. Department of Agriculture: http://www.nedc.nrcs.usda.gov/isd/isd5.html)

Performance Conditions

The performance conditions specify the circumstances under which the constituent skill must be performed (in the swimming diploma example this was "fully clothed" as the condition for "treading water"). They may include safety risks (e.g., if the skill has to be carried out in a critical working system), time stress (e.g., delay or slow work could cause major problems), workload (e.g., in addition to tasks already being carried out which cannot be transferred to others), environmental factors (e.g., amount of noise, light, weather conditions), time-sharing requirements (e.g., if the skill has to be performed simultaneously with other skills), social factors (e.g., in a hostile group/environment or a friendly team), and so forth. This is often called the *transfer of training* problem.

Consider the surgeon who is usually trained under optimal conditions (i.e., sterile operating room, good lighting, modern tools, and a full staff of assistants). If she is a military surgeon who might be sent to a hostile zone, she will also have to perform that same surgery under less than optimal conditions (e.g., battlefield hospital, poor lighting, limited tools, and with minimal staff). Often, relevant conditions have already resulted from the design of the learning tasks and the sequencing of the task classes:

- *Simplifying conditions:* In order to build an easy-to-difficult sequence of task classes, simplifying conditions may be used (Chapter 5.1). The more complex conditions under which learners should be able to work *after* the training program will be especially relevant to the formulation of performance objectives.
- *Other conditions:* In order to ensure that learners work on a varied set of learning tasks, dimensions are determined on which tasks differ from each other in the real world (Chapter 4.5). One dimension pertains to the conditions under which the task is performed. These conditions are also relevant to the formulation of performance objectives.

Simplifying conditions or other conditions that resulted from previous Steps will typically be related to the whole complex skill - and not to a particular constituent skill. For instance, the "clarity of the patent application" was identified as an important simplifying condition for the complex skill "examining patent applications". If the performance objectives are formulated, "clarity" may only be listed as a relevant condition in the performance objective for the constituent skill "analyzing applications" (and be *inherited* by objectives for lower-level skills). The objective then reads: "after the training program, employees are able to analyze both clear and unclear [condition] patent applications..." The formulation of performance objectives may also reveal additional conditions not previously identified. This may be a reason to repeat a number of previous Steps.

Tools and Objects

The tools and objects necessary to perform a particular constituent skill are specified in the performance objective for that skill. On one hand, the necessary objects and tools must be documented so that a learning environment can be developed that is suitable for practicing and, thus, learning to carry out the tasks. All objects and tools, or - low or high fidelity - simulations or imitations of them, must be available in this task environment. On the other hand, because some tools and objects may quickly change from year to year (such as computer hardware, input devices, and software programs; medical diagnostic equipment; tax codes and regulations; etc.) it is also important to document which performance objectives and which related constituent skills are affected by the introduction of new objects and tools. This will greatly simplify updating existing training programs as well as designing programs for re-training.

Standards: Criteria, Values, and Attitudes

Performance objectives should contain standards for acceptable performance, including the relevant criteria, values, and attitudes. *Criteria* refer to minimum requirements that must be met in terms of accuracy, speed, productivity, percentage of errors, tolerances and wastes, time requirements, and so forth (in the swimming example how many seconds the child has to tread water). This will answer any question such as "How many?" "How fast?" "How well?" Examples of criteria are: "at least 5 will be produced", "within 10 minutes", or "without error".

Values typically do not specify a - quantifiable - minimum requirement, but indicate that the constituent skill should be performed according to appropriate rules, regulations, or conventions (in the swimming example there are conventions of how to turn along one's body axis when going from the crawl to the backstroke). For example "taking the ICAO safety regulations into account", "without violating the traffic rules", or "in accordance with the European Patent Convention".

Attitudes are also treated as a standard. Like knowledge structures, attitudes are handled as subordinate to, but fully integrated with, constituent skills. For example, you neither specify that a librarian must have a "client-centered attitude" nor that the complex skill "searching for research literature" requires such an attitude. Librarians do not need to be client-centered outside working hours or when they perform constituent skills that do not involve clients. But assignable constituent skills such as "translating the research question into relevant search terms", may require a client-centered attitude if it is to be performed in an acceptable fashion. It is only necessary to specify the attitude in the performance objective for these relevant constituent skills. If possible, all observable behaviors that indicate or demonstrate the attitude should be formulated or specified in a way that they are observable! The standard "with a smile on your face" is more concrete, and thus more observable, than "friendly", "regularly performing checks" is more concrete, and thus more observable, than "punctual", and "frequently giving relevant arguments on the topic" is more concrete, and thus more observable, than "persuasive".

After the relevant actions, conditions, tools/objects, and standards for a constituent skill have all been specified, the performance objective for this skill can finally be formulated. The performance objective at the top of the skill hierarchy is a specification of the overall learning goal. It is also called the *terminal objective*. Lower-level objectives formulate the desired exit behavior in more and more detailed terms. An example of a terminal objective for "searching for research literature" is (please refer back to Figure 2.2):

> After following the training program, learners are able to search for relevant research literature by selecting appropriate bibliographical databases such as Psycinfo® and ERIC© [objects]; formulating the search query in close cooperation with [condition] and by in-depth questioning of the client [standard], performing the search with PICA© and FreeSearch© [tools], and selecting the results from the output of the searches [object] on the basis of their relevance [standard] to the research question.

An example of a lower-level performance objective for a training program for learning to examine and evaluate patent applications is related to the constituent skill "preparing search reports" (please refer back to Figure 5.3):

> After following the training program employees are able to individually [condition] prepare a search report [object] according to the regulations of the European Patent Convention [standard] using CAESAR© [tool],

and to draft a communication or vote [objects] using CASEX[©] [tool] on the basis of documents found and the substantive examination.

6.3 Classifying Performance Objectives

Classifying constituent skills and their related performance objectives is very important for designing the training blueprint. This classification takes place on three dimensions. These dimensions are related to whether a constituent skill:

1 *will or will not be taught.* By default, constituent skills are classified as skills that will be taught.
2 *is treated as non-recurrent, recurrent, or both.* By default, constituent skills are classified as non-recurrent, involving schema-based problem solving and reasoning after the training and requiring the availability of supportive information during the training.
3 *needs to be automated or not.* By default, recurrent constituent skills are classified as skills that do not need be automated. Non-automated skills involve the application of rules after the training and require the presentation of procedural information during the training. If recurrent constituent skills are classified as skills that need to be automated, they may also require additional part-task practice during the training program (Step 10).

Classification on the three dimensions eventually results in five classes of constituent skills with related performance objectives (see Table 6.1). The skills and objectives are discussed in the following sections in an order that gives priority to the default classifications, namely: (a) non-recurrent constituent skills, (b) recurrent constituent skills that do not need to be automated, (c) recurrent constituent skills that need to be automated, (d) constituent skills that are both non-recurrent and recurrent, and (e) constituent skills that will not be taught.

Table 6.1 A classification of constituent skills and the main characteristics of related performance objectives.

Constituent Skills To-Be-Taught				Constituent Skills Not-To-Be-Taught
Non-recurrent Constituent Skills	Recurrent Constituent Skills		Double Classified Constituent Skills	
	Not-To-Be-Automated	To-Be-Automated		
Performance objective relates to schema-based problem solving and reasoning	Performance objective relates to the application of rules or the use of a procedure	Performance objective relates to the availability of a routine	Performance objective relates to the ability to recognize when a routine does not work and to switch to a problem solving and reasoning mode	Not applicable

Non-Recurrent Constituent Skills

The terminal objective (i.e., at the top of the skill hierarchy) is always classified as non-recurrent, because a complex cognitive skill - by definition - involves schema-based problem solving and reasoning. Thus, a top-level skill can *never* be recurrent. By default, its constituent skills are also classified as non-recurrent. A skill is classified as being recurrent only if particular aspects of that skill will be performed on the basis of specific cognitive rules after the training. Performance objectives for non-recurrent constituent skills describe exit behaviors that vary from problem situation to problem situation, but that are quite effective because they are guided by cognitive schemas that steer the problem-solving behavior (i.e., use cognitive strategies) and because they allow for reasoning about the domain (i.e., use mental models). After the training, learners should have the schemas necessary to find a solution, whereby their behavior is both efficient and flexibly adaptable to new and often unfamiliar situations. In the context of patent examination, for example, the constituent skill "determining novelty and inventive steps" (see Figure 5.3) is classified as non-recurrent because this process is different for each new patent application. The skills enabled by this particular non-recurrent constituent skill (i.e., those constituent skills that are higher in the hierarchy such as "writing pre-examination results" and "preparing search reports") are also non-recurrent skills. In the training blueprint, non-recurrent constituent skills require the availability of supportive information for their development (Step 4).

Recurrent Constituent Skills

Non-recurrent constituent skills may contain particular aspects that can be performed by applying cognitive rules. These aspects, which typically appear lower in the skill hierarchy, are classified as *recurrent constituent skills*. Performance objectives for recurrent constituent skills describe exit behavior that is highly similar from problem situation to problem situation, and which is driven by the application of domain-specific rules or the use of step-by-step procedures for the linking of particular characteristics of the problem situation to particular actions that need to be carried out. After the training, learners should possess the cognitive rules that allow them to relatively quickly and with very few or no errors come up with a solution. *Consistent* skills, for which the learner can make the same response to a particular situation every time the situation occurs (as opposed to *variable* skills; Fisk & Gallini, 1989; Myers & Fisk, 1987), will typically be classified as being recurrent. In the context of patent examination, the constituent skill "using search tools" (see Figure 5.3) will be classified as recurrent because the tools are always operated in the same manner - irrespective of the patent for which the search is being conducted. By definition, the *prerequisite skills* for a particular recurrent constituent skill (i.e., the related constituent skills that are lower in the hierarchy) must also be recurrent: A recurrent constituent skill can *never* have non-recurrent aspects! In the training blueprint, recurrent constituent skills require for their development the availability of procedural information (Step 7).

Take note: Classifying a constituent skill as non-recurrent or recurrent requires careful analysis of the desired exit behavior, including the conditions and standards of performance. The same constituent skill can be non-recurrent for one training program and recurrent for another! A poignant example is military aircraft mainte-nance training. In peacetime, a standard might be "reach a highly specific diagnosis so that repairs can take place in the most economical way". Time, here, is not criti-cal and possible errors in the diagnosis can be corrected via thorough testing proce-dures. Thus, maintaining aircraft in peacetime will probably be classified as a non-recurrent skill. In wartime, the standard is to "diagnose the component that is not functioning as quickly as possible so that the whole component can be replaced". Speed is of the utmost importance and economic considerations are much less im-portant. Thus, maintaining aircraft in wartime will probably be classified as a recur-rent skill. Consequently, a training program for aircraft maintenance in peacetime will be different from a training program in wartime!

To-Be-Automated Recurrent Constituent Skills

By default, recurrent constituent skills need not be automated and are only prac-ticed in learning tasks. A special subset of recurrent constituent skills is skills that need a very high level of automaticity after the training. These skills may be addi-tionally trained through *part-task practice* (Step 10), so that after the training they can effortlessly be performed as a routine. For many training programs, such as the training program for examining patent applications, there are no constituent skills that need to be automated. For other training programs, a very high level of auto-maticity may be desired, namely for constituent skills that:

- *enable the performance of many other constituent skills higher in the hierar-chy.* Musicians, for example, continually practice the musical scales in order to automate those constituent skills that are most basic to performing. In the same way, children practice multiplication tables so as to automate constitu-ent skills basic to many arithmetic tasks.
- *have to be performed simultaneously with many other constituent skills.* Process operators in the chemical industry, for example, may automate read-ing display panels because this coincides with their diagnosis of the situation [a skill] and students may automate note taking because this is performed si-multaneously with active listening [a skill].
- *are critical in terms of loss of capital, danger to life, or damage of equip-ment.* Air traffic controllers, for example, automate the detection of danger-ous in-flight situations from a radar screen and naval navigation officers automate the performance of standard maneuvering procedures on large ves-sels.

If a recurrent constituent skill needs to be automated because it meets one or more of the requirements just described, the question that then needs to be answered is: Is this automation practically feasible? From a *theoretical* point of view, all recurrent skills can be automated because they are consistent; a given situation always and uniquely triggers the same response (Fisk & Lloyd, 1988; Myers & Fisk, 1987). But in instructional design, one often does not focus on the specific mappings be-tween situations and responses, but on higher-level or global consistencies that link enormous or even infinite amounts of situations to particular responses (Fisk, Lee, & Rogers, 1991; Fisk, Oransky, & Skedsvold, 1988). This may, from a *practical* point of view, make reaching full automaticity highly unlikely because reaching it could normally take the learner a whole lifetime to achieve. Suppose that the adding of number-pairs less than 1000 is practiced. Underlying this skill is a simple procedure, but with regard to its automation it is not the difficulty of the procedure that counts, but the number of situation-response mappings. Here, the possible situations refer to all number pairs from $0 + 0$ to $999 + 999$, or one million different situations (1000×1000). If 100 practice-items, each with duration of 5 seconds, are necessary to reach full automaticity for each situation-response pair, then 100,000,000 items and thus 500,000,000 seconds are needed for a training program. This is approximately 139,000 hours, 17,360 eight-hour working days, or more than 70 years (excluding vacations) to reach full automaticity. This explains why most people compute the sum of $178 + 539$ instead of automatically responding with the answer 717.

An example of a recurrent skill that is relatively easy to automate is steering a car. Suppose that keeping the car on-track on a pretty straight highway is practiced. The situation that the learner is confronted with can be seen as the angle that the front of the car makes with the lines on the highway. With an accuracy of 1°, and assuming that the maximum correction is 45° to the left or to the right (sharper curves are highly uncommon on a highway), there are 90 different situations. If 100 practice items of 1 second each are necessary to automate each situation-response pair, we need 9,000 items or 9,000 seconds. This is only 2½ hours and explains why most people have little trouble keeping a car going in a straight line on the highway - even during a conversation with passengers.

Double Classified Constituent Skills

The decision as to whether a recurrent skill needs to be automated balances, thus, between the desirability of automation and its feasibility. There are, however, rare situations in which lack of speed and/or making errors might cause great loss, danger, or damage, so that skills that would normally be classified as not-to-be automated or even as non-recurrent are still classified as to-be-automated recurrent skills (i.e., it must be *double classified*). "Safely shutting down a nuclear power plant in case of danger", for example, will be performed in many various ways depending on the specific circumstances and would, essentially, involve strategic problem solving and reasoning about the working of the system. Nevertheless, it may be classified as a to-be-automated recurrent skill because lack of speed or making errors could and probably will be catastrophic. The instructional designer will pay a very high price for this classification. Performing an algorithmic analysis of the skill will be very expensive and will entail a tremendous amount of work, more often than not requiring a team of technical specialists to work on this for months or even years. The time required for training will also increase exponentially, sometimes demanding thousands of hours of training (often with the help of a high fidelity simulation environment).

A common problem with this special category of to-be-automated constituent skills is that there may always be situations in which a developed routine does not work. Even after substantial analyses and extensive training, task performers can be confronted with situations that no one has anticipated. It is often these unforeseen situations or faults, or unforeseen combinations of situations or faults, which cause calamities or near-calamities. Because of this, this special class of skills can be classified as both "non-recurrent" and "to-be-automated recurrent". In general, learners should be explicitly taught that this is the case and be trained to switch from an "automated mode" to a "problem solving and reasoning mode" if an impasse occurs while performing a learned routine. In Chapter 2, this ability was described as *reflective expertise*. The double classification and its resulting training design are then expected to maximize the chance that both familiar and unfamiliar problem situations will effectively be dealt with.

Constituent Skills Not-To-Be-Taught

Finally, there may also be reasons *not* to teach particular constituent skills. An instructional designer may, for example, decide only to deal with those performance objectives for which learners have shown performance deficiencies, thus excluding all other performance objectives from the training program. Alternatively, the designer may, due to training-time constraints, include only those objectives that are particularly important, difficult, or unfamiliar to the target learners. The designer, however, should be very careful when making the decision to exclude particular objectives from the training program because, explicitly taught or not, they are always part of a highly interrelated set of constituent skills. If learners have already mastered a particular constituent skill in an isolated manner, this is no guarantee that they can carry it out in the context of whole-task performance. Performing a particular constituent skill in isolation is completely different from performing it in the context of a whole task (Elio, 1986), and automaticity of a constituent skill that has been developed through extensive part-task practice is often not preserved in the context of whole-task performance (Schneider & Detweiler, 1988). Thus, if someone is taking driving lessons and is able to properly use the clutch and shift smoothly when driving on a straight and empty road, it does not guarantee that this same person will be able to use the clutch and shift smoothly when driving through an unfamiliar city in heavy traffic. Also, a particular skill might not be very important per se (e.g., adjusting the rearview mirror), but might enable the performance of other important constituent skills (e.g., monitoring those vehicles driving in the same direction behind the vehicle so as to change lanes safely). Thus, the instructional designer should be aware that not training one or more constituent skills might have the same effect as removing one or more building blocks from a wobbly tower.

Using Performance Objectives

In many instructional design models, performance objectives are the basis for training design. As already stated, this is certainly not the case for the Ten Steps where real-life tasks are the starting point for good design. Nevertheless, the complete and interrelated set of constituent skills and associated performance objectives may fulfill several important functions in the design process. A complete and interrelated set of performance objectives for the "skills to-be-taught" provides a concise description of the global contents of the training program, which is a good basis for discussing it with all relevant stakeholders. The skill hierarchy describes how different aspects of complex task performance are interrelated. Well-defined performance objectives give a clear picture of what learners will be able to do after completing the training program (i.e., what their exit behavior should be). In addition, the classification of objectives as recurrent and non-recurrent gives a further specification of exit behavior, and also greatly affects the further design process because supportive information will be designed for non-recurrent aspects and procedural information for recurrent aspects of the whole complex skill.

Performance objectives also provide valuable input for further analysis and design activities. In-depth task and knowledge analyses may be necessary if instructional materials for supportive and/or procedural information need to be developed from scratch. In this situation, performance objectives for constituent skills classified as non-recurrent provide important input for the analysis of cognitive strategies (Chapter 8) and mental models (Chapter 9), while performance objectives classified as recurrent provide similar input for the analysis of cognitive rules (Chapter 11) and prerequisite knowledge (Chapter 12). These analysis activities provide specific descriptions of supportive and procedural information that are helpful for reaching a highly detailed training blueprint. Furthermore, the standards that are part of the performance objectives provide a basis for the development of scoring rubrics that allow for assessment of the performance on learning tasks.

6.4   Performance Assessment

Performance objectives specify the standards for acceptable performance consisting of relevant criteria, values, and attitudes. These standards are necessary because they give learners needed information on the expected quality of their performance on learning tasks. It is a kind of *performance assessment* because it is a form of testing that requires learners to perform a task rather than select an answer from a ready-made list. This section focuses on *formative* performance assessment; assessment of learner progress with the sole goal of improving learning. The assessment might be performed by:

- *The learner*. If learners assess their own performance this is called self-assessment. The main aim of the assessment is to identify constituent skills or aspects of performance that do not yet satisfy their standards and are thus "points for improvement".
- *A peer learner*. If learners assess the performance of their learners this is called peer-assessment. Again, the aim of such assessment is to identify important "points of improvement" for the assessed learner. An added benefit is that peer-assessment is also a valuable learning experience for the assessor (see Step 4).

- *Some other instructional agent.* The assessment may also be performed by the teacher, a practitioner or an expert from the professional field, the instructor, an examiner, and so forth.

Good self-assessment, peer-assessment, and expert critiques carried out by an instructional agent are based on clear standards provide learners with important information on the quality of their performance and on their opportunities for improvement. According to the Ten Steps, whole tasks are used throughout the training program. Consequently, an identical set of standards might be used for the assessment of all learning tasks. The standards are typically included in an assessment form or *scoring rubric*, which contains an indication of each aspect or constituent skill to be assessed, the standards for acceptable performance of this skill, and a scale of values on which to rate each standard. In addition, a scoring rubric may also include definitions and examples to clarify the meaning of constituent skills and standards. Table 6.2 provides an example of a small part of a scoring rubric.

The Table contains aspects of performance that have been classified as non-recurrent, recurrent not-to-be-automated, and recurrent to-be-automated. They are all constituent skills of the complex skill "searching for relevant research literature" (please refer back to the skill hierarchy in Figure 2.2). For non-recurrent aspects of performance such as "translating the client's research question into relevant search terms", standards will not only take the form of criteria, but also of attitudes and values. While criteria relate to minimum requirements which are either met or not met (yes/no), values and attitudes typically require narrative reports or, at least, more scale values with qualitative labels (e.g., insufficient, almost sufficient, just sufficient, good, excellent). Each point on the scale should be clearly labeled and defined. The rule-of-thumb is to best avoid scales with more than six or seven points (such scales give a false sense of exactness and it is often hard for assessors to make such subtle assessment decisions) and to use only as many points as are necessary to adequately cover the range from very poor to excellent performance. Standards are relatively firm for recurrent, not-to-be-automated aspects of performance. In contrast to non-recurrent aspects, the accuracy of recurrent aspects can thus be judged more often with a simple correct or incorrect (i.e., either according to the specified rules or not). And the same is true for recurrent, to-be-automated aspects of performance.

Table 6.2   An example of a partial scoring rubric (assessment form) for the complex skill "searching for relevant research literature".

Performance aspect / constituent skill	Standards as specified in the performance objective	Scale of values
	Attitude: Communication with the client in order to clarify and specify the research question is correct, in service and pleasant	Unable to begin effectively Begins, but fails to complete task with required attitude Minor flaws but satisfactory Acceptable behavior Exemplary behavior *Please explain your answer:* ...
	Criterion: All proposed search terms are listed in the applicable Thesauri	Yes/no
Translating client's question into relevant search terms (*non-recurrent*)	*Value*: Relevance of the proposed search terms has been checked with the client according to the normal working procedures	No Partly Complete *Please explain your answer:* ...
	Criterion: Time between receiving the research question from the client and checking the relevance of proposed search terms is not more than five working days	Yes/no
Operating search program (*recurrent not-to-be-automated*)	*Criterion:* Operating the search program is faultless and does not interfere with the search task itself	Yes/no
	Value: Shortcuts rather than mouse-driven menu choices are used to prevent RSI	No Mostly Always
Using Boolean operators (*recurrent to-be automated*)	*Criterion:* Use of Boolean operators (AND, OR, NOR) is faultless and very fast	Yes/no
To be continued for all other relevant aspects of performance...		

Judgments on only one or a few aspects of performance provide learners with little detail about how he or she can improve performance. Therefore, a well-designed scoring rubric will pay attention to most or all aspects of performance, and typically contain more than one standard for each constituent skill (Baartman, Bastiaens, Kirschner, & van der Vleuten, 2006). For a training program designed according to the Ten Steps, the same scoring rubric can be used for the whole training program because whole tasks are used from the very beginning (an exception is when part-task sequencing is used; see Chapter 5.3). An important decision relates to the level of detail chosen for judging: a global level pertains to constituent skills that are high in the skill hierarchy and is best used for skills that have already been mastered; a detailed level pertains to constituent skills that are low in the skill hierarchy and is best used for skills that have not yet been mastered. Alternatively, a hierarchical computer-based menu system might be used allowing the assessor to judge the global aspects first and, only if desired, unfold these global aspects to judge the more specific aspects, and so forth until the highest level of detail (i.e., the bottom of the hierarchy) is reached. This offers the opportunity to use a high level of detail for judging new or problematic aspects of the task and, at the same time, use a low level of detail for judging aspects of the task that have already been mastered.

Ideally, the assessor judges all aspects of performance using the same scoring rubric for all learning tasks. Obviously, this is an extremely labor-intensive job for a teacher or instructor and impossible if there are many students. Therefore, the Ten Steps promotes the use of self-assessment and peer-assessment (Sluijsmans, Brand-Gruwel, van Merriënboer, & Bastiaens, 2003; Sluijsmans, Brand-Gruwel, van Merriënboer, & Martens, 2004). The whole collection of performance assessments, for all learning tasks, can then be gathered in a *development portfolio*. At each point in time, this portfolio contains an overview of: (a) all learning tasks that have been performed by the learner, (b) the performance of the learner on specific task aspects as well as "points for improvement" (i.e., vertical evaluation), and (c) the overall performance of the learner on the tasks (i.e., horizontal evaluation). In *on-demand education*, the learner uses this portfolio to select the next learning task(s) that he or she will work on. For instance, if the overall performance on learning tasks with support is high, the given level of support might be decreased for the next task(s); if the performance on specific task aspects is low, the next task(s) may focus on those aspects or points that need to be improved, and if the overall performance on learning tasks without support (conventional problems) is high, the learner might switch to a next, more difficult task class. The use of development portfolios for self-directed learning and on-demand education is further discussed in Chapter 15.

To conclude, it should be clear that this section only focused on the formative use of performance assessments. They may also be used in a summative fashion. The results of summative assessments are not primarily used to inform students about their progress and the quality of their performance, but to make grading decisions, pass/fail decisions, or decisions on certification. In this case, it is inevitable that a teacher or other expert assessor fills out the scoring rubric. Furthermore, these summative assessments of performance will typically be based only on conventional learning tasks that students perform *without* any support, that is, tasks at the end of a task class. A formal decision might be that the student may or may not proceed to the following task class or level of difficulty, or that the student can or cannot be certified.

6.5   Summary of Guidelines

- If you set performance objectives for a training program, then you need to start from an overall learning goal and first describe all relevant constituent skills and their relationships in a skill hierarchy.
- If you construct a skill hierarchy, then you need to make a distinction between a vertical relationship where skills lower in the hierarchy are enabling or prerequisite for skills higher in the hierarchy, and a horizontal relationship where skills adjacent to each other are ordered in time.
- If you specify a horizontal relationship in a skill hierarchy, then you need to make a distinction between a temporal relation where the order of skills performance is from left to right; a simultaneous relation where skills are performed at the same time, and a transposable relation where skills can be performed in any desired order.
- If you specify a performance objective for a constituent skill, then you need to clearly state what the learners are able to do after the training (action verb), under which conditions they are able to do it, which tools and objects they must use, and which standards apply for acceptable performance.
- If you specify the standards for acceptable performance in a performance objective, then you need to make a distinction between criteria that must be met (e.g., minimum requirements for speed and accuracy), values that must be taken into account (e.g., satisfying particular rules, conventions, and regulations), and attitudes that must be exhibited by the task performer.
- If you classify performance objectives, then you need to make a distinction between non-recurrent constituent skills (involving problem solving and reasoning), recurrent constituent skills (involving application of rules or use of procedures), and skills that are both non-recurrent and recurrent (recognizing when rules/procedures do not work so as to switch to a problem-solving and reasoning mode).
- If you classify performance objectives as recurrent, then you need to make a distinction between not-to-be automated constituent skills (requiring presentation of procedural information) and to-be-automated constituent skills (possibly also requiring part-task practice).
- If the learner's performance on learning tasks is assessed, then this is best done on the basis of a scoring rubric with all relevant aspects of performance, the standards for those aspects, and the scales that enable the assessor to give a judgment for all standards.
- If a scoring rubric is used for formative assessment, then ask the learner and/or peer learners to fill out the scoring rubric.

7
STEP 4: DESIGN SUPPORTIVE INFORMATION

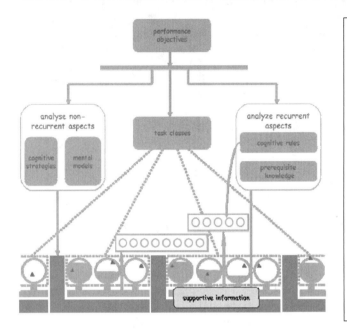

Necessity

Supportive infor-mation is one of the four design components and helps learners to perform the non-recurrent aspects of the learning tasks. It is strongly recommended to perform this step.

Having designed the learning tasks, the next step is designing supportive informa-tion for carrying out the learning tasks. This chapter presents guidelines for this. It concerns the second design component and bridges the gap between what learners already know and what they should know to fruitfully work on the non-recurrent aspects of learning tasks in a particular task class. Supportive information refers to (a) general information on how to solve problems within the task domain, including information on the organization of the domain, (b) examples that illustrate this do-main-specific information, and (c) cognitive feedback on the quality of the task performance. All instructional methods for the presentation of supportive informa-tion promote schema construction by means of *elaboration*. In other words they help learners establish meaningful relationships between newly presented informa-tion elements and between the newly presented elements and their prior knowledge. This process of elaboration yields rich cognitive schemas that relate many elements to many other elements. Such schemas allow for deep understanding and increase the availability and accessibility of task-related knowledge in long-term memory.

The structure of this chapter is as follows. First, the nature of general informa-tion about how to solve problems in the task domain (Systematic Approaches to Problem-solving - SAP) and about the organization of the domain (domain models) is discussed. For this general information, expository methods that help students establish meaningful relationships between information elements on the one hand,

and those elements and existing prior knowledge on the other, are presented. This is followed by a description of the use of modeling examples to illustrate SAPs and the use of case studies to illustrate domain models. Then, presentation strategies for combining the general SAPs and domain models with specific modeling examples and case studies are discussed. Here, the focus is on the use of inquisitory methods that promote active processing of the information by the learners. Fourth, guidelines are presented for providing cognitive feedback on the quality of the non-recurrent aspects of task performance. Finally, positioning the supportive information in the training blueprint is discussed. The chapter concludes with a brief summary.

7.1   Providing SAPs and Domain Models

Learners need information in order to work fruitfully on - non-recurrent aspects of - learning tasks and to genuinely learn from those tasks. This supportive information provides the bridge between what learners already know and what they need to know to work on the learning tasks. It is the information that teachers typically call "the theory" and which is often presented in study books and lectures. Because the same body of knowledge underlies the ability to perform all learning tasks in the same task class, supportive information is not coupled to individual learning tasks, but to task classes as a whole. The supportive information for each subsequent task class is an addition to or an elaboration of the previous supportive information, allowing the learners to do new things that could not be done before.

Supportive information reflects two types of knowledge. First, it concerns the cognitive strategies that allow one to perform tasks and to solve problems in a systematic fashion. A cognitive strategy may be analyzed as a *Systematic Approach to Problem-solving* (abbreviated as SAP; see Chapter 8), which specifies the phases that an expert typically goes through while carrying out the task as well as the rules-of-thumb that may be helpful to successfully complete each of the phases. An educational or pedagogic specification of a SAP may either be directly presented as supportive information, where the learner studies it as helpful information to perform the learning tasks within one particular task class, or be rewritten into a *process worksheet* that "guides" the learner through performing a particular task (for an example of this kind of problem-solving support, refer back to Chapter 4.3).

In addition to this, supportive information also reflects the mental models that allow one to reason within the task domain. Mental models may be analyzed in different kinds of *domain models* (see Chapter 9), which specify what the different and particular things in a domain are (i.e., conceptual models), how they are organized (i.e., structural models), and how they work (i.e., causal models). Clearly, mental models of how a task domain is organized are only helpful for solving problems if learners also apply useful cognitive strategies. Moreover, cognitive strategies are only helpful if learners possess good mental models of the domain. Thus, there is a bi-directional relationship between cognitive strategies and mental models: The one is of little use without the other. The presentation of SAPs and domain models is discussed in the next sections.

Presenting Systematic Approaches to Problem Solving (SAPs)

SAPs tell students how they can best solve problems in a particular task domain. To this end they provide an overview of the phases and sub phases needed to reach particular goals and sub goals; they clearly depict the temporal order of these phases and sub phases, and also indicate how particular phases and sub phases may be dependent upon the outcomes of former phases. In addition, rules-of-thumb or heuristics are provided to the learners that may be helpful to reach the goals for each phase or sub phase.

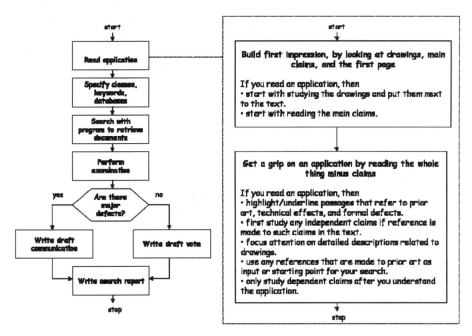

Figure 7.1   Example of a SAP for examining patents. It describes phases in problem solving (see left part), as well as sub phases and rules-of-thumb that may help to complete each (sub) phase (see right part).

Figure 7.1 gives an example of a SAP for a training program for patent examiners. The left part describes the problem-solving phases that can be distinguished for one of the task classes in the skill cluster "preparing search reports" (see Chapter 5.3). This SAP is presented as a flowchart (also called a SAP-chart) in which particular phases are dependent upon the success or failure of preceding phases. According to this SAP, "writing a draft communication" occurs only if defects have been found in the patent application; otherwise, the patent examiner has to "write a draft vote" (i.e., a proposal to the examining division to grant the patent). The SAP on the right side of Figure 7.1 is a further specification of the first phase ("read application") of the SAP on the left, and is divided into two sub phases. Usually, you will present global SAPs for early task classes and increasingly more detailed SAPs, with more specific sub phases, for later task classes.

The SAP on the right side of Figure 7.1 also provides some helpful *rules-of-thumb* for building a first impression of the application (goal of phase 1) and to get a good grip on the application (goal of phase 2). It is best to provide a prescriptive formulation of the rules-of-thumb such as "in order to reach [...], you should try to do [...]" - and to discuss *why* these rules should be used, *when* they should be used, and *how* they should be used (Newby & Stepich, 1990). Furthermore, it may be helpful to give the SAP a name (e.g., Systematic Search, Split Half Method, Methodical Medical Acting) so that it can easily be referred to in instructional materials and discussions with students.

Instructional methods for presenting SAPs must help learners establish, in a process of elaboration, meaningful relationships between newly presented information elements (e.g., phases, goals, rules), and meaningful relationships between those new information elements and already available prior knowledge. For the phases in a SAP, the chosen method or methods should stress the *temporal organization* of the goals and sub goals that must be reached by the task performer. For instance, when learners study a SAP, the instruction should explain why particular phases need to be performed before other phases (e.g., a solution must be heated to a certain temperature before the reagent is added because the chemical reaction is temperature dependent) or indicate the effects and problems of re-arranging phases (e.g., if you first add the reagent to the solution and then heat it, it will cause the reagent to bind to a specific molecule and loose its function). When presenting rules-of-thumb, instructional methods should stress the *change-relationship* between an "effect" - the goal that must be reached - and its "cause" - what must be done by the task-performer in order to reach this goal. For instance, the instruction may explain how particular rules-of-thumb bring about particular desired states-of-affairs (e.g., if you add a certain reagent to a solution, then the calcium will precipitate out of the solution) or they may predict the effects of the use, or lack of use, of particular rules-of-thumb (e.g., if you don't heat the solution, then the reagent will not function, because the working of the reagent is temperature dependent).

Presenting Domain Models

Domain models indicate how things are organized in the world, specifying the relevant elements in a domain as well as the relationships between those elements. A distinction can be made between three types of models, namely conceptual models, structural models, and causal models.

Conceptual models are the most common type of model encountered. These have concepts as their elements and allow for the classification or description of objects, events, and activities. Conceptual models help learners to answer the question: What is this? For instance, knowledge about several types of stocks and/or bonds, and how these differ from each other, helps a financial analyst determine the risks associated with different portfolios. Knowledge of the contents of many different patent databases helps a patent examiner decide which databases should be searched for the proper evaluation of a particular patent application. Analog to instructional methods for presenting SAPs, methods for presenting domain models should help learners establish meaningful relationships between newly presented elements. Table 7.1 summarizes some popular methods for establishing such relationships.

Table 7.1   Eight popular instructional methods stressing meaningful relationships in the presentation of supportive information.

Instructional method	Highlighted relationship(s)[a]
1. Analyze a particular idea into smaller ideas	Subordinate kind-of or part-of relation
2. Provide a description of a particular idea in its main features or characteristics	Subordinate kind-of or part-of relation
3. Present a more general idea or organizing framework for a set of similar ideas	Superordinate kind-of or part-of relation
4. Compare and contrast a set of similar ideas	Coordinate kind-of or part-of relation
5. Explain the relative location of elements in time or space	Location relation
6. Re-arrange elements and predict effects	Location relation
7. Make a prediction of future states	Cause-effect or natural process relation
8. Explain a particular state of affairs	Cause-effect or natural process relation

[a]   The different types of relationships are further explained in Chapters 8–9.

Important methods include (see methods 1–4 in Table 7.1):

- *Analyze a particular idea into smaller ideas.* If a conceptual model of electric circuits is discussed you can distinguish typical kinds of electric circuits such as parallel or a series (kind-of relation) and/or state the typical components of an electric circuit such as a switch, resistor, or battery (part-of relation).
- *Provide a description of a particular idea in its main features or characteristics.* When presenting a conceptual model of a human-computer interface you can give a definition (i.e., a list of features) of virtual reality helmets and data gloves (a kind-of relation, because helmets and gloves provide a particular kind of interface) and/or give a definition of the concept "dialogue box" (a part-of relation, because a dialogue box is a part of an interface).
- *Present a more general idea or organizing framework for a set of similar ideas.* If a conceptual model of process control is to be presented you can state what all controllers (e.g., temperature controllers, flow controllers, level controllers) have in common. This is often more inclusive, more general, and more abstract than each of the specific elements. If such an organizing framework is presented beforehand it is called an *advance organizer* (Ausubel, 1960).
- *Compare and contrast a set of similar ideas.* If a conceptual model of iterative computer code is discussed, you can compare and contrast the working of different kinds of looping constructs (e.g., WHILE loops, REPEAT UNTIL loops, FOR loops, etc.).

Structural models describe how objects, events or activities for reaching particular goals or effects are related to each other in time or in space. Such models help learners answer the question: How is this organized? Models that indicate how activities or events are related in time are also called *scripts*. Structural models help the learner to understand and predict behavior (What happens when?). In biology, for example, knowledge about stereotyped sequences of events occurring in a particular species of birds at a certain time of year enables a biologist to predict and understand the ritual of mating behavior.

Models that indicate how objects are related in space are called *templates* and help the learner to understand and design artifacts (How is this built?). In software engineering, for example, knowledge about stereotyped patterns of programming code or programming templates, and how these patterns fit together, helps computer programmers understand and write the lines of code for computer programs. The same methods used to stress relationships as for conceptual models can also be used for structural models. Additional methods for presenting structural models include (see methods 5 and 6 in Table 7.1):

- *Explain the relative location of elements in time or space.* If a structural model of scientific articles is presented you would want to explain how the main parts of an article (i.e., title, abstract, introduction, method, results, and discussion) and sub parts (i.e., participants, materials, procedure, etc.) are related to each other so that the article will reach its main goals (i.e., comprehensibility, replicability).
- *Rearrange elements and predict effects.* When presenting a structural model of computer programs you could indicate the effects of re-arranging particular pieces of code on the behavior and the output of programs.

Causal models focus on how objects, events or activities affect each other and help the learner to interpret processes, give explanations, and make predictions. Such models help learners answer the question: How does this work? The simplest causal model that relates an action or event to an effect is usually called a *principle*. A principle allows the learner to draw implications by predicting a certain phenomenon that is the effect of a particular change, or to make inferences by explaining a phenomenon as the effect of a particular change. Principles may refer to very general change relationships, in which case they often take the form of *laws* (e.g., the Law of supply and demand - see Figure 7.2) or to highly specific relationships in a particular technical system (e.g., opening valve C leads to an increase of steam supply to component X).

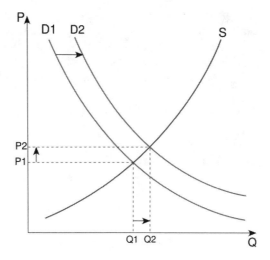

Figure 7.2   The law of supply and demand describes how prices vary as a result of a balance between product availability at each price (supply) and the desires of those with purchasing power at each price (demand).

Models that explain natural phenomena by means of an interrelated set of principles are called *theories*; models that explain the working of engineered systems are called *functional models*. For instance, knowledge about how components of a chemical plant function, and how each component affects all other components, helps process operators with their troubleshooting task. For the presentation of causal models, additional methods to stress relationships are (see methods 7 & 8 in Table 7.1):

- *Make a prediction of future states.* If a meteorological model is discussed, you may give weather forecasts in different given situations.
- *Explain a particular state of affairs.* If a theory of why particular objects are subject to corrosion is discussed, you could state the factors causing corrosion for one metal object such as iron and not causing corrosion for another metal object such as stainless steel.

It should be noted that the *expository methods* in Table 7.1 do not provide any kind of "practice" to the learners, who are not explicitly stimulated to actively process the new information. The methods are typically used in expository texts and traditional lectures, where the most common way to increase the learners' understanding is *paraphrasing*, where learners have to express the meaning of the newly presented information in their own words. There is an enormous amount of educational literature on writing instructional texts and preparing instructional presentations that discusses many more explanatory methods than the ones presented in Table 7.1 (e.g., Hartley, 1994). In this book, Chapter 9 presents more information on meaningful relationships, different types of domain models, and related analysis techniques, making clear that complex domain models may include combinations of conceptual, structural, and causal models. The remainder of this chapter will focus on two issues that must always be taken into account if a learner needs to understand the supportive information, namely illustrating SAPs and domain models with modeling examples and case studies, and the need for prior-knowledge activation and elaborative processing of newly presented information.

7.2   Illustrating SAPs and Domain Models

A particularly important meaningful relationship is the experiential relationship, which relates the general, abstract information discussed in the previous section (i.e., an educational specification of SAPs and domain models) to concrete, familiar examples that illustrate this information. According to the Ten Steps, you should never present SAPs or domain models without illustrating them with relevant examples. This position is taken because cognitive strategies and mental models may not only contain general, abstract knowledge represented by SAPs and domain models, but also contain memories of concrete cases that exemplify this knowledge. When people perform real-life tasks, they may use both their general knowledge of how to approach problems in that task domain and of how the domain is organized as well as their specific memories of concrete cases that refer to similar tasks. In a process of cased-based reasoning, the memories may be used as an analogy for solving the problem at hand. And in a process of inductive learning (refer back to Box 2 (in Chapter 4) for a short description of this basic learning process), they may be used to refine the general knowledge.

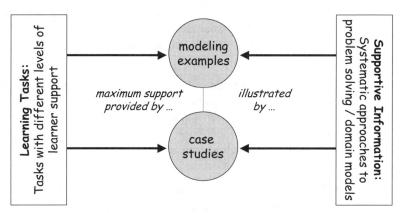

Figure 7.3   Modeling examples and case studies as a bridge between learning tasks and supportive information.

In instructional materials, modeling examples and case studies are the external counterparts of internal memories, providing a bridge between the supportive information and the learning tasks. For providing supportive information, modeling examples illustrate SAPs and case studies illustrate domain models while these same two approaches may be seen as learning tasks with maximum task support (see Figure 7.3). They are important for learners at all levels of expertise, ranging from beginners to true experts. For instance, it is known that Tiger Woods (at the time of this writing the best golf player in the world) still extensively studies video-tapes of his opponents to develop cognitive strategies on how to approach problems during the match, and meticulously studies the layout of golf courses around the world to develop mental models of how they should best be played. In other words, even expert task-performers further develop their cognitive strategies and mental models through the study of examples.

Modeling Examples

Designing modeling examples and case studies has already been discussed as part of the design of learning tasks in Chapter 4, because they can be seen as learning tasks with maximum task support. Modeling examples that illustrate SAPs may show a professional performing a non-trivial task and simultaneously explaining why she has made particular decisions and why she has taken particular actions (e.g., by thinking-aloud). Modeling examples bring the hidden mental processes that a professional carries out to solve a problem out into the open; they show how thinking processes are consciously controlled in order to attain meaningful goals. Learners are allowed to see how professionals reason through difficult, problematic situations to overcome impasses, rather than simply observing a smooth progression toward a correct solution. In a training program aimed at "searching for relevant research literature", for example, learners may study how an experienced librarian constructs search queries - including situations where things go wrong - so that they themselves can develop more effective search strategies. Psychology students, for example, may study videotaped therapeutic sessions in order to study how experienced therapists use SAPs to guide their conversations so that they can better learn to distinguish the phases in a bad news conversation (i.e., tell the client the bad news, deal with the client's emotions, search for solutions) and use a wide range of rules-of-thumb to cope with their clients' emotional states (Holsbrink-Engels, 1997).

Case Studies

There are a number of different kinds of case studies that can be used, depending on the domain model they exemplify. Case studies that illustrate *conceptual models* will typically describe a concrete object, event, or activity exemplifying the model. Students learning to search for literature may study a thesaurus in order to develop a sense of relevant fields of study, noting the search terms themselves, the broader, narrower, and related terms, et cetera. Students in the field of human-computer interaction may study a successful human-computer interface to develop mental models of concepts such as direct manipulation, user friendliness, desktop metaphors, dialogue boxes, and so on.

Case studies that illustrate *structural models* may be artifacts or descriptions of those artifacts designed to reach particular goals. Students learning to carry out a literature search may study different bibliographical databases in order to find out how they are organized. A more elaborated model of how databases are organized may help them to construct better search queries. Students of architecture may visit an office building to study how particular goals have or have not been met by the use of certain - often-prefabricated - templates or elements together in particular ways. An improved model of possible construction techniques may help the learner to design better buildings.

Case studies that illustrate *causal models* may be real-life processes or technical systems. Students learning to carry out a literature search may study how a particular query system works. A more detailed mental model of how a query system works may help them to improve their searches. Architecture students may study a detailed description of the sequence of events that led to a disaster or near disaster in an office building. A better mental model of possible fault trees may help them to identify weaknesses in building processes or even to design safer buildings.

7.3   Presentation Strategies

An important question is now how specific modeling examples and case studies are combined with general SAPs and domain models. Three basic presentation strategies can be distinguished, namely a deductive strategy, an inductive strategy, and a guided discovery strategy.

Deductive Strategy

A *deductive presentation strategy* works from the general, abstract information presented in SAPs and domain models toward concrete illustrations of this information. Typically, the first learning task(s) will take the form of a modeling example or a case study and will be used to illustrate the presented SAPs and domain models. For instance, in a biology program one may train students to categorize animals as birds, reptiles, fish, amphibiae, or mammals. The general information might then include a conceptual model of mammals, indicating that they have seven vertebrae in the neck, are warm blooded, have body hair, and give birth to living young who are nourished by milk secreted by mammary glands. The first learning task may then be a case study illustrating this model and, for instance, asking the learners to study interesting mammals like giraffes, whales, and human beings. In the schematic representation of the training blueprint, we use:

 *Deductive strategy*

In many training programs, this deductive strategy is used by default, probably because it is most time-effective. The "theory" is presented first, after which students must "apply" this theory to the learning tasks. The strategy also, however, has some important drawbacks. Learners with little or no relevant prior knowledge whatsoever may have great difficulties understanding the general information that has been presented to them. Another limitation is that learners are not invited to elaborate on the presented information, nor are they stimulated to connect it to what they already know. There is a clear risk that the newly presented information is "above the learners' head". Therefore, a deductive strategy can best be used if instructional time is limited, if learners have already some experience in the domain, and/or if a deep level of understanding is not strictly necessary.

Inductive Strategy

An *inductive presentation strategy* works from the concrete illustrations or examples toward the general, abstract information (SAPs and domain models). Thus, modeling examples or case studies are used as steppingstones for the presentation of the general information. In this strategy, case studies of the behavior and manifestation of mammals (apes, tigers, giraffes, human beings) will be given before the conceptual model. In the schematic representation of the training blueprint, we use:

 *Inductive strategy*

Whereas the general information, including meaningful relationships, is explicitly presented to the learners, it is often worthwhile to guide them to this general information by asking them *leading questions*, which is indicated by the question mark in the diagram. Such questions help learners to process the examples actively and especially, to process the relationships between pieces of information illustrated in the examples. Instead of the expository methods for information presentation presented in Table 7.1, *inquisitory methods* are used that ask the learners to produce or construct the meaningful relationships themselves from what they already know and from the modeling examples and case studies presented to them.

Useful leading questions that stimulate learners to activate their relevant prior knowledge may ask the learners to come up with analogies and counter-examples or they may be constructed by adding the prefix "ask the learners to...". to the methods discussed in Section 7.1 (see Table 7.2 for some examples of leading questions). Case studies and modeling examples can be interspersed with such leading questions that require learners to critically think about and thoughtfully analyze the organization of the illustrated task domain and the demonstrated problem-solving process. Scattered throughout the description, or possibly at the end of it, are questions that require learners to examine the ideas, the evidence and counter evidence, and the assumptions that are relevant to the example. These questions help learners to work from what they already know, to "self-explaining" the new information (Chi, de Leeuw, Chiu, & LaVancher, 1994; Renkl, 1997), and to stretch their knowledge toward a more general understanding.

Table 7.2   Inquisitory methods that help learners activate their prior knowledge and establish meaningful relationships in presented supportive iinformation.

Inquisitory method	Example leading question
1. Ask the learner to present a familiar analogy for a particular idea	Can you think of something else that stores energy as heath?
2. Ask the learner to present a counter-example for a particular idea	Are there any fish that do not live in the water?
3. Ask the learner to analyze a particular idea into smaller ideas	Which elements may be part of an electronic circuit?
4. Ask the learner to provide a description of a particular idea in its main features	What are the main characteristics of amphibiae?
5. Ask the learner to present a more general idea or organizing framework for a set of similar ideas	To which family belong apes, tigers, giraffes, and human beings?
6. Ask the learner to compare and contrast a set of similar ideas	What have human beings and whales in common?
7. Ask the learner to explain the relative location of elements in time or space	Why do most vehicles steer with their front wheels?
8. Ask the learner to re-arrange elements and predict effects	Will this machine still function when the plus and min pole are reversed?
9. Ask the learner to explain a particular state of affairs	Why are the summers cool and wet in the Netherlands?
10. Ask the learner to make a prediction of future states	Will this kettle of water still be boiling tomorrow?

An inductive strategy is somewhat less time-effective than a deductive strategy, due to the fact that if you first present the general information, as is the case for a deductive strategy, this can often be well illustrated with only one or two examples. However if you first present examples, as is the case for an inductive strategy, then you will typically need more examples in order to point out the commonalities that are central in the general information. And this increases, as the concept becomes abstracter. The concept "dog" will need fewer examples than "mammal", which will need fewer examples than "justice". If leading questions are used, students also need time to process and answer those questions. However, an advantage of an inductive strategy is that its early use of concrete examples works well for learners with little prior knowledge. Any leading questions also promote the activation of relevant prior knowledge and elaboration of the presented information. Students are stimulated to find meaningful relationships on their own, which may help their understanding. Therefore, the Ten Steps suggest using this approach by default.

Guided Discovery Strategy

Both the deductive strategy and the inductive strategy at some point explicitly present the general information to the learners. This is not the case for a *guided discovery strategy*, where the learners have to independently determine and articulate the general information and meaningful relationships that are illustrated in the modeling examples and case studies:

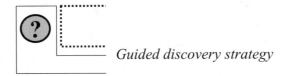

Guided discovery strategy

Guided discovery is time consuming and difficult, because the learners do not know beforehand what they are required to discover. On the other hand, if learners have well-developed knowledge and skills, this strategy builds heavily on that knowledge and offers them good opportunities for using their elaboration skills, that is, embedding new information in already available cognitive schemas (McDaniel & Schlager, 1990). Moreover, just as might be done in the inductive strategy, leading questions are used to guide the learners to the discovery of the general information. Whereas many authors argue that pure discovery is ineffective for learning and should be avoided as an instructional method (for an overview, see Kirschner, Sweller, & Clark, 2006), guided discovery may be a usable method if there is ample time available, if learners have well-developed knowledge and skills, and if a deep level of understanding is necessary.

Table 7.3 summarizes the main factors for selecting a deductive strategy, an inductive strategy, or a guided discovery strategy; default is an inductive strategy. Thus, as a rule one should start with the presentation of one or more modeling examples or case studies and then explicitly present SAPs and domain models illustrated by those examples. Note that especially for SAPs, a large number of modeling examples may be necessary to enable the learners to discover and articulate the relevant phases and rules-of-thumb. This is due to the highly abstract and sometimes counter-intuitive character of SAPs (Clark & Taylor, 1992; Taylor & Clark, 1992).

Table 7.3 Relevant factors for the selection of an optimal presentation strategy for supportive information.

Deductive Strategy	Inductive Strategy	Guided Discovery Strategy
Only if:		*Only if:*
- available time is very limited		- there is ample instructional time available
- learners have ample relevant prior knowledge	Default Strategy	- learners have well-developed discovery skills and little relevant prior knowledge
- a deep level of understanding is not strictly necessary		- a deep level of understanding is necessary

To conclude this section, it should be noted that the use of leading questions as well as other methods that promote the activation of prior knowledge and the elaboration of new information are especially important to present supportive information that is novel and/or difficult for the learners. Collins and Ferguson (1994; see also Sherry & Trigg, 1996; Shaffer, 2006) developed *epistemic games* as a promising approach. Epistemic games are knowledge-generating activities that ask learners to structure and/or restructure information and provide them with new ways of looking at supportive information. They are often sets of moves, entry conditions, constraints, and strategies that guide the building of the epistemic form. The rules may be complex or simple, implicit or explicit. Another useful approach can be found in cognitive flexibility theory (Jonassen, 1992; Spiro, Coulson, Feltovich, & Anderson, 1988), which takes into account that ideas are linked to other ideas with many different relationships, enabling one to take *multiple viewpoints* upon a particular idea. For instance, if a case study describes a particular piece of machinery, the description may be given from the viewpoint of the designer of the device, the user of the device, the engineer that has to maintain the device, the salesperson that has to sell the device, and so on. Comparing and contrasting the different viewpoints helps the learner better process and understand the supportive information. A common aspect of these approaches is that they provide a kind of "practice" to the learners, which is aimed at attaining a better or deeper understanding of the information that may be helpful to perform the learning tasks and, eventually, the target skills of the training program. It may be called *vicarious experience*, as opposed to the direct experience that is provided by the learning tasks.

Box 3 - Elaboration and Supportive Information

Well-designed supportive information provides a bridge between what learners already know and what might be helpful for them to know to perform, and learn to perform the learning tasks. Its presentation should provoke elaboration of new information, that is, those cognitive activities that integrate new information with cognitive schemas already available in memory. Together with induction (see Box 2), elaboration is a major learning process responsible for the construction of cognitive schemas.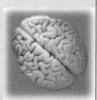

Meaningful Learning
The best way to increase learners' memory for new information is to have them elaborate on the instructional material. This involves having them enrich or embellish the new information with already existing knowledge. When learners elaborate, they first search their memory for general cognitive schemas that may provide a cognitive structure for understanding the information in general terms, and for concrete memories that may provide a useful analogy ("Oh, I came across something like this before"). These schemas are connected to the new information, and elements from the retrieved schemas that are not part of the new information are now related to it. It is a form of meaningful learning because the learners consciously connect the new material with one or more schemas that already exist in memory. Thus, learners use what they already know about a topic to help them structure and understand the new information.

Structural Understanding
The main result of elaboration is a cognitive schema that is an embellishment of the new infor-

mation, with many interconnections both within the schema itself as well as from that schema to other schemas. This will facilitate the retrievability and usability of the schema because multiple retrieval routes to particular information become available. In short, the result of elaboration is a rich knowledge base that provides structural understanding of subject matter. The knowledge base is suitable to be operated upon by controlled processes, that is, it may be interpreted to guide problem-solving behavior and to reason about the domain.

Elaboration Strategies

Like induction, elaboration is a strategic and controlled cognitive process requiring conscious processing from the learners. It can be learned, and includes sub processes such as exploring how new information relates to things learned in other contexts, explaining how new information fits in with things learned before (self-explanation), or asking how the information might be applied in other contexts. Collaboration between learners and group discussion might stimulate elaboration. In a collaborative setting, learners often must articulate or clarify their ideas to the other member(s) of their group, helping them to deepen their own understanding of the domain. Group discussions may also benefit activating relevant prior knowledge and so facilitate elaboration.

Tacit Knowledge

Cognitive schemas that result from elaboration (or induction) can be interpreted to guide problem-solving behavior or to reason about a domain. However, if a cognitive schema is consistently and repeatedly practiced, cognitive rules may be formed that eventually directly produce the effect of the use of the cognitive schema without referring to this schema anymore (the development of such cognitive rules is discussed in Box 4 (in Chapter 10)). For many schemas, this will never occur. For instance, a troubleshooter may have constructed a schema of the behavior of a system with a particular malfunction based on one or two experiences. When confronted with a problem situation, he might use this - concrete - schema to reason about the system ("Oh yes, I had something like this seven or eight years ago"). This schema will never become automated because it is not used frequently enough. However, people may also construct schemas that are repeatedly applied afterwards. This may yield tacit knowledge (literally: silent or not spoken; also called implicit knowledge or "tricks-of-the-trade"), which is characterized by the fact that it is difficult to articulate and of a heuristic nature; you "feel" that something is the way it is. The explanation is that people construct advanced schemas through elaboration or induction, and then form cognitive rules of these as a function of direct experience. Afterwards, the schemas quickly become difficult to articulate because they are no longer used as such. The cognitive rules directly drive performance but are not open to conscious inspection.

Further Reading

Chi, M. T. H., de Leeuw, N., Chiu, M. H., & LaVancher, C. (1994). Eliciting self-explanations improves understanding. *Cognitive Science, 18*, 439–477.

Reigeluth, C. M. (1983b). Meaningfulness and instruction: Relating what is being learned to what a student knows. *Instructional Science, 12*, 197–218.

Stark, R., Mandl, H., Gruber, H., & Renkl, A. (2002). Conditions and effects of example elaboration. *Learning and Instruction, 12*, 39–60.

Willoughby, T., Wood, E., Desmarais, S., Sims, S., & Kalra, M. (1997). Mechanisms that facilitate the effectiveness of elaboration strategies. *Journal of Educational Psychology, 89*, 682–685.

Van Boxtel, C., van der Linden, J., & Kanselaar, G. (2000). Collaborative learning tasks and the elaboration of conceptual knowledge. *Learning and Instruction, 10*, 311–330.

7.4   Cognitive Feedback

A particularly important type of supportive information for learners is feedback on the quality of their performance. This so-called *cognitive feedback* (Balzer, Doherty, & O'Connor, 1989; Butler & Winne, 1995) refers to the non-recurrent aspects of performance only. It consists of information (including prompts, cues, and questions) that helps learners to construct or reconstruct their cognitive schemas in such a way that future performance is improved (McKendree, 1990). All methods for the presentation of supportive information - and especially elaboration - share this focus on schema construction with each other (see Box 3 mentioned earlier for a description of this basic learning process).

Cognitive feedback stimulates learners to reflect on the quality of both their personal problem-solving processes and the solutions that they have found, so that more effective cognitive strategies and mental models can be developed. In contrast to corrective feedback, the main function of cognitive feedback is not to detect and correct errors, but rather to foster reflection in the receiver's mind. This reflection is essential to *double-loop learning* (Argyris & Schön, 1978; see Figure 7.4) which occurs when ineffective behaviors are detected and improved in ways that involve the modification of the learner's underlying strategies, mental models, attitudes, and related criteria.

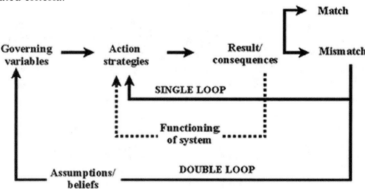

Figure 7.4   Single loop and double loop learning (Adapted from Argyris in Allen, 2001).

The central role that the Ten Steps attribute to reflection is shared with *cognitive apprenticeship learning* (Collins, Brown, & Newman, 1989; Kluger & DiNisi, 1998) which acknowledges that for complex learning, there is no such thing as correct behavior. The best a task performer can do is apply a SAP and make good use of domain knowledge to find an acceptable solution.

Obviously, it is difficult for an instructional designer to fully plan the cognitive feedback in advance, primarily because the feedback is to a certain extent dependent on the learner's idiosyncratic problem-solving process. Cognitive Feedback

(CF) is provided after learners have completed a learning task and is represented in the schematic training blueprint as follows:

A basic method for promoting reflection is to ask learners to critically compare and contrast their own problem-solving processes and - intermediate - solutions with those of others (cf. method 6 in Table 7.2). For instance:

- Learners can be asked to compare their own *problem-solving processes* with SAPs presented in the instructional materials, with modeling examples that illustrate those SAPs, or with the problem-solving processes reported by other learners. Often, this requires that learners document their own problem-solving process in a process report or video recording.
- Learners can be asked to compare their own *solutions*, or intermediate solutions, with solutions presented in case studies, with expert solutions, with the solutions of previous encountered problems, or with solutions reported by other learners.

Comparing one's own models and solutions with the models and solutions of "experts" may be especially useful if the learners start out with *intuitive cognitive strategies* and/or naive mental models. In this way, the learners can then "build" on their original models and strategies and slowly develop more effective knowledge in a process of conceptual change. The inquisitory methods presented in Table 7.2 (i.e., leading questions) are a good way to promote reflection. Collins and Stevens (1983; see also Collins & Ferguson, 1994) propose many additional methods that provide *feedback by discovery*, such as selecting counter-examples, generating hypothetical cases, and entrapping students. An example of this is if a student in the field of patent examination has applied a particular method to classify patent applications, he could be made aware of a counter-example of a situation in which this method will not work well or could be presented with a task in which the strategy he has used leads to a wrong decision. In another example, if a medical student decides that a patient has a particular disease because she has particular symptoms, one might present a hypothetical patient who has the same symptoms that have arisen as a side effect of medication, not because of the diagnosed disease. Comparisons with models and solutions provided by peer-learners may be especially useful in later phases of the learning process. Group presentations and group discussions typically confront learners with a wide range of alternative approaches and solutions, offering a degree of variability that can help them to reach a more general understanding of the task domain.

7.5 Supportive Information in the Training Blueprint

In the training blueprint, SAPs, domain models, modeling examples, and case studies are specified per task class. They enable learners to perform the non-recurrent aspects of the learning tasks at the level of difficulty that is characteristic for the task class under consideration. For each subsequent task class, the supportive information is an extension or elaboration of the information presented for the previous task classes, allowing students to perform more difficult versions of the task under more complex conditions. Thus, each new task class attempts to bring the learners' knowledge, skills, and attitudes to a higher plane. This approach resembles both Bruner's (1960) conception of a spiral curriculum and Ausubel's (1968) ideas about progressive differentiation.

Positioning General Information and Examples

The position of general information within a task class depends on the chosen presentation strategy. In a deductive strategy, students first study the general information (in SAPs and domain models) by reading textbooks, going to lectures, and so forth. This information is then illustrated in the first learning tasks, which will usually take the form of modeling examples and case studies. Obviously, the general information will not only be available to the learners before they start to work on the learning tasks, but is also available while they work on those tasks. Thus, during practice they may consult their textbooks, teachers, Internet sites, or any other background material containing relevant general information for performing the tasks.

In an inductive strategy, the default strategy in the Ten Steps, learners begin by studying modeling examples and case studies that lead them to the general information relevant for performing the remaining learning tasks. As in a deductive strategy, the general information is explicitly made available to the learners and can be consulted at any time. The difference is that for a deductive strategy, the general information is usually presented in a ready-made form such as lectures, prescribed textbooks, or readers, while for an inductive approach it is not uncommon that learners are required to *search* for the general information in the library, in a "study landscape", or on the Internet. This approach may be particularly useful if learners need to develop information literacy or to gain information problem-solving skills. The general information is then made available in a wide collection of "resources", and therefore this approach is sometimes called *Resource Based Learning* (RBL; Hill & Hannafin, 2001).

In a guided discovery strategy, students begin by studying modeling examples and case studies that help them to identify and articulate the SAPs and domain models relevant for performing any remaining learning tasks. The general information is never presented to the learners in a ready-made form, but must be articulated and described by them in a presentation or report.

To conclude, it should be clear that the selection of a presentation strategy is not a single design choice, but rather a decision that needs to be made for each task class. It is quite common that learners have no relevant prior knowledge when they start a training program, which would be a reason to apply an inductive strategy (or even a highly guided discovery strategy) in the first task classes. As learners acquire some of the necessary relevant knowledge of the task domain during the training, it becomes possible to apply a more time-effective deductive strategy in later task classes.

Positioning Cognitive Feedback

Cognitive feedback on non-recurrent aspects of task performance is only provided after the students have finished a learning task. Because there is no clear distinction between correct and incorrect behaviors and between correct and incorrect solutions, it is not possible to provide "immediate" feedback while the students are working on the learning tasks (note that this *is* advisable for recurrent aspects of performance!) For reasoning and problem-solving aspects of a task, learners must be allowed to experience the advantages and disadvantages of applying particular approaches and rules-of-thumb. For instance, it is clearly impossible to provide feedback on errors for learners composing a search query, because there is no single procedure or list of search-terms that will lead to a correct solution. Instead, many approaches are possible and the learner might apply many rules-of-thumb in order to reach a more or less adequate solution. Feedback can only be given - and fully be designed - retrospectively.

To conclude this chapter, Table 7.4 presents one task class out of a training blueprint for the moderately complex skill "searching for research literature" (you may refer back to Table 5.2 for a description of the other task classes). A specification of the supportive information has been added to the specification of the task class and the learning tasks. As can be seen, part of the supportive information is made available to the learners before they start to work on the learning tasks (a case study and an inquiry for structural models) and part is presented after they finish (cognitive feedback). See Appendix 2 for the complete training blueprint.

Table 7.4   A preliminary training blueprint for the moderately complex skill "searching for relevant research literature". For one task class, a specification of the supportive information has been added to the learning tasks.

Task Class 2

Learners are confronted with situations where the concepts in the to-be-searched domain are clearly defined. A large number of articles have been written about the subject, but only in one field of research. Therefore, the search needs only to be performed on titles of articles in one database from the particular field of research. However, many search terms need to be interconnected with Boolean operators to limit the otherwise large amount of articles the search can yield.

Supportive Information: *Case study*

Learners receive three (good) worked-out examples of literature searches. Each example contains an elaborate search query in which Boolean operators are used.

| **Supportive Information:** *Inquiry for mental models* |
| Learners are asked to identify templates of search queries describing Boolean combinations of search terms that can be used to make search queries more specific. |

| **Learning Task 2.1:** *Imitation + constraint* |
| Learners receive a worked-out example of a research question, a list of articles, and an elaborate Boolean search query to produce the list of articles. They receive a similar research question, and a goal to produce a list with a limited amount of relevant articles. By imitating the given example, they must then formulate the search query, perform the search and select relevant articles. They can only perform the search after the search query is approved. |

| **Learning Task 2.2:** *Completion* |
| Learners receive a research question and a list of search terms. They have to formulate a search query by combining the given search terms using different Boolean operators. |

| **Learning Task 2.3:** *Conventional* |
| Learners receive a research question. They have to perform a literature search for the 10 most relevant articles. |

| **Supportive Information:** *Cognitive feedback* |
| Learners receive feedback on their approach to solve the problem in Learning Task 2.3. |

7.6   Summary of Guidelines

- If you design supportive information, then you need to make a distinction between general information, illustrations, or examples of this general information, and cognitive feedback.
- If you design general information, such as Systematic Approaches to Problem solving (SAPs) and domain models, then you need to use instructional methods that stress meaningful relationships between elements to help students understand the information.
- If you design SAPs, then you need to take a prescriptive perspective (what the learner should do) and clearly indicate the problem-solving phases and the rules-of-thumb that may help the learner to complete each phase.
- If you design domain models, then you need to take a descriptive perspective (how the domain is organized) and make a distinction between conceptual, structural, and causal models.
- If you present general information, then you need to illustrate this information with modeling examples (for SAPs) and case studies (for domain models).
- If you illustrate general information with modeling examples and case studies, then you need to use - by default - an inductive strategy that works from the examples, which are best interspersed with leading questions, to the general information.

- If you design cognitive feedback, then you need to ask students to critically compare and contrast their own problem-solving processes and solutions with those of others.
- If you specify supportive information in the training blueprint, then you need to make sure that the supportive information for a new task class builds on the information for the previous task classes and is an extension or embellishment of it.
- If you specify supportive information in the training blueprint, then you need to keep in mind that students acquire more expertise during the training program, which might be a reason to shift from inductive to deductive presentation strategies.

8
STEP 5: ANALYZE COGNITIVE STRATEGIES

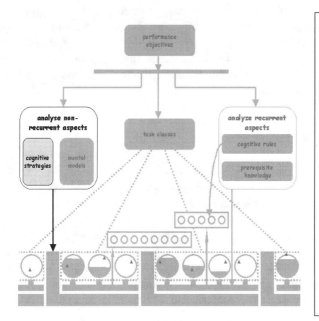

Necessity

Analysis of cognitive strategies provides the basis for the design of supportive information, in particular, Systematic Approaches to Problem solving (SAPs). This step should only be performed if this information is not yet available in existing materials.

We all have previously encountered a problem or have had to carry out a task that looks familiar and for which we think we've had quite a lot of experience. Unfortunately, while solving the problem or carrying out the task, we come across some aspect of it that we never saw before. At this point, our procedural knowledge is not enough and we have to make use of a different type of knowledge - strategic knowledge - to solve the problem or carry out the task. Such strategic knowledge helps task performers systematically approach new problems and efficiently marshal the necessary resources for solving them. This chapter focuses on the analysis of cognitive strategies for dealing with the *unfamiliar* aspects of new tasks. The results of the analyses take the form of Systematic Approaches to Problem solving. They specify how competent task performers organize their own behaviors, that is, which phases they go through while solving problems, and which rules-of-thumb they use to successfully complete each phase. Systematic descriptions of how to approach particular problems in a subject matter domain are sometimes already available in the form of existing job descriptions, instructional materials, or other documents. If this is the case, then there is no need to perform the activities described in this chapter. In all other cases, the analysis of cognitive strategies may be important for designing problem-solving support for learning tasks (e.g., process worksheets), for refining a chosen sequence of task classes, and, last but not least, for designing an important part of the supportive information.

The structure of this chapter is as follows. First, the specification of SAPs is discussed, including the identification of phases in problem solving and the rules-of-thumb that may help to successfully complete each phase. Second, the analysis of intuitive cognitive strategies is briefly discussed because the existence of such strategies may interfere with the acquisition of more effective strategies. Third, the use of SAPs in the design process is discussed because SAPs are helpful for designing problem-solving guidance, refining a sequence of task classes, and designing supportive information. For each of those activities, the existence of intuitive strategies may affect the selection of instructional methods. The chapter concludes with a summary of the main guidelines.

8.1 Specify SAPs

SAPs are prescriptive plans that specify the goals and sub goals to be reached by learners when solving problems in a particular domain, plus the rules-of-thumb that may help them to reach each of those goals and sub goals. Thus, SAPs describe the control structures that steer the performance of competent task performers. It is important to note that SAPs are always heuristic. Thus, though they may help a learner to solve problems in the task domain, their application does not *guarantee* the solution of the problem. Although they are less powerful than algorithmic procedures, power is exchanged for flexibility because SAPs may be helpful in many more different problem situations than a solution algorithm. For designing instruction, analyzing cognitive strategies for inclusion in SAPs serves three goals:

1 provide the basis for the development of problem-solving guidance; such as, in the form of process worksheets (see Chapter 4.3).
2 help refine a sequence of task classes; such as, by identifying a progression from simple to more complicated cognitive strategies (see Chapter 5.1).
3 provide the basis for the development of an important part of the supportive information (see Chapter 7.1).

The analysis of phases and rules-of-thumb will typically be based on interviewing and observing experts who work on concrete, real-life tasks. Asking them to think aloud may help identify the phases they go through and the rules-of-thumb they apply. Foregoing document study may help the analyst (i.e., the instructional designer) properly prepare the interviews and interpret the observations. In order to keep the analysis process manageable, it best progresses from (a) relatively simple tasks from early task classes to more difficult tasks from later task classes, and (b) from general phases and associated rules-of-thumb to more specific sub phases and rules-of-thumb.

According to this stepwise approach, the analyst first confronts a competent task performer with a relatively simple task. If task classes have been defined as part of Step 2, it is best to start with tasks from the first task class. The expert's high-level approach is described in terms of phases and related goals, and applied rules-of-thumb that may help to reach the goals are identified for each phase. Then, each phase may be further specified into sub phases and, again, rules-of-thumb may be identified for each sub phase. After the analysis has been completed for tasks at a particular level of difficulty, the analyst confronts the task performer with more difficult tasks. These tasks will typically require additional phases and/or additional rules-of-thumb. This continues as an iterative process until the analysis of the most difficult tasks has been completed. At each level of iteration, phases in problem solving and rules-of-thumb are identified.

Identifying Phases in Problem Solving

SAPs describe the successive phases in a problem-solving process as an ordered set of goals to be reached by the task performer so that they can systematically be used to approach problems through optimally sequencing actions and decisions in time. The ordered set of phases with their associated goals, and sub phases with their associated sub goals, are also called plans or prescriptive scripts. Some SAPs are ordered in a linear fashion, while others are ordered in a non-linear fashion by taking particular decisions made during problem solving into account. A highly familiar linear sequence of five phases in the field of instructional design is, for example, the *ADDIE* model:

- *Phase 1:* Analyze - the goal of this phase is to analyze the context in which the training takes place, the characteristics of the target group, and the task or content to-be-taught.
- *Phase 2:* Design - the goal of this phase is to devise a blueprint or lesson plan for the training program.
- *Phase 3:* Develop - the goal of this phase is to develop or produce the instructional materials to be used in the training program.
- *Phase 4*: Implement - the goal of this phase is to implement the training program in the organization, taking the available resources and organizational structures into account.
- *Phase 5*: Evaluate - the goal of this phase is to evaluate the training program and gather information that may be used to improve it.

Obviously, these phases may be further specified into sub phases. For instance, sub phases for the first phase include: (a) analyze the context, (b) analyze the target group, and (c) analyze the task or content domain. Sometimes, the sub phases need to be further specified into sub-sub phases, and so forth.

Figure 8.1 provides an example of a non-linear sequence of phases for solving thermodynamics problems (Mettes, Pilot, & Roossink, 1981). Each non-shaded box corresponds with a goal or sub goal to be reached, and particular decisions made during problem solving are taken into account (indicated by the diamond boxes). This kind of SAP takes the form of a flowchart (see Chapter 11) and may be called a *SAP-chart* (see Chapter 7) and is typically used when particular goals are dependent on the success or failure of reaching previous goals. In this particular thermodynamics SAP, the phase "reformulate the problem" is only relevant if the problem is *not* a standard problem. Furthermore, this phase may be further specified into the sub phases "identify key relationships", "convert to standard problem", and "introduce alternate processes".

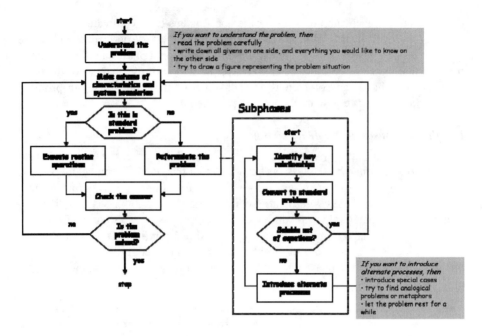

Figure 8.1   SAP for solving thermodynamics problems, showing phases, sub phases and examples of rules-of-thumb (shaded boxes) for one phase and one sub phase.

Identifying Rules-of-Thumb

Rules-of-thumb take the general form: "If you want to reach X, then you may try to do Y" and are often used by competent task performers for generating a solution to a particular problem that is appropriate for dealing with the given situation and its particular set of circumstances. Rules-of-thumb are also called heuristics (Schoenfeld, 1979) or prescriptive principles, and may be separately analyzed in a principle transfer analysis (Reigeluth & Merrill, 1984). The basic idea is that some of the principles that apply in a particular domain may be formulated in a prescriptive way to yield useful rules-of-thumb. For instance, one well-known principle in the field of learning and instruction is:

> There is a positive relationship between the amount of practice and the level of performance

This principle can also be formulated in a prescriptive format as a rule-of-thumb:

> If you want learners to reach a high level of performance, then you may consider providing them with a large amount of practice

If one thinks of a continuum with highly domain-specific, algorithmic rules at one extreme and highly domain-general problem-solving methods at the other, rules-of-thumb would typically be situated in the middle. While they are still linked to a particular domain, they merely indicate a good direction to search for a solution (i.e., generate a procedure) rather than algorithmically specifying a part of this solution (i.e., perform a procedure; see Chapter 11). Some other examples of rules-of-thumb are:

- If you are driving a car and have difficulties with curves, then estimate the angle of the curve and turn the steering wheel appropriate to that angle.
- If you are playing computer games in which you have to deal with fast moving objects, then try not to look at the objects but rather at their after-image on the screen.
- If you are controlling air traffic, then try to control the aircraft by making as few corrections as possible.
- If you are giving a presentation at a conference, then try to adjust the amount of information that you present to the prior knowledge of your audience.

As part of a SAP analysis, the analysis of rules-of-thumb is conducted for each phase, and may be repeated for each sub phase. Each specified goal may then be used to define a category of rules-of-thumb dealing with similar causes and effects. The if-sides typically refer to the general goal of the phase under consideration but may also include additional conditions. For instance, the shaded boxes in Figure 8.1 list some rules-of-thumb that may help the learner to understand the problem (the first main phase) and help to introduce alternate processes (one of the sub phases within the main phase "reformulate the problem"). Mettes, Pilot, and Roossink (1981) give three guidelines for the specification of such rules-of-thumb:

- Provide only rules-of-thumb not yet known by the learners and limit them to those rules-of-thumb necessary for performing the most important tasks.
- Formulate rules-of-thumb in a readily understandable way for learners and use the imperative to make clear that they are directions for desired actions.
- Make the text as specific as possible, but at the same time remain general enough to ensure the appropriateness of the rules-of-thumb for all situations to which they apply.

8.2 Analyzing Intuitive Cognitive Strategies

The Ten Steps focus on the analysis of effective cognitive strategies in SAPs. This is a rational analysis because it describes how the tasks *should* be performed. In addition to this, the designer may analyze which cognitive strategies are currently being used by the target learners. This is an empirical analysis because it describes how the tasks are *actually* performed. There may be large differences between SAPs which describe an effective approach that is applied by competent task performers, and intuitive or naive cognitive strategies used by the learners and identified in an empirical analysis.

A common intuitive strategy for solving design problems is, for instance, to follow a *top-down depth-first* approach. When novices write a scientific article or a computer program, they typically decompose the problem into sub problems that are dealt with in separate sections or subroutines. The detailed solution is then fully implemented for each sub problem before continuing with the next sub problem. In the two problems just presented, the complete text is written for one section or the full programming code is developed for one subroutine. As a result, novices easily loose track of the relationships between sections or subroutines, and spend large amounts of time linking pieces of text or code, repairing suboptimal texts or codes, and rewriting pieces of text or code afterwards. Experts, on the other hand, follow a *top-down breadth-first* approach. They decompose the problem into sub problems (sections, subroutines), then decompose all sub problems into sub-sub problems, and so forth until the final solution is specified at the text or code level. Developing extensive and detailed outlines generates the solution in its full breadth.

With regard to rules-of-thumb, there may also be large differences between intuitive heuristics used by learners and the rules-of-thumb identified in a SAP analysis. We refer back to the rules-of-thumb presented in the previous section to make this point clear. The intuitive counterpart for the rule-of-thumb for going around curves with an unfamiliar vehicle by estimating the angle is to steer by lining up the hood ornament to the road stripe, a strategy that requires many more decisions and leads to a higher workload. The intuitive counterpart for the rule-of-thumb for playing computer games by focusing on the after-images of fast moving objects is to focus directly on the objects themselves, a strategy which has a negative effect on game performance because distracting movements are not suppressed. The intuitive counterpart of the rule-of-thumb to control air traffic by making corrections only if this is necessary to prevent dangerous situations is to make many small corrections, a strategy that may work when only a few aircraft are on the radar screen, but which is not suitable for handling larger numbers of aircraft. And finally, the intuitive counterpart of the rule-of-thumb to adjust the amount of presented information to the prior knowledge of the audience is to provide the audience with as much information as possible in the available time, a strategy that clearly does not work because the audience becomes overloaded.

8.3 Using SAPs to Make Design Decisions

Step 5 will only be performed if information on systematic approaches to problem solving is not yet available in existing instructional materials. If the Step is performed, the produced analysis results provide the basis for a number of different design activities. In particular, specified SAPs may help set up problem-solving guidance, further refine an existing sequence of task classes, and design part of the supportive information. Furthermore, the identification of intuitive strategies may affect several design decisions.

Designing Problem-Solving Guidance

SAPs can be used to design problem-solving guidance in the form of process worksheets or performance constraints (see Chapter 4.3). A process worksheet clearly indicates the phases to go through when carrying out the task. The rules-of-thumb may either be presented to the learners as statements (e.g., "if you want to improve your understanding of the problem, then you might try to draw a figure representing the problem situation") or as guiding questions ("what activities could you undertake to improve your understanding of the problem?").

Also, *performance constraints* can be applied to ensure that learners cannot perform actions irrelevant for the phase they are working on and/or cannot continue to the next phase before successfully completing the current one. Problem-solving guidance for learning tasks in difficult task classes will often be more elaborate or more extensive than guidance for tasks in easy task classes. In such cases, a progression from simple-to-complex SAPs can be used to design guidance for different task classes.

Refining Task Classes through a Progression of SAPs

SAPs can be used to refine an existing sequence of task classes, using a method known as *knowledge progression* (see Chapter 5.1). The easiest version of the task (i.e., the first task class) will usually be equivalent to the simplest or shortest path through a SAP-chart. Increasingly, paths that are more complex and that correspond to more complex task classes can subsequently be identified in a process known as *path analysis* (P. Merrill, 1980, 1987). In general, more complex paths contain more decisions to be made and/or more goals to be reached than less complex paths. In addition, more complex paths usually contain the steps of simpler paths, so that a hierarchy of paths can be organized in order to refine a sequence of task classes. For example, three paths may be distinguished in the SAP-chart shown in Figure 8.1:

1   The shortest path occurs for a standard problem. Thus, the question "is this a standard problem?" is answered with "yes". Consequently, the first task class contains standard problems in thermodynamics.

2   The next shortest path occurs for a non-standard problem that can be transformed into a standard problem if the identification of key relations yields a solvable set of equations. Thus, the question "is this a standard problem?" is answered with "no" and the question "is this a solvable set of equations?" is answered with "yes". Consequently, the second task class contains non-standard problems that can easily be converted to standard problems.

3   The most difficult path occurs for a non-standard problem that cannot be transformed into a standard problem through the identification of key relations. In this situation, the question "is this a standard problem?" is answered with "no" and the question "is this a soluble set of equations?" is also answered with "no". Consequently, the third and final task class contains non-standard problems that can only be transformed into standard problems by the use of reformulations, special cases, or analogies.

127

Designing Supportive Information

SAPs provide the basis for designing the part of the supportive information related to cognitive strategies. First, SAPs can explicitly be presented to learners because they tell them how to best solve the problems in a particular task domain (see Chapter 7.1). Often, an instructional specification is needed after the analysis to ensure that the phases and the rules-of-thumb are formulated in such a way that they are clearly understandable for the learners for whom the instruction is designed. Second, SAPs can drive the search or design of modeling examples that give concrete examples of their application (see Chapter 7.2). Such modeling examples may be seen as either learning tasks with maximum *process-oriented support* or illustrations of cognitive strategies. Finally, SAPs can be used to provide cognitive feedback to learners (see Chapter 7.4). For instance, learners can be asked to compare their own problem-solving process with a presented SAP, or with modeling examples illustrating this SAP.

Dealing with Intuitive Strategies

The identification of intuitive strategies may affect decision making for the three design activities discussed. With regard to designing *problem-solving guidance*, the existence of intuitive strategies may be a reason to provide extra guidance to learners working on the learning tasks. This extra guidance prevents unproductive behaviors and mistakes that result from using the intuitive strategy. Providing particular aids such as process worksheets and structured answer forms can help learners stay on track and apply useful rules-of-thumb. Performance constraints can block the use of intuitive strategies and can force learners to apply a more effective systematic approach. In a course on scientific writing, for example, learners could be forced or coerced into fully decomposing their manuscript into ideas and sub ideas with associated headings and subheadings (i.e., to use a top-down breadth-first approach), before they are allowed to start writing the text. Certain word processors have this function (i.e., the outline function) built into them.

With regard to *refining task classes*, the existence of intuitive strategies can be a reason for providing additional task classes, that is, to work slowly from easier learning tasks toward more difficult learning tasks. This allows the learner to carefully compare and contrast, at each level of difficulty, his or her intuitive approach to problem solving with a more effective approach. Ideally, the intuitive approach will then gradually be replaced - although it should be noted that some intuitive strategies are highly resistant to change.

With regard to *designing supportive information*, the existence of intuitive strategies can be a reason to make use of particular instructional methods. For the coupling of SAPs and modeling examples, an inductive strategy working from the study of modeling examples to the discussion of the general SAP is prescribed as the default strategy (see Chapter 7.3). To deal with intuitive strategies, more modeling examples should be provided and the inductive strategy is best replaced by a guided discovery strategy, which offers even better opportunities for learners to interconnect the newly presented phases and rules-of-thumb to their already existing, intuitive ideas. For using cognitive feedback (see Chapter 7.4), the existence of intuitive strategies makes it of utmost importance that learners carefully compare and contrast their own intuitive approaches and the resulting solutions with the SAPs, modeling examples, and expert solutions presented.

8.4   Summary of Guidelines

- If you analyze cognitive strategies, then observe and interview competent task performers to identify both the phases and sub phases in a systematic problem-solving process and the rules-of-thumb that may help to complete each phase successfully.
- If you identify phases and sub phases in a systematic approach to problem solving, then specify an ordered set of (sub) goals that should be reached by the task performer and, if necessary, the decisions that must be made because particular goals are dependent upon the success or failure of reaching previous goals.
- If you identify rules-of-thumb that may help to successfully complete one problem-solving phase, then list the conditions under which the rule-of-thumb may help to solve the problem (if...) and the action that could be taken by the learner (then...).
- If you analyze intuitive cognitive strategies, then focus on the discrepancies between the problem-solving phases and rules-of-thumb applied by competent task performers and those applied by a naive learner.
- If you use SAPs to design problem-solving guidance, then design process worksheets or performance constraints in such a way that the learner is guided through all relevant problem-solving phases and prompted to apply useful rules-of-thumb.
- If you use a SAP to refine a sequence of task classes, then identify simple to increasingly more complex paths in the SAP-charts and define associated task classes.
- If you use SAPs to design supportive information, then formulate the phases and rules-of-thumb in such a way that they are clearly understandable for your target group and select or design modeling examples that can be used to illustrate them.
- If you are teaching a cognitive strategy to learners who are inclined to use an ineffective intuitive strategy, then provide extra problem-solving guidance, let task difficulty progress slowly, and let the learner critically compare and contrast his or her intuitive problem-solving strategy with more effective strategies.

9
STEP 6: ANALYZE MENTAL MODELS

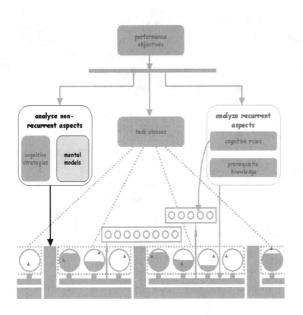

Necessity

Analysis of mental models provides the basis for designing supportive informa- tion, particularly, conceptual, struc- tural, and causal models. This step should only be per- formed if this infor- mation is not yet available in existing materials.

What we know determines what we see and not the other way around. A geologist walking in the mountains of France will see geological periods and rock forma- tions. A bicyclist walking in those same mountains will see gear ratios and climb- ing percentages. Each of these people see the same thing (in terms of their sensory perception), but interpret what they see in very different ways. In this respect, we say that the two people have very different mental models.

Mental models help task performers understand a task domain, reason in this domain, and give explanations and make predictions (Gentner & Stevens, 1983; Van Merriënboer, Seel, & Kirschner, 2002). This chapter focuses on the analysis of mental models that represent how a domain is organized. The results of such an analysis is a domain model, which can take the form of a conceptual model (what is this?), a causal model (how does this work?), and a structural model (how is this built?). Mental models specify how competent task performers mentally organize a domain in such a way that they can reason about it to support their problem solving. Quite often, extensive descriptions of relevant domain models are already available in existing instructional materials, study books, and other documents. If this is the case, then there is no need to perform the activities described in this chapter. In all other cases, the analysis of mental models may be important to refine a chosen se- quence of task classes and, in particular, to design an important part of the suppor- tive information.

The structure of this chapter is as follows. First, the specification of domain models is discussed, including the identification of conceptual models, structural models, and causal models. Second, the empirical analysis of intuitive mental models is briefly discussed because the existence of such models may easily interfere with the construction of more effective and scientific models. Third, the use of domain models for the design process is discussed. Domain models are helpful for refining a sequence of task classes and for designing an important part of the supportive information. For both activities, the existence of intuitive mental models may affect the selection of instructional methods. To conclude, the analysis of mental models is briefly compared with the analysis of cognitive strategies and the main guidelines are presented.

9.1 Specify Domain Models

Domain models are defined as rich descriptions of how the world is organized in a particular task domain that allow the interconnection of facts and concepts to each other through the definition of meaningful relationships. This process may result in highly complex networks representing rich cognitive schemas that enable learners to interpret unfamiliar situations in terms of their general knowledge, or to "understand new things". For the design of instruction, the analysis of mental models into domain models:

1   helps refine a sequence of task classes, for example, by identifying a progression from simple toward more complicated mental models underlying the performance of increasingly more difficult learning tasks (see Chapter 5.1).
2   provides the basis for the development of an important part of the supportive information for each task class (see Chapter 7.1).

The analysis of mental models will typically be based on document study and interviews of competent task performers who explain which models they use when working in a particular domain (i.e., talking about the domain, classifying and analyzing things, giving explanations, and making predictions). In order to keep the analysis process manageable, it best progresses from analyzing the mental models that underlie the performance of simple tasks from early task classes, to analyzing the mental models that underlie the performance of more difficult tasks from later task classes. Having done this, the analyst then confronts a task performer with relatively simple tasks, and assists her/him in describing a mental model helpful to performing those tasks. This process is repeated for each new task class with tasks at increasingly higher levels of difficulty.

   At each level of task difficulty, the analysis of mental models is an associative process. The analyst establishes meaningful relationships or associations between facts and/or concepts that could *possibly* be helpful in carrying out the problem solving and reasoning aspects of the task at the given level of difficulty - but this is not *necessarily* true. Simply said, this reflects the common belief that the more you know about a domain and more or less related domains, the more likely it is that you will be able to solve problems in this domain effectively. A severe risk here is to proceed with the associative analysis process for too long. In a sense, everything is related to everything, and thus the analyst can build seemingly endless networks of interrelated pieces of knowledge. Therefore, new relationships must not be added if a competent task performer cannot clearly explain *why* newly associated facts or concepts improve her or his performance.

However, this is certainly not an easy decision to make. For instance, should students in information science know how a computer works in order to program a computer? Should students of art know about the chemistry of oil paints in order to be able to paint? Should students in educational technology know how people learn in order to produce an effective or efficient instructional design?

When is enough, enough? The number of different types of relationships that can be distinguished in domain models is theoretically unlimited. According to the prominent types of relationships, three basic kinds of models may be distinguished: conceptual models, structural models, and causal models.

Identify Conceptual Models

The basic elements in conceptual models are *concepts*, which represent a class of objects, events or other entities by their characteristic features (also called *attributes* or *properties*). A concept can be viewed as a node with links to propositions or "facts" that enumerate the features of the concept (see Chapter 12). Concepts enable one to identify or classify concrete things as belonging to a particular class. Most words in a language identify concepts, and most concepts are arbitrary, meaning that things can be grouped or classified in many different ways. For instance, a computer can be classified according to its nature (an "electronic device"), its color ("black"), its age ("old"), and so on.

However, in a particular task domain, some concepts are more useful for performing a task than others. Obviously, classifying computers by their color is not very useful to a service engineer, while classifying them by type of processor is. However, for an interior designer, classifying them by color does make sense.

Conceptual models interrelate concepts with each other. They allow one to answer the basic question: *What is this?* Conceptual models are particularly important for carrying out tasks that have to do with categorization, description, and qualitative reasoning because they allow the person carrying out the task to compare things with each other, analyze things in their parts or kinds, search for examples and analogies, and so on.

There are many different types of relationships that can be used in constructing a conceptual model. A particularly important relationship is the *kind-of* relationship, which indicates that a particular concept is a member of another more abstract or more general concept. For instance, both the concepts "chair" and "table" have a kind-of relationship with the concept "furniture", because they both belong to this same general class. Kind-of relationships are often used to define a hierarchy of concepts called taxonomy. In a taxonomy, concepts that are more abstract or more general are called *superordinate*, concepts at the same level of abstraction or generalization are called *coordinate*, and concepts that are more concrete or more specific are called *subordinate*. Superordinate concepts provide a context for discussing ideas lower in the hierarchy; coordinate concepts provide a basis for comparing and contrasting ideas, and subordinate concepts provide a basis for analyzing an idea in its kinds. Table 9.1 provides examples of superordinate, coordinate, and subordinate kind-of relations between concepts.

Table 9.1   Examples of superordinate, coordinate, and subordinate kind-of relationships (taxonomy) and part-of relationships (partonomy).

	Kind-of relationships	Part-of relationships
Superordinate *Provide* *context*	• The concept "animal" is superordinate to the concept "mammal" • The concept "non-fiction" is superordinate to the concept "cook book"	• The concept "body" is superordinate to the concept "leg" • The concept "book" is superordinate to the concept "chapter"
Coordinate *Compare &* *contrast*	• The concept "mammal" is coordinate to the concept "bird" • The concept "study book" is coordinate to the concept "travel guide"	• The concept "leg" is coordinate to the concept "arm" • The concept "chapter" is coordinate to the concept "preface"
Subordinate *Analyze*	• The concept "human" is subordinate to the concept "mammal" • The concept "self-study guide" is subordinate to the concept "study book"	• The concept "foot" is subordinate to the concept "leg" • The concept "section" is subordinate to the concept "chapter"

Another important association is the *part-of* relationship, which indicates that a particular concept is part of another concept. The concepts "keyboard" and "monitor", for example, have a part-of relationship with the concept "desktop computer", because they are both part of a desktop computer. Part-of relationships are often used to define a hierarchy of concepts that is called *partonomy*. The right column of Table 9.2 provides some examples of superordinate, coordinate, and subordinate part-of relationships between concepts.

Taxonomies and partonomies are examples of *hierarchically* ordered conceptual models. Alternatively, each concept in *heterarchical* models may have relationships with one or more other concepts, yielding network-like structures. A heterarchical model in which the relationships are not labeled is called a *concept map*. In such a map, specified relationships mean nothing more than "concept A is in some way related to concept B", "concept A is associated with concept B", or "concept A has something to do with concept B". Sometimes, a distinction is made between unidirectional relationships (indicated by an arrow from concept A to concept B) and bi-directional relationships (indicated by either a line without an arrowhead or a double-headed arrow between the concepts A and B). Figure 9.1 provides an example of a concept map indicating relationships between concepts that may help to reason about the pros and cons of vegetarianism.

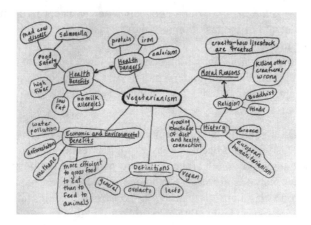

Figure 9.1   Example of a concept map.

One problem with the unlabeled relationships in a concept map is that their meaning may be misinterpreted or remain obscure. An alternative is a semantic network (see Figure 9.2), which may be seen as a concept map in which the relationships or links are explicitly labeled.

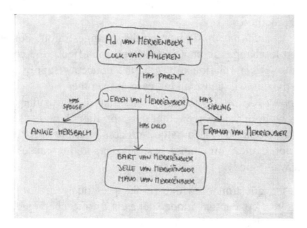

Figure 9.2   Example of a semantic network.

135

In addition to the kind-of and part-of relationships discussed, other meaningful relationships that may be used to label the links in a semantic network include:

- *Experiential relationship*, which connects a new concept to a concrete example, which is already familiar to the learners: a "car alternator" exemplifies the concept "generator".
- *Analogical relationship*, which connects a new concept to a similar, familiar concept outside of the task domain: the "human heart" is said to be similar to an "HS pump".
- *Prerequisite relationship*, which connects a new concept to another, familiar concept that enables the understanding of that new concept: understanding the concept "prime number" is enabled by understanding the prerequisite concept "division".

The experiential, analogical, and prerequisite relationships permit a deeper understanding of the task domain because they explicitly relate the conceptual model to what is already known by the learner. They are particularly important when inductive instructional methods are used for novice learners (see Chapter 7.3), because these relationships may help the learners to construct general and abstract models from their own prior knowledge. Other meaningful relationships include:

- *Location-in-time relationship*, indicating that a particular concept has a particular relation in time (i.e., before, during, after) with another concept: in a military context, the concept "debriefing" has an after-relation with the concept "operation".
- *Location-in-space relationship*, indicating that a particular concept has a special relation in space (e.g., in, on, under, above, etc.) with another concept: in a typical scientific article, the concept "results section" is located in space under the "method section".
- *Cause-effect relationship*, indicating that changes in one concept (the cause) are related to changes in another concept (the effect): the concept "demand" has a cause-effect relationship with the concept "supply", because an increase in the one will cause an increase in the other.
- *Natural-process relationship*, indicating that one particular concept typically coincides with, or follows, another concept, though no causality implied: the concept "evaporation" has a natural-process relation with "condensation" (in a distillation cycle, you cannot say that evaporation causes condensation or the other way round).

The answer to the question of which of the previously mentioned relationships should be used in a conceptual model depends on the characteristics of the task domain and, especially, on the learning tasks that will have to be carried out in this domain. To keep the analysis process manageable, conceptual models that allow for qualitative reasoning in a task domain best use a *parsimonious* set of relationships. Furthermore, one may explicitly focus on location relationships in structural models, or on cause-effect and natural-process relationships in causal models. The next sections discuss these special models.

Identify Structural Models

Structural models are domain models where location-in-time and/or location-in-space relations between concepts are dominant and together form *plans* allowing learners to answer the question "how is this built?" or "how is this organized?" Plans organize concepts in time or space. Plans that organize concepts in time are also called *scripts*. Scripts describe a stereotyped sequence of events or activities using location-in-time relationships. For instance, in biology the following script is seen as typical for the mating behavior of the male catfish:

- Chasing, followed by
- Clinging, followed by
- Enfolding while squeezing

This script allows a biologist to interpret the observation of male catfish acting in a certain way while in the vicinity of a female catfish as the start of a catfish mating ritual. It allows the biologist to understand what is going on, because the mating behavior of other fish is quite different from that of catfish. Furthermore, scripts allow the prediction of future events or of finding a coherent account for disjointed observations. For example, if a biologist observes a male catfish chasing and clinging, she can then predict that the male catfish will then enfold while squeezing.

Plans that organize concepts in space rather than time are also called *templates*, which describe a typical spatial organization of elements using location-in-space relationships. Early research in the field of chess, for example, showed that expert chess players have better memory for meaningful problem states than novices because they have templates available that refer to patterns of chess pieces on the board (De Groot, 1966). As a more practical example, in the field of scientific writing the following template is seen as typical for an empirical journal article:

- Introduction which is positioned in the article before the
- Method, which is positioned in the article before the
- Results, which is positioned in the article before the
- Discussion, which is positioned in the article before the
- References

This template helps a researcher to understand empirical articles quickly because they all adhere to the same basic structure. It also helps the researcher to write such articles because the templates steer the writing process. In the same way, templates in other fields help task performers to design artifacts: computer programmers use stereotyped patterns of arranging programming code, architects use typical building-block solutions for designing buildings, and electrical engineers build complex circuits from standard components.

Structural models often do not consist of just one plan, but rather of an interrelated set of plans that helps understand and design artifacts. Different kinds of relationships might be used to associate plans with each other. Figure 9.3 provides a structural model helpful for writing scientific articles. As another example in the field of computer programming, more general and abstract plans may refer to the basic outline of a program (e.g., heading, declaration, procedures, main program).

These plans are related to less abstract plans providing a general representation of basic programming structures such as procedures, looping structures, and decision structures. These, in turn, are related to concrete plans providing a representation of structures that are close to the actual programming codes, such as specific templates for looping structures (e.g., WHILE-loops, FOR-loops, REPEAT-UNTIL loops), conditions (e.g., IF-THEN, CASE), and so on.

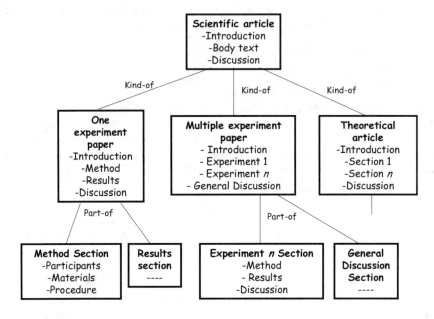

Figure 9.3   Structural model for writing scientific articles.

Identify Causal Models

Causal models are domain models in which cause-effect and natural-process relations between concepts are dominant, forming *principles* which allow learners to answer questions as "how does this work?" or "why doesn't this work?" Principles relate changes in one concept to changes in another concept, with either a cause-effect or a natural-process relationship. Cause-effect relationships may be deterministic, indicating that one change always implies another change. For instance, "a decrease in the volume of a vessel holding a gas always yields an increase in gas pressure", or, "a greater amount of carbon dioxide (CO_2) and/or ozone (O_3) in the atmosphere leads to more smog". The relationships may also be probabilistic, indicating that one change sometimes implies another change. For instance, "working hard can lead to success", or, "smoking can cause cancer". Natural-process relationships are used when one event typically coincides with another event (A occurs simultaneously to B; A occurs before B, or B follows A) - without causality implied. The relationship is thus merely correlational. For instance, "the sun rises each morning" (is it morning because the sun rises, or does the sun rise because it is morning?), or, "overweight people exercise little".

Causal models typically do not consist of one principle, but of an interrelated set of principles that apply in a particular domain. Causal models allow task performers to understand the working of natural phenomena, processes, and devices and to reason about them. Given a cause, the model enables making predictions and drawing implications (i.e., given a particular state, predict what effect it will have) and given an effect, the model enables giving explanations and interpreting events (i.e., given a particular state, explain what caused it). If a causal model describes the principles that apply in natural phenomena, it is called a *theory*. For instance, a theory of electricity may be used to design an electric circuit that yields a desired type of output, given a particular input (i.e., a large source of electricity running through a thin resistor makes the resistor very hot: this is how a light bulb functions). If a causal model describes the principles that apply in engineered systems, it is called a *functional model*. Such a model describes the behavior of individual components of the system by stating how they change in response to changes in input and how this affects their output, and it describes the behavior of the whole system by describing how the outputs of one device are connected to the inputs of other devices (i.e., "how it works").

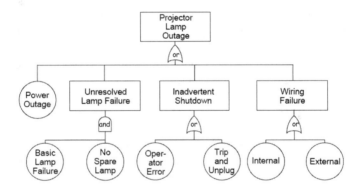

Figure 9.4   A fault tree for projector lamp outage.

Given a desired effect, a well-developed functional model of an engineered system allows someone who is performing a task to identify and arrange the causes that bring about the desired effect. This approach may be particularly helpful for carrying out operating tasks. Given an undesired effect (e.g., a fault or an error), a well-developed functional model allows a task-performer to identify the causes that might have brought about the undesired effect (i.e., make a diagnosis) and, eventually, to re-arrange those causes to reach a desired effect (i.e., make a repair). This may be particularly helpful when performing troubleshooting tasks. *And/or-graphs* are suitable representations for linking effects to multiple causes, and *fault trees* are a specific type of and/or-graph that may help the user to perform troubleshooting tasks because they identify all of the potential causes of system failure (Wood, Stephens, & Barker, 1979). Figure 9.4 provides a simple example of a fault tree for diagnosing projector-lamp outage. It indicates that failure of the lamp may be the result of power outage (the circle on the second level indicates that this is a basic event not developed further) *or* an unresolved lamp failure *or* an inadvertent shutdown *or* a wiring failure. An unresolved lamp failure, in turn, results from a basic lamp failure *and* the absence of a spare lamp. It should be clear that fault trees for large technical systems might become extremely complex.

Combining Different Types of Models

Structural models and causal models are special kinds of conceptual models, and provide a particular perspective on a task domain. Complex domain models may combine them into semantic nets, which try to represent the whole mental model enabling the performance of a complex cognitive skill. However, to keep the analysis process manageable, it might be worthwhile to focus first on only one type of model. Different task domains have different dominant structures: Structural models are particularly important for domains that focus on analysis and design, such as mechanical engineering, instructional design, or architecture; causal models are particularly important for domains that focus on explanation, prediction and diagnosis, such as the natural sciences or medicine, and general conceptual models are particularly important for domains that focus on description, classification and qualitative reasoning, such as history or law. The analyst should start with an analysis of the dominant type of model, or, "organizing content" in the domain of interest (Dijkstra & van Merriënboer, 1997; Reigeluth & Stein, 1983). In later stages of the analysis process, other models that form part of the mental model may then be linked to this organizing content.

9.2   Analyzing Intuitive Mental Models

The Ten Steps focus on the analysis of effective mental models that help solve problems and carry out tasks in the domain. This is a "rational" analysis because the identified domain models rest on generally accepted conceptions, plans, and laws in the domain. In addition to this rational analysis, the instructional designer can and should analyze the mental models of novice learners in the field. This is an "empirical" analysis because it describes the actual models used by the target group. There may be considerable differences between domain models which describe the effective mental models used by competent task performers and the intuitive or naive mental models of novice learners in that domain. Such intuitive or naive mental models are often fragmented, inexact, and incomplete; they may reflect misunderstandings or *misconceptions*, and the learners are typically unaware of the underlying relationships between the elements. Figure 9.5, for example, provides examples of novice learner's intuitive conceptual models of the earth (Vosniadou & Brewer, 1992). An example of an intuitive structural model is that of the Internet as a centralized system, in which all computer systems are connected to one central server. An example of an intuitive causal model is that the tides are exclusively caused by the revolution of the moon.

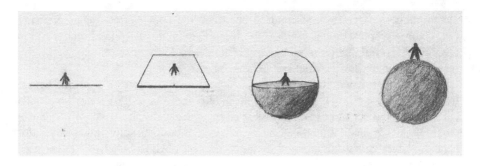

Figure 9.5   Examples of child's naive mental models of the Earth (Vosniadou & Brewer, 1992).

Intuitive mental models are often very hard to change. One approach is to begin the instruction with the existing intuitive models (i.e., using inductive teaching methods) and slowly progress toward increasingly more effective models in a process of *conceptual change* (Schnotz, Vosniadou, & Carretero, 1999). Another approach is to use instructional methods that help learners question the effectiveness of their intuitive model, such as by contrasting it with models that are more accurate or by taking multiple perspectives on it. These approaches are briefly discussed in the next section.

9.3   Using Domain Models to Make Design Decisions.

Step 6 is only performed if information on domain models is not available in existing documentation and instructional materials. If it is performed, the resulting analysis results provide the basis for a number of design activities. In particular, specified domain models may help the further refining of an existing sequence of task classes by using a progression of mental models, and the designing of an important part of the supportive information. In addition, the identification of intuitive mental models may affect several design decisions.

Refining Task Classes through a Progression of Mental Models

Domain models can be used for refining an existing sequence of task classes, using the method of *mental model progression* (see Chapter 5.1). The first task class is defined as a category of learning tasks that can be correctly performed based on the simplest domain-model. This model already contains the concepts that are most representative, fundamental, and concrete and should be powerful enough to enable the formulation of non-trivial learning tasks that learners may work on. Increasingly more difficult task classes correspond one-to-one with increasingly more complex domain models. In general, models that are more complex contain more - different types of - elements and more relationships between those elements than earlier models that are less complex. They either add complexity or detail to a part or aspect of the former models and become elaborations or embellishments of them or they provide alternative perspectives on solving problems in the domain. In a mental model progression, all models thus share the same essential characteristics: Each more-complex model builds upon the previous models. This process continues until a level of elaboration and a set of models offering different perspectives is reached that underlies the final exit behavior.

Table 9.2 provides an example of a mental model progression in the field of troubleshooting electrical circuits (White & Frederiksen, 1990). Each model enables learners to perform learning tasks that may also occur in the post-instructional environment. In this domain, causal models describe the principles that govern the behavior of electrical circuits and their components such as batteries, resistors, capacitors, and so forth. Three simple-to-complex causal models are:

- *Zero-order models* containing principles relating the mere presence or absence of resistance, voltage, and current to the behavior of a circuit. They can be used to answer a question like "will the light bulb be on or off?"
- *First-order models* containing principles that relate changes in one thing to changes in another. They can be used to answer a question like "is there an increase in voltage when the resistance is lowered?"
- *Quantitative models* containing principles that express the laws of electricity, such as Kirchov's law and Ohm's law. They can be used to answer a question like "what is the voltage across the points X and Y in this circuit?"

Table 9.2   A mental model progression in the domain of electronics troubleshooting (White & Frederiksen, 1990).

Model Progression	Content of Model	Corresponding Task Class
Zero-order model	• Basic circuit principles • Types of conductivity • Current and absence/presence of resistance	Learning tasks requiring understanding of how voltages, current flows and resistances are divided
First-order model	• Concept of feedback • Analog circuits • Relating voltage, current and resistance	Learning tasks requiring detecting and understanding feedback
Quantitative model	• Kirchov's law • Ohm's law • Wheatstone bridges	Learning tasks requiring computing voltages, currents and resistances across points

Designing Supportive Information

Domain models provide the basis for designing the part of the supportive information related to mental models. First, they may be explicitly presented to learners because they tell them how things are labeled, how things are built, and how things work in a particular domain (see Chapter 7.1). An educational specification is often needed to ensure that the domain model is formulated in such a way that it is clearly understandable for the learners for whom it is designed. Second, domain models may help the instructional designer to find case studies that give concrete examples of the classification, organization, and working of things (see Chapter 7.2). Those case studies may be seen either as learning tasks with maximum *product-oriented support* or as illustrations of mental models. Third, domain models may fulfill a role in providing cognitive feedback to learners because learners can then be asked to compare their own solutions with a presented domain model (see Chapter 7.4). If learners, for example, have written a scientific article they may then compare the structure of their own article with a given structural model (cf. Figure 9.3) or with a specific article from a scientific journal in that domain. If a learner has reached a diagnosis of a particular error he or she can then check the credibility of his or her own diagnosis with a given fault tree (cf. Figure 9.4). Such reflective activities help learners to elaborate on the supportive information.

Dealing with Intuitive Mental Models

The identification of intuitive models that novice learners possess may affect decision making for the design activities discussed previously. With regard to refining task classes, the existence of intuitive models may be a reason to start from those existing models and to provide a relatively large number of task classes, that is, to work slowly from the intuitive, ineffective models, via more effective but still incomplete and fragmented models, toward more effective, more complete, and more integrated models. This allows learners to carefully compare and contrast, at each level of difficulty, the new and more powerful models with previous, less powerful models. Ideally, the scientific models of experts then gradually replace the intuitive models of novice learners. It should, however, be stressed that intuitive mental models may be highly resistant to change.

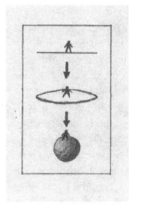

With regard to *designing supportive information*, the existence of strong intuitive mental models might be a reason to select instructional methods that explicitly focus on the elaboration of new information. First, with regard to case studies, it is desirable to present a relatively large number of case studies to illustrate the domain model and to present those case studies from *multiple viewpoints*. For instance, when teaching a model of the earth, the supportive information may be in the form of satellite images of the earth from different perspectives (always showing a sphere but with different continents), and when teaching the working of the tides, case studies may show that the tides are stronger in the Atlantic Ocean than in the Mediterranean Sea and are thus not only affected by the relative location of the moon and the sun to the earth but also by their shape, size, and boundaries. Second, *inductive methods* and *guided discovery methods* should be preferred above *deductive methods*. The former two methods help learners refine their existing models and construct models that are more effective. Questions such as "why do ships disappear beyond the horizon?" and "what happens if you start walking in a straight line and never stop?" may help refine a model of the earth, Questions such as "when is it spring tide?" and "when is it neap tide?" may help build a model of how the tides work. Third, *feedback by discovery* should stimulate learners to critically compare and contrast their own models with more effective or more scientific models. Here, learners could compare their own model of the earth with a globe, and they could compare their own predictions of the tides with the actual measurements provided by the coast guard.

Analyzing Mental Models Versus Analyzing Cognitive Strategies

Mental models describe how the world is organized and cognitive strategies (Chapter 8) describe how task performers' actions in this world are organized. The Ten Steps assume a *reciprocal relationship* between mental models and cognitive strategies, indicating that the one is of little use without the other. The better a learner's knowledge about a particular domain is organized in mental models, the more likely it is that the use of cognitive strategies will lead to a sound solution. The reverse of this is also true. The more powerful the mental models are, the more likely it is that cognitive strategies help find solutions. Therefore, well-designed instruction should always ensure that the development of domain models goes hand in hand with the development of SAPs.

According to the Ten Steps, the difference between cognitive strategies and mental models is primarily in their *use* rather than in the *way* they are represented in human memory. Cognitive strategies, for example, use location-in-time relationships to describe task performer's actions while mental models use the same relationships to describe particular events in the world and cognitive strategies use cause-effect relationships to describe rules-of-thumb while mental models use the same relationships to describe principles that apply in a particular domain. In essence, the same representation can be and is used in different ways. A geographical map provides a useful metaphor. On one hand, it provides an impression of what a geographical area looks like (cf. a mental model), while on the other hand it can be used to plan a route for traveling from A to B (cf. a cognitive strategy).

The Ten Steps suggest analyzing cognitive strategies (Step 5) before analyzing mental models (Step 6). The reason for this is that SAPs are often underspecified or even completely absent in existing documentation and instructional materials. In traditional instruction, it is common to focus first on "what-is questions" and only then to focus on "how-to questions". The Ten Steps reverse this. Nevertheless, there is no fixed order for analyzing cognitive strategies and mental models. If the learning tasks under consideration are best described as applying SAPs (e.g., design skills) it is probably easiest to start with an analysis of cognitive strategies, but if they are best described as reasoning with domain models (e.g., diagnosis skills) it is probably easiest to start with an analysis of mental models.

9.4   Summary of Guidelines

- If you analyze domain models, then study relevant documents and interview competent task performers to identify the dominant knowledge elements and relationships between those elements that may help to qualitatively reason in the task domain.

- If you identify conceptual models that allow for description and classification, then focus on kind-of-relationships and part-of relationships between concepts.
- If you want to relate new conceptual models to the prior knowledge of your learners, then use experiential, analogical, and prerequisite relationships.
- If you identify structural models, then focus on location-in-time and/or location-in-space relationships.
- If you identify causal models, then focus on cause-effect and/or natural-process relationships.
- If you analyze intuitive mental models, then focus on the discrepancies between the elements and relationships between elements distinguished by a competent task performer and those distinguished by a naive learner.
- If you use a domain model to refine a sequence of task classes, then identify simple to increasingly more complex models and define corresponding task classes.
- If you use a domain model to design supportive information, then formulate the domain model in such a way that it is clearly understandable for your target group and select or design case studies that can be used to illustrate the model.
- If you are teaching a domain model to learners who are inclined to use an ineffective intuitive mental model, then present case studies from different viewpoints, use inductive or guided discovery strategies, and provide feedback by discovery.
- If you need to analyze cognitive strategies and mental models, then start with the analysis that is easiest to perform in your task domain.

10
STEP 7: DESIGN PROCEDURAL INFORMATION

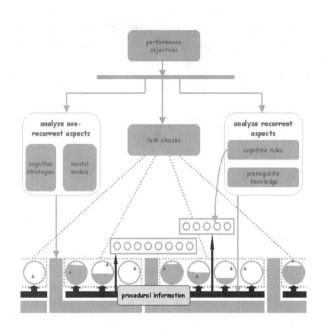

Necessity

Procedural information is one of the four design components and enables learners to perform the recurrent aspects of learning tasks as well as part-task practice items. It is strongly recommended to perform this step.

Much that we do in our lives is partly based upon fairly fixed "routines". We have routines when we get up in the morning, when we go to work or school during the week, when we do our weekly shopping at the supermarket, when we cook certain dishes, and even when we study for examinations. We have these routines and use them for carrying out those task aspects or performing those acts that are basically the same every time we do them. In other words, we follow fixed procedures.

This chapter presents guidelines for designing procedural information. It concerns the third blueprint component, which specifies how to perform the recurrent aspects of learning tasks (Step 1) or how to carry out part-task practice items (Step 10) which are always recurrent. Procedural information refers to (a) *just-in-time (JIT) information displays* providing learners with the rules or procedures that describe the performance of recurrent aspects of a complex skill as well as knowledge prerequisite for correctly carrying out those rules or procedures, (b) *demonstrations* of the application of those rules and procedures as well as instances of the prerequisite knowledge, and (c) *corrective feedbac*k on errors. All instructional methods for presenting procedural information promote *knowledge compilation*, a process through which new knowledge is converted into highly specific cognitive rules. These cognitive rules drive the recurrent aspects of performance without the need of interpreting cognitive schemas. After extensive training, which may sometimes take the form of part-task practice (see Chapter 13), the rules can even become fully automated (routines) and drive the recurrent aspects of performance without the need for conscious control.

The structure of this chapter is as follows. First, the design of JIT information displays is discussed. These displays should be modular, use simple language, and prevent split attention effects. Then, the use of demonstrations and instances is described. Presented rules and procedures are best demonstrated in the context of the whole learning tasks. This is followed by three presentation strategies for procedural information, namely unsolicited presentation by an instructor or computer system, on-demand presentation in a manual, help system, or job aid, and presentation in advance so that the learners can memorize it before they start to work on the learning tasks. Fourth, guidelines are given for providing corrective feedback on the recurrent aspects of performance. Finally, the positioning of procedural information in the training blueprint is discussed. The chapter concludes with a brief summary of guidelines.

10.1 Providing Just-In-Time Information Displays

Learners need procedural information to carry out the recurrent aspects of learning tasks. *Just-in-time information displays* specify how to carry out those tasks at a level of detail that can be immediately understood by all learners. It is often called "how-to instruction", "rule-based instruction", or "step-by-step instruction" and is often presented by an instructor or made available in manuals, (on-line) help systems, job aids, quick reference guides, and so forth. Because the procedural information is identical for many, if not all, learning tasks that appeal to the same recurrent constituent skills, it is typically provided along with the first learning task for which the recurrent aspect is relevant. For subsequent learning tasks, it is quickly diminished as learners gain more expertise and no longer need the help (this principle is called *fading*).

Just-in-time (JIT) information combines two types of knowledge. First, it reflects the cognitive rules that allow one to carry out particular recurrent aspects of performance in a correct, algorithmic fashion. The analysis of those rules, or of procedures that combine those rules, is discussed in Chapter 11. Second, it concerns those things that the learner should know in order to be able to apply those rules correctly (i.e., prerequisite knowledge or concepts). The analysis of those prerequisite knowledge elements, such as facts, concepts, plans, and principles is discussed in Chapter 12. Clearly, there is a *unidirectional* relationship between cognitive rules and prerequisite knowledge: prerequisite knowledge is pre-conditional to correct use of the cognitive rules, but not the other way round.

Both cognitive rules and prerequisite knowledge are best presented during practice, precisely when learners need it. When learning to play golf and making your first drives on the driving range, your instructor will probably tell you how to hold your club (a rule), what a "club" is (a concept prerequisite to the use of the rule), how to take your stance (a rule), how to swing the club and follow through with your swing (a rule), and what "following through" is (a concept prerequisite to the use of the rule). Although it is possible to present all of this information beforehand in a classroom lesson or in a textbook, it makes more sense to present it exactly when it is needed, because its activation in short-term working memory during task performance helps learners to construct appropriate cognitive rules in their long-term memory.

Partitioning the Information in Small Units

JIT information has a *modular structure* and is organized in small displays where each display corresponds with one rule or one procedure for reaching a meaningful goal. The displays are clearly separated from each other according to a principle called *closure*, which indicates that the displays are clearly distinct from each other and self-contained (i.e., they can be fully understood without consulting additional information sources). Organization of the information in small units is essential because only by presenting relatively small amounts of new information at the same time can we prevent processing (i.e., cognitive) overload when learners are working on the learning tasks.

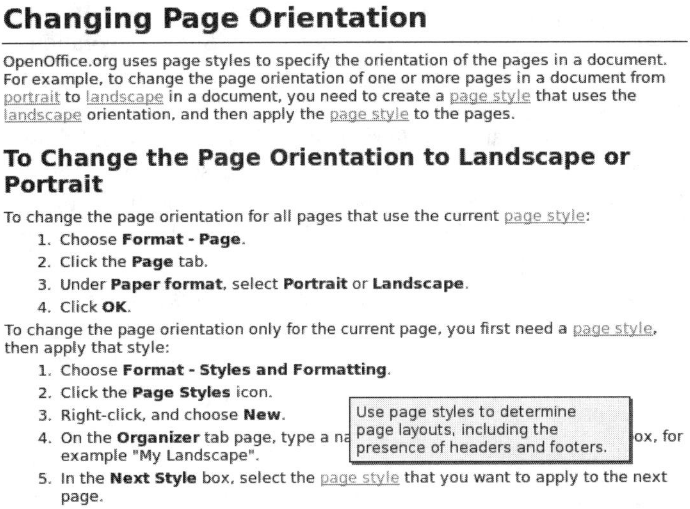

Changing Page Orientation

OpenOffice.org uses page styles to specify the orientation of the pages in a document. For example, to change the page orientation of one or more pages in a document from portrait to landscape in a document, you need to create a page style that uses the landscape orientation, and then apply the page style to the pages.

To Change the Page Orientation to Landscape or Portrait

To change the page orientation for all pages that use the current page style:

1. Choose **Format - Page**.
2. Click the **Page** tab.
3. Under **Paper format**, select **Portrait** or **Landscape**.
4. Click **OK**.

To change the page orientation only for the current page, you first need a page style, then apply that style:

1. Choose **Format - Styles and Formatting**.
2. Click the **Page Styles** icon.
3. Right-click, and choose **New**.
4. On the **Organizer** tab page, type a name ... box, for example "My Landscape".

   > Use page styles to determine page layouts, including the presence of headers and footers.

5. In the **Next Style** box, select the page style that you want to apply to the next page.

Figure 10.1   Example of a JIT Information display presenting the procedure for changing document orientation (based on OpenOffice.org Writer).

Figure 10.1 provides a familiar example of a JIT information display presented on a computer screen. The display is clearly oriented towards one goal, namely, "changing the page orientation of a document". It provides the procedure to reach this goal, and each instruction corresponds with one procedural step. Some steps may require prerequisite knowledge, such as knowledge of the concepts 'page style', 'portrait', and 'landscape'. In the example, these are hot, clickable words with a different color than the main text and linked to certain concept-specific or action-specific information. The box in Figure 10.1 shows the concept definition that appears if the learner or user clicks the link 'Page Style'. Clicking the other links will yield similar concept definitions. Finally, this example shows that some goals may refer to lower-level sub goals with their own procedures, for instance, applying the page style to a single page or applying the page style to all subsequent pages.

Formulating JIT Information

The most important requirement for formulating JIT information is that each rule or procedural step is specified at the *entry level* of the learners. Ideally, even the lowest-level ability learners must be able to apply the presented rules, or carry out the presented actions, without making errors - under the assumption that they already possess the prerequisite knowledge. This requirement is directly related to the main distinguishing characteristic between a SAP and a procedure: In a SAP, success is not guaranteed because the phases merely guide the learner through a heuristic problem-solving process, but in a procedure success *is* guaranteed because the steps provide an algorithmic description of how to reach the goal (Note: It is always possible to apply a rule or carry out an action incorrectly and have the procedure fail). Because each step or rule is formulated at a level that it is directly understandable for each learner, no particular reference has to be made during the presentation to related knowledge structures in long-term memory. Since elaboration is of importance to reach understanding of supportive information, it is superfluous if the given information is immediately comprehensible.

It is important to use an action-oriented writing style for JIT information displays, which entails using the active voice, writing in short sentences, and not spelling everything out. If a procedure is long and complex, it is better presented graphically. Moreover, when procedures specify the operation of complex machinery, it may be helpful to depict *physical models* of those devices in exploded views or via other graphical representations. The analysis of tools and objects into physical models is briefly discussed in Chapter 12.1. There are many more guidelines for micro-level message design and technical writing that will not be discussed in this book (see Alred, Brusaw, & Oliu, 2003; Fleming & Levie, 1993; Hartley, 1994).

Preventing Split Attention

When making use of JIT information, learners must divide their attention between the learning task they are working on and the JIT information that is presented to specify how to perform the recurrent aspects of this task. In this situation, learners must continuously switch their attention between the JIT information and the learning task in order to integrate the two mentally. This continuous switching between mental activities (i.e., carrying out the task and processing the JIT information) may increase extraneous cognitive load (see Box 1) and hamper learning. Compare this with trying to hit a golf ball while at the same time the golf pro is giving you all types of pointers on your stance, your grip, the angle of your arms, and so forth. This *split attention effect* has been well documented in the literature (for an overview, see Chandler & Sweller, 1992; Sweller, van Merriënboer, & Paas, 1998). To prevent the split attention effect, it is of utmost importance to integrate the JIT information fully with the task environment and to replace multiple sources of information with a single, integrated source of information. This physical integration removes the need for mental integration, reduces extraneous cognitive load, and has positive effects on learning.

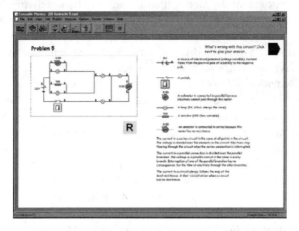

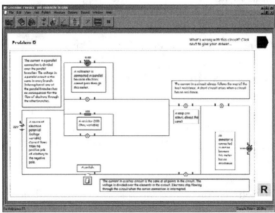

Figure 10.2   An electrical circuit with non-integrated JIT information (above) and integrated JIT information (below).

Figure 10.2 provides an example of a task environment in which students learn to troubleshoot electrical circuits with the aid of a computer simulation. In the upper figure, the diagram of the electrical circuit on the left side of the screen is separated from the JIT information on the right side of the screen, causing split attention because the learner must constantly move back and forth between the circuit and its components on the left-hand side of the screen and the information about the components on the right-hand side. In the lower figure, the exact same JIT information is fully integrated into the diagram of the electrical circuit such that the learner does not have to split his/her attention between a component in the circuit and the information about that component. The integrated format has been shown to have positive effects on learning (Kester, Kirschner, & van Merriënboer, 2004a, 2004b, 2005).

A special type of split attention occurs with paper-based manuals (or checklists, quick reference guides, etc.) containing procedural information which relates to a real-life task environment. In such a situation, it may be impossible to integrate the information in the task environment. For instance, if a medical student is diagnosing a patient or if a process operator is starting up a distiller, the relevant procedural information cannot be integrated into the task environment. One option to prevent that learners have to divide their attention between the task environment and the procedural information here is to include representations of the task environment in the manual. For instance, if the task environment is a computer-based environment, then you can include screen-captures in the manual (Chandler & Sweller, 1996), and if the task environment is an operating task for a particular machine, then you can include pictures of the relevant parts of the machine in the manual. It is, after all, the splitting of the learner's attention between the task environment and the manual that creates the problem, not the use of the manual per se. This split attention problem, thus, can be solved by either integrating the JIT information in the task environment or, vice versa, by integrating relevant parts of the task environment in the manual. In the future, new modes of presentation such as *augmented reality* may even make this problem smaller. To use the example previously mentioned, the process operator could wear a pair of glasses that present the JIT information at the time and place that the operator is looking.

10.2   Exemplifying Just-In-Time Information

JIT information can best be exemplified using concrete examples in the context of whole tasks. *Demonstrations* exemplify the use of procedures and the application of rules, whereas *instances* exemplify prerequisite knowledge elements.

Demonstrations

The rules and procedures presented in JIT information-displays can be *demonstrated* to the learners. It is not, for example, uncommon that on-line displays like the one presented in Figure 10.1 contain a "show me"-link, which animates the corresponding cursor movements and menu selections giving the learner or user the opportunity to observe how the rules are applied or how the steps are performed in a concrete situation. The Ten Steps strongly suggest providing such demonstrations in the context of whole, meaningful tasks. Thus, demonstrations of recurrent aspects of a skill ideally coincide with modeling examples or other suitable types of learning tasks. This allows learners to see how a particular recurrent aspect of a task fits within meaningful whole-task performance.

Going back to students learning to search for relevant research literature, at some point in their training they will receive JIT information on how to operate the search program. A particular JIT information display might present the step-by-step procedure for limiting a search to particular publication types (e.g., books, journal articles, dissertations, etc.) or years. This procedure is preferably demonstrated in the context of the learning task, showing how to limit the search to publication types relevant for the task at hand, instead of dreaming up a demonstration for an imaginary situation. Another situation is where a complex troubleshooting skill requires executing a standard procedure to detect when a specific value is out of range. This standard procedure is best demonstrated as part of a modeling example for the whole troubleshooting skill, where the learner's attention is focused on those recurrent aspects spotlighted in the demonstration.

Instances

Linked to the demonstration of procedures or rules ("show me"), it may be helpful to give concrete examples or instances (Merrill, 1983) of possible knowledge elements (i.e., facts, concepts, plans, and principles) that are prerequisite to correctly using the rules or procedural steps. Just like demonstrations of rules and procedures, instances are best presented in the context of the learning tasks. Thus, if a concrete page layout is presented as an instance of the concept "page style" (see the box in Figure 10.1), this should be a set of specifications that is as relevant as possible for the specific task at hand (here changing the page orientation). In the case where students learn to search for relevant research literature, a JIT information display on how to limit the search to particular publication types would provide concept definitions of those publication types. Again, if a concrete instance is shown of one particular type of publication, this should preferably be a publication that is relevant for the search-task at hand.

Van Merriënboer and Luursema (1995) describe a programming tutor in which all procedural information is presented and demonstrated in a just-in-time manner. The system uses completion tasks, in which the learners have to complete partially written computer programs. When a particular piece of programming code is used for the first time in part of a to-be-completed program, an on-line JIT information display presents a rule describing when and how this pattern of code should be used. At the same time, the instantiated code is highlighted in the given part of the computer program, offering a concrete instance exemplifying the use of the code in a realistic computer program.

Combining JIT Information Displays with Demonstrations and Instances

JIT information is always specified at the level of the lowest-ability learners, suggesting the use of a deductive strategy for information presentation (cf. Table 7.3). This means that the instructional designer works from the general procedural steps and condition-action pairs in the JIT information-displays to the concrete examples of those steps and pairs, namely the demonstrations and instances. This strategy is time-effective and takes maximum advantage of the fact that learners already possess the prior knowledge necessary to understand the given information easily. The use of an inductive strategy to promote elaboration is superfluous here. Ideally, JIT information-displays are presented *simultaneously* with those demonstrations and instances that are part of the same learning task as the displays are connected. This was already illustrated in Figure 10.2. There, the JIT information-displays are not only integrated with the learning task in space, preventing *spatial split attention* effects, but also integrated in time, preventing *temporal split attention* effects. In this way, the JIT information is best positioned in the context of the whole task.

Concluding, it should be noted that more demonstrations of a rule or procedure, and/or more instances of its prerequisite knowledge elements might be desirable to fully exemplify a JIT information-display. These demonstrations and instances must be *divergent* for all situations the JIT information applies. A demonstration will typically show the application of only one version of a procedure. For instance, the procedure for changing the page orientation (Figure 10.1) may be used to change the orientation of one page or the whole document. Therefore, the procedure may be demonstrated by changing the layout of one page, but it may also be demonstrated by changing the layout of the whole document. Ideally, the whole set of demonstrations given to the learner is *divergent*, that is, representative for all situations that can be handled with the procedure. Likewise, an instance only concerns one example of a concept, plan, or principle. If an instance is presented to exemplify the concept "page style", the instance may show different footers, headers, and orientations. As for demonstrations, the whole set of instances should ideally be representative for all entities covered by the concept, plan, or principle.

10.3   Presentation Strategies

Procedural information should be active in learners' working memory when learning tasks are practiced so that it can be converted into cognitive rules in a process of *knowledge compilation* (see Box 4 in this Chapter). Optimal availability of procedural information during practice must be ensured. To this end, the timing of the information presentation is important because the new information must be active in working memory when it is needed to carry out the task. Three presentation strategies are:

1   *Unsolicited presentation.* Procedural information is spontaneously presented to the learners by the instructor or by a computer system, providing step-by-step instructions that are simultaneously acted upon by the learners. In the case of unsolicited presentation, the learners have no control over the presentation. The relevant procedural steps are thus directly activated in the learners' working memory.

2   *On-demand presentation.* Procedural information is actively solicited by the learners and provided by the instructor or by specialized instructional materials (e.g., manuals, help systems, job aids, quick reference guides) during task performance when the learner requests it. In the case of on-demand presentation, the relevant procedural steps are only activated in the learners' working memory after they have been located in specially designed and easily accessible instructional materials.

3   *Memorization in advance.* Learners memorize the procedural information before they need to use it when performing a learning task for the first time. During task performance, the procedural steps are easily accessible in the learners' long-term memory and readily activated in working memory.

Unsolicited Information Presentation

The most familiar type of *unsolicited presentation* of JIT information is given by an instructor, who is acting like an "Assistant Looking Over Your Shoulder" (ALOYS; see Figure 10.3) and who gives specific directions on how to perform recurrent aspects of learning tasks. This form of *contingent tutoring* (Wood & Wood, 1999) is exhibited, for example, by the teacher who closely watches individual students while they work on learning tasks in a laboratory and who gives directions like "no, you should hold this equipment this way…" or "alright, and now you must divide this number by that one…", or by the coach who observes her players from the side of the playing field and shouts directions like "remember to bend your knees…" or "no, keep your eye on the ball…" These how-to directions involve the recurrent aspects of performance rather than the more complex conceptual and strategic issues (i.e., supportive information). Nevertheless, it is extremely difficult to determine when to present what type of JIT information. The instructor must continuously monitor whole-task performance of individual students and interpret this performance to "predict" when particular JIT information is needed by a particular learner in a particular situation. There have been attempts to automate the unsolicited presentation of JIT information in the field of intelligent tutoring and intelligent help systems, but this has proven to be very difficult if learners perform complex and open-ended learning tasks. This is only possible if learners only perform one recurrent aspect of a complex task as part-task practice (see Chapter 13).

Figure 10.3   The assistant looking over your shoulder.

Because an instructor is often not available and because the automation of contingent tutoring is extremely difficult, the Ten Steps suggest explicitly presenting JIT information-displays together with the first learning task for which they are relevant as a default presentation strategy. This is also called *system-initiated help* (Aleven, Stahl, Schworm, Fischer, & Wallace, 2003). The JIT information is connected to a learning task that, if possible, also demonstrates the use of the new rule or procedure. The information presented is more or less gradually diminished for subsequent learning tasks. One example of this approach would be when JIT information is explicitly displayed together with the first learning task for which it is relevant, when it is presented on the learner's request for a few subsequent learning tasks, and where it is withheld for the final learning tasks. Whereas this approach works well under most circumstances, one requirement is that the designer has a certain degree of control over which learning tasks the learner will be confronted. If this is not the case, it may not be feasible to connect the JIT information displays to the learning tasks. If training takes place on the job, it is not uncommon for the learner to be confronted with authentic but arbitrary problems that cannot be foreseen by the designer. A good example of this is when a medical student is in training at a hospital. In this situation, there is no real control over the order in which he or she will encounter different patients with different symptoms and different diseases. This makes system-initiated help impossible. In such situations, use is sometimes made of decision support systems; computer-based information systems that are used for supporting decision-making (Turban, 1995).

On-Demand Information Presentation

The unsolicited presentation of procedural information, precisely when students need it, is the best way to facilitate knowledge compilation (Aleven et al., 2003; Anderson, 1993). Such contingent tutoring, however, is very difficult to implement if no human tutor is available. System-initiated help, on the other hand, is very difficult to implement if the designer has no control over the learning tasks that the learners will be confronted with. The question also exists as to when exactly "precisely when students need it" is and who should determine that moment. In these situations, on-demand presentation of JIT information in a manual, (on-line) help system, or checklist is a viable alternative. Whereas the JIT information is not presented directly and explicitly when it is needed for the learning tasks, it is at least easily available and readily accessible for the learners during practice.

There are three basic guidelines for the unsolicited presentation of JIT information-displays and all three are equally important for *on-demand information presentation*. The guidelines are: (a) present small modular units, (b) write in an action-oriented style, and (c) prevent split attention.

With regard to *modular* structure, well-designed on-demand materials ideally should support random access. Thus, JIT information-displays should be as independent of one another as possible, so that learners can jump around in any direction. Whereas complete independence may be impossible to realize, displays should be as independent as possible by providing *closure*, meaning that they can be understood without consulting "outside" information because they are written for the lowest-level ability learner.

With regard to *action-oriented writing*, it is important that the learner is actually invited to perform the recurrent aspects of the learning task. Van der Meij (2003) gives an example of an uninviting and ineffective invitation to act:

> • You can choose the REMOVE command
> The text has now been removed
>
> Note: Instead of the REMOVE command, you could also use [DELETE] or [BACKSPACE].

This writing is uninviting because there are no words that prompt the learner to act. The user is stimulated to read rather than to act. The word "note" refers to a remark on the side, an addendum. The learner cannot really act or explore, because there are no alternatives that can be tried out. In an action-oriented style, the words clearly prompt the learner to act and the invitation comes just at the right moment. There are no side notes, but rather true alternatives that can be tried out, as in the following display inviting learners to browse a text:

> Quickly browsing a text
> • Press the ↓ key a number of times to see what happens
>
> The → key and ← key work in almost the same way. Try them out!

With regard to *preventing split attention*, instructional materials for the on-demand presentation of JIT information should take into account that information-seeking activities bring about additional cognitive load that may negatively affect learning. Even if the information is useful, learning may be reduced because simultaneously dealing with the learning task and the procedural information imposes too much cognitive load on the learners. Consulting additional information when cognitive load is already high due to the characteristics of the learning task easily becomes a burden for learners as indicated by the saying "when all else fails, consult the manual…".

In the field of *minimalism* (Carroll, 1998; Carroll, Smith-Kerker, Ford, & Mazur-Rimetz, 1988; Lazonder & van der Meij, 1993), additional guidelines have been developed for the design of *minimal manuals* that provide procedural information on demand. Minimalism explicitly focuses on supporting learners, or users in general, who are working on meaningful tasks. The three main guidelines for this approach pertain to:

1   *Goal directedness.* Use an index system allowing learners to search for recognizable goals they may be trying to reach rather than functions of the task environment. In other words, design in a task-oriented rather than system-

oriented fashion. Learners' goals, thus, provide the most important entrance to the JIT information-displays (see Table 10.1).

2   *Active learning and exploration.* Allow learners to continue their work on whole, meaningful learning tasks, to explore things. Let them try out different recurrent task aspects for themselves.

3   *Error recovery.* When learners try out the recurrent task aspects, things may go wrong. Error recognition and error recovery must be supported on the spot, by including a section "What to do if things go wrong?" in the JIT information-display (Lazonder & van der Meij, 1994, 1995).

Table 10.1   Goal-oriented versus system-oriented titles of JIT information displays (van der Meij & Carroll, 1995).

Goal-oriented titles (*correct*)	System-oriented titles (*incorrect*)
Starting up the class browser	Using keyboard messages
Finding the application game	The Format menu
Creating an application instance	Macros
Sending messages to the application instance	Using Convert
Exploring other objects and messages used by the application class	Displaying hidden codes

Memorization in Advance

In addition to unsolicited and on-demand information presentation, a third, traditional approach has learners memorize procedural information before they start to work on the learning tasks. By doing this, learners store information in long-term memory so that it may be activated in working memory when needed for performing the recurrent aspects of learning tasks. The procedural information is already specified at a level that it is immediately understandable by all learners, so that mindful elaboration of the information (i.e., deliberately connecting it to what is already known) is not critical. Instead, instructional methods typically encourage learners to maintain the new information in an active state by repeating it, either aloud or mentally, in order to store it in memory. This repetition of information is also called rehearsal. The use of *mnemonics* (e.g., phrases, acronyms, visual imagery, tricks) and the formation of more or less meaningful information clusters with a relatively small size may facilitate memorization. Two of the better-known mnemonics are "i before e, except after c or when sounded as 'ay' as in neighbor and weigh" and "Roy G Biv" (red, orange, yellow, green, blue, indigo, violet for remembering the colors of the spectrum and their sequence). As an example of clustering, suppose that knowledge of shorthand airport destinations (JFK for New York, AMS for Amsterdam, etc.) is necessary for handling airfreight, useful clusters would be "destinations in Europe", "destinations in South America", and so forth.

Prior memorization is *not* recommended by the Ten Steps for two reasons. First, such memorization makes it impossible to demonstrate a presented rule or procedure, or to give instances of its prerequisite knowledge elements in the context of whole learning tasks. For instance, if learners need to memorize that a particular software package uses function keys F9 to synchronize folders, Alt-F8 to edit macros, and Alt-F11 to go to Visual Basic *before* they work with the package, how function keys actually work cannot be simultaneously demonstrated in the context of working with the package. This hinders the development of an integrated knowledge base in which the non-recurrent and recurrent aspects of working with the software are interrelated (Van Merriënboer, 2000). In other words, memorization in advance can easily lead to fragmented knowledge that is hard to apply in real-life tasks. Second, memorization is a dull activity for learners and adds nothing to some more active JIT-approaches such as unsolicited and on-demand information presentation.

10.4   Corrective Feedback

As stated, procedural information consists of JIT information-displays, demonstrations and instances, and *corrective feedback* given on the recurrent aspects of performance. In contrast to cognitive feedback, the main function of corrective feedback is not to foster reflection, but rather to detect and correct errors. This concerns a direct effect on actions and is essentially *single-loop learning* (Argyris & Schön, 1978); an error is detected and corrected, so that the learner can carry on her or his present work in a more efficient, effective, or correct manner. If the rules or procedures that algorithmically describe effective performance are not correctly applied, the learner is said to make an "error". At this point, information is presented that helps the learner recognize that an error has been made. It may also explain why there is an error and give a hint for how to reach the desired goal. Like the presentation of all procedural information, this feedback should promote the compilation of newly acquired knowledge into cognitive rules (see Box 4).

Well-designed feedback should inform the learner that there was an error and why there was an error, but without simply saying what the correct action is (Balzer, Doherty, & O'Connor, 1989). It should take the goals that learners may be trying to reach into account. If the learner makes an error that conveys an incorrect goal, the feedback should explain why the action leads to the incorrect goal and should provide a suggestion or a *hint* as to how to reach the correct goal. Such a hint will often take the form of an example or demonstration. An example of such a suggestion or hint is "when trying to solve that acceleration problem, applying this formula does not help you to compute the acceleration. Try using the same formula used in the previous example". If the learner makes an error that conveys a correct goal, the feedback should only provide a hint for the correct step or action to be taken and not simply give away the correct step or action, because "learning by doing" is critical to the formation of cognitive rules. An example of such a suggestion or hint is "When trying to solve that acceleration problem you might want to consider substituting certain quantities for others". Simply telling the learner what to do is ineffective. The learner must really execute the correct action while the critical conditions for performing this action are active in working memory.

If a learner has made an error, it may be necessary to give her or him information on how to recover from the results of this error before giving any other information. This will be relatively straightforward if an instructor gives the feedback, but the inclusion of this type of error information in manuals or help systems is more difficult. One aspect of minimalist instruction is to support learners' error recovery by giving error information on the spot by combining the JIT information-displays with a section on "what to do if things go wrong?" In order to include such a section, it is necessary to make an analysis of the *typical errors* made by the target learners, so that the detection, diagnosis, and correction of most frequent errors can be supported (see Chapter 11.2 for the analysis of typical errors). The error information should contain:

- a description of the situation that results from the error, so that it can be recognized by the learner;
- information on the nature and the likely cause(s) of the error, so that it can possibly be avoided in the future, and
- action statements for correcting the error.

An example of well-designed error information given when a student is not successful in "selecting" a sentence in a word processor is (van der Meij & Lazonder, 1993):

> If you cannot select the sentence as a whole, the cursor was not positioned at the start of the sentence when you chose the SELECT command. Press the F1 key to undo the select function and start again.

With regard to the timing of feedback on errors, it should preferably be presented *immediately* after performing an incorrect step or applying an incorrect rule (Kulik & Kulik, 1988). It is necessary for the learner to preserve information about the conditions for applying a particular rule or procedural step in working memory until feedback (right/wrong) is obtained. Only then can a cognitive rule that attaches the correct action to its critical conditions be compiled. Obviously, any delay of feedback may hamper this process, but as was the case for the unsolicited presentation of JIT information, the presentation of immediate feedback typically requires an instructor who is closely monitoring the learner's whole-task performance, diagnosing errors in its recurrent aspects, explaining the errors, and providing hints. For diagnosing errors, instructors will typically use their knowledge about the typical errors that learners make. In the field of e-learning, immediate feedback on errors is relatively easy to realize for part-task practice, where only one recurrent constituent skill is practiced (e.g., in drill-and-practice). Unfortunately, this is hard to realize if learners perform relatively complex, open-ended learning tasks.

Box 4 - Knowledge Compilation and Procedural Information

Well-designed procedural information enables learners to perform, and learn to perform, the recurrent or routine aspects of learning tasks. The presentation of procedural information should simplify embedding it in cognitive rules that directly steer behavior, that is, that evoke particular actions under particular conditions. Together with strengthening (see Box 5), knowledge compilation is the major process responsible for rule automation. Anderson's Adaptive Control of Thought theory (ACT - 1993; Anderson & Lebiere, 1998) is currently the most comprehensive theory describing the learning processes responsible for the automation of rules.

Weak Methods

In the early stages of learning a complex skill, the learner may receive information about the skill by reading textbooks, listening to lectures, studying examples, and so on. The general idea is that this information may be encoded in memory and be interpreted by weak methods in order to generate behavior. Weak methods are problem-solving strategies that are independent of the particular problem, and are generally applicable such as means-ends analysis, forward-checking search, analogy, and so forth. According to ACT, weak methods are innate and can be used to solve problems in any domain. However, this process is very slow, takes up many cognitive resources, and is prone to errors. Learning, on one hand, involves the construction of cognitive schemas by means of induction (see Box 2) and elaboration (see Box 3), which makes performance much more efficient and effective because acquired cognitive strategies and mental models may be interpreted to guide the problem-solving process. On the other hand, it also involves the automation of rules that directly steer behavior - without the need for interpretation. The first step in this process of automation is called knowledge compilation.

Knowledge Compilation

Weak methods that are applied on newly acquired knowledge yield an initial solution; compilation is the process that creates highly specific cognitive rules from this solution. After the knowledge is compiled, the solution is generated by those new rules instead of by the weak methods. The term "compilation" is used by analogy to a computer program that translates source code into machine code. Essentially this is a piece of text that may be written in any word processor, but that may be compiled into executable program code. Knowledge compilation includes the sub processes proceduralization and composition.

Proceduralization

This sub process refers to the incorporation of knowledge into new domain-specific rules. As a simple illustration, suppose you use the following fictitious rule to make phone calls:

    IF
    your goal is to call person X
    THEN
    move X's phone number into your working memory
    and set as a sub goal dialing the phone number

If you regularly make phone calls to your partner, whose phone number is 6345789, proceduralization will embed this knowledge in the rule, yielding:

    IF
    your goal is to call your partner
    THEN
    set as a sub goal dialing 6345789

Composition

This sub process chunks rules together that consistently follow each other in performing particular tasks. Thus, a sequence of rules is collapsed into a single rule that does the work of the sequence. Suppose that another rule used to make phone calls is:

IF

your goal is to dial a phone number

THEN

pick up the receiver

dial the phone number

set as a sub goal starting to converse

Again, if you regularly make phone calls with your partner, composition will chunk this rule with the former rule, resulting in:

IF

your goal is to dial your partner

THEN

pick up the receiver

dial 6345789

set as a sub goal starting to converse

Forgetting

Knowledge compilation greatly speeds up performance, but it does not need to eliminate (a) the weak methods, (b) the knowledge that is now embedded in the rules, or (c) the smaller rules from which the larger rules are built. The original knowledge remains available to apply in situations in which the compiled rules cannot. However, if this knowledge is not used any more, it might be forgotten. So, if you call your partner several times a day, there is a chance that you won't remember the phone number unless you pick up the phone and actually dial the number. The same process may be responsible for the development of "tacit knowledge" (see Box 3).

Further Reading

Anderson, J. R. (1983). *The architecture of cognition*. Cambridge, MA: Harvard University Press.

Anderson, J. R. (1987). Skill acquisition: Compilation of weak-method problem solutions. *Psychological Review, 94*, 192–210.

Anderson, J. R. (1993). *Rules of the mind*. Hillsdale, NJ: Lawrence Erlbaum Associates.

Anderson, J. R., & Lebiere, C. (1998). *The atomic components of thought*. Mahwah, NJ: Lawrence Erlbaum Associates.

LePlat, J. (1990). Skills and tacit skills: A psychological perspective. *Applied Psychology: An International Review, 39*, 143–154.

10.5 Procedural Information in the Training Blueprint

In the training blueprint, procedural information is specified per learning task, enabling learners to perform the recurrent aspects of those tasks. A distinction can be made between JIT information-displays that spell out appropriate rules or procedures on one hand and their prerequisite knowledge elements, examples of the information given in the displays (i.e., demonstrations and instances), and corrective feedback on the other. At the very least, JIT information-displays are coupled to the *first* learning task for which they are relevant, though they may also be coupled to subsequent learning tasks that involve the same recurrent aspects. The JIT information-displays are best exemplified by elements of the learning task itself, so that learners see how demonstrations and/or instances fit into the context of the whole task. This requires the use of learning tasks that present a part of the problem-solving process or of the solution (e.g., modeling examples, case studies, completion tasks, etc.) and indicates the use of a deductive strategy where the JIT information-displays are illustrated by *simultaneously* presented examples. Corrective feedback on recurrent aspects of task performance is best given immediately after misapplication of a rule or procedural step. Whereas JIT information-displays and related examples can often be designed before learners actually participate in an educational program, this may be impossible for corrective feedback because it depends on the behaviors of each individual learner. Nevertheless, some preplanning might be possible if typical errors and misconceptions of the target group have been analyzed beforehand.

Fading

If procedural information is not only coupled to the first learning task for which it is relevant, but also to subsequent tasks, this is done via a process of *fading*. Fading ensures that the procedural information is repeatedly presented, but in ever decreasing amounts until learners no longer need it. For instance, a help system may first systematically present relevant JIT information-displays, then only those displays requested by the student, ending with no information at all. A particular task environment may first present informational feedback (i.e., explaining *why* there is an error), then present only right/wrong feedback, and finally provide no corrective feedback at all. Fading not only insures that learners receive procedural information as long as they need it, but also provides better opportunities to present a divergent set of demonstrations and/or instances. Ideally, the whole set of examples should be representative for all situations that the presented rules or procedures deal with.

Dealing with Typical Errors and Misconceptions

Based on their prior experience and intuition, learners may be inclined to make typical errors when they have to apply particular rules or carry out particular procedural steps (the analysis of such typical errors is described in Chapter 11.2). Furthermore, *misconceptions* may occur with regard to the knowledge that is prerequisite to a correct use of rules or procedures (the analysis of such misconceptions is described in Chapter 12.2). A typical error for switching off a desktop computer is to press its power button, rather than applying the rule "if you want to shut down the computer, then click <Start> and then click <Shut Down>". A related misconception is that <Start> only applies to starting up new programs, whereas it also applies to changing settings, searching documents and, indeed, shutting down applications. The existence of typical errors and misconceptions may affect the presentation of procedural information in the following ways:

1   Focus the learners' attention on steps and prerequisite knowledge elements that are liable to typical errors or misconceptions. Unsolicited information

presentation, relatively slow fading of presented information, and the use of many demonstrations and instances can help.

2 Use, if possible, multiple representations in JIT information-displays (e.g., text and pictures). Graphical representations of procedures and physical models of tools and objects that must be manipulated by the learners can help.

3 Stimulate learners to compare and contrast correct steps and prerequisite knowledge elements with their incorrect counterparts, that is, with "malrules" and misconceptions.

4 Include error recovery information in presented JIT information-displays so that learners can undo and repair the undesired consequences of errors once they have been made.

Concluding this chapter, Table 10.2 presents one task class out of the training blue-print for the moderately complex skill "searching for research literature" (you may refer back to Table 5.2 for a description of the other task classes).

A specification of the procedural information has been added to the specification of the task class, the learning tasks, and the supportive information. As you can see, the procedural information is presented when learners work on the first learning task for which it is relevant. See Appendix 2 for the complete training blueprint. As a final remark, procedural information is not only relevant to performing the learning tasks, but may also be relevant to part-task practice. Special considerations for connecting procedural information to part-task practice will be discussed in Chapter 13.

Table 10.2   A preliminary training blueprint for the moderately complex skill "searching for relevant research literature". For one task class, a specification of the procedural information has been added to the learning tasks.

Task Class 1
Learners are confronted with situations where the concepts in the to-be-searched domain are clearly defined. Only a small number of articles are written about the subject and articles are only written in one field of research. Therefore, the search needs only to be performed on titles of articles in one database from the particular field of research. There are only a few search terms needed for performing the search and the search will yield a limited amount of articles.

Supportive Information: *Modeling example*
Learners watch an expert perform a literature search and explain his or her actions while doing so.

Supportive Information: *Presentation of cognitive strategies*

- SAP of the four phases involved in performing a literature search: (a) selecting an appropriate database, (b) formulating a search query, (c) performing the search, and (d) selecting results.
- SAPs for quickly scanning the relevance of scientific articles.

Supportive Information: *Presentation of mental models*
- Conceptual model of literature search concepts.
- Structural model of how databases are organized and can be used.
- Conceptual model of different types of scientific articles and how they are organized.

Learning Task 1.1: *Case study*

Learners receive three worked-out (good) examples of literature searches. Each example describes a different research questions in the same subject matter domain, the search query and the produced list of articles. The learners have to study the examples and explain why the different search queries produced the desired results.

Learning Task 1.2: *Completion*	**Procedural information**
Learners receive a research question and an incomplete search query that produces a list containing irrelevant items. They must refine the search query using additional search terms, perform the search, and select the relevant articles.	- Procedures for operating the search program. - Procedures for using a thesaurus.
Learning Task 1.3: *Conventional*	**Procedural information**
Learners receive a research question. They have to perform a literature search for the 10 most relevant articles.	- Procedures for operating the search program (fading). - Procedures for using a thesaurus (fading).

10.6   Summary of Guidelines

- If you design procedural information, then you need to make a distinction between JIT information displays, demonstrations and instances, and corrective feedback.
- If you design JIT information displays, then you need to use small self-contained units that spell out one rule or procedure and its prerequisite knowledge elements, use simple language, and physically integrate the displays with the task environment to prevent split attention.
- If you exemplify JIT information-displays with demonstrations of rules or procedures, or instances of prerequisite knowledge elements, then you need to give those examples in the context of the whole learning tasks and make sure they are divergent.
- If you present procedural information and there is an instructor available, then you need to use an unsolicited presentation strategy in which the instructor spells out how to perform the recurrent aspects during whole task performance (i.e., contingent tutoring).
- If you present procedural information and there is no instructor available, then you need to use an unsolicited strategy in which JIT information-displays are explicitly presented with the first learning task for which they are relevant (i.e., system-initiated help).
- If you present procedural information and there is no control over the learning tasks, then you need to use an on-demand presentation strategy and make

JIT information-displays available in a (minimal) manual, help system, or job aid that can be consulted by the learners during task performance.

- If you design corrective feedback, then help the learner to recognize that there is an error, explain the cause of the error, and give a hint for how to reach the correct goal.
- If you specify procedural information in the training blueprint, then you need to couple it to the first learning task for which it is relevant and fade it away for subsequent learning tasks.

11
STEP 8: ANALYZE COGNITIVE RULES

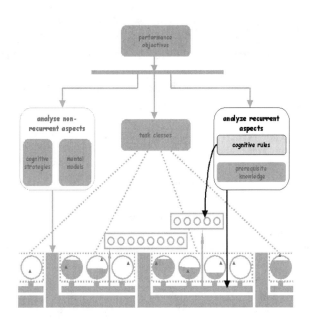

Necessity

The analysis of cognitive rules provides the basis for the design of an important part of the procedural information and, if applicable, part-task practice. This step should only be performed if a specification of rules and procedures is not yet available in existing instructional materials.

When multiplying or dividing two numbers, if both numbers have the same sign, then the product or quotient is positive whereas if the numbers have different signs, the product or quotient is negative. When simplifying an equation we first multiply the numbers adjacent to the multiplication sign before adding (e.g., $3\times6+2=20$ $(18+2)$ and not 24 (3×8)). These are examples of cognitive rules that we all learned when we were learning arithmetic. Such cognitive rules enable task performers to carry out recurrent aspects of learning tasks in a correct way. We do not have to multiply or divide all of the numbers that there are or simplify all equations; we can apply the multiplication/division rule to any two numbers we encounter in a problem and the precedence procedure to equation.

This chapter focuses on the analysis of cognitive rules for solving *familiar* aspects of new tasks. The results of the analyses take the form of if-then rules or procedures. They specify how competent task performers carry out those aspects of real-life tasks that are identical from task to task, and from problem to problem situation. Sometimes, relevant if-then rules and/or procedures for a particular task domain are already available in existing job aids, instructional materials, and other documents. Then, there is no need to analyze cognitive rules. In all other cases, the analysis of cognitive rules yields input for the analysis of prerequisite knowledge (Chapter 12): Together with the analysis results for prerequisite knowledge, it provides the basis for the design of the procedural information. If applicable, the analysis of cognitive rules also provides that basis for the design of part-task practice (Chapter 13).

The structure of this chapter is as follows. First, the specification of if-then rules in a rule-based analysis, and the specification of procedures in an information processing analysis, is explained. Both analysis methods stress that the final specification should be at the level of the target group's lowest-ability learner. Second, the analysis of so-called "malrules" and typical errors are briefly discussed because these incorrect rules and procedural steps can interfere with the acquisition of their correct counterparts. Third, the use of if-then rules and procedures on behalf of the instructional design process is discussed. The identified rules and procedures are helpful for analyzing prerequisite knowledge, designing procedural information, and designing part-task practice. For the design activities, the existence of typical errors and malrules may affect the selection of instructional methods. The chapter concludes with a summary of the main guidelines.

11.1   Specify If-Then Rules and Procedures

If-then rules and *procedures* describe how the recurrent aspects of a complex task, or recurrent constituent skills, are correctly performed. Like SAPs (Chapter 8), rules and procedures organize the task performers' actions in the domain of interest. In contrast to SAPs, which have a heuristic nature, rules and procedures are *algorithmic*, indicating that using the applicable rules or performing the procedural steps in the specified order guarantees that the task is correctly performed and its goal will be reached. The rules and procedures discussed in this chapter, thus, are examples of "strong methods". Their strength, however, is counterbalanced by their limited flexibility: Highly domain-specific rules ensure that familiar aspects of tasks can be correctly performed, but they are not at all useful for unfamiliar task aspects in new problem situations. For the design of instruction, the analysis of cognitive rules into if-then rules or procedures serves three goals:

1   It yields input for the analysis of prerequisite knowledge, which describes what learners need to know in order to correctly apply the rules or correctly perform the procedural steps (see Chapter 12).
2   Along with the analysis results of prerequisite knowledge, it provides the basis for the design of procedural information.
3   If part-task practice needs to be developed, the analysis of cognitive rules provides the basis for its design (see Chapter 13).

Analyzing cognitive rules is a laborious task, with much in common with computer programming. The analyst usually lets one or more competent task performers execute the task and simultaneously talk about their performance ("talk aloud") or mentally walk through the task. All actions and decisions are recorded in a table or task outline. This process is repeated for all different versions of the task that involve different decisions, in order to make sure that all possible if-then rules or all different procedural paths are included in the analysis results. Moreover, the analysis of recurrent constituent skills is always a hierarchical process: It is reiterated until it reaches an elementary level where the rules can be applied, or the steps can be performed, by the lowest-ability learners from the target group - assuming that they have already mastered the prerequisite knowledge.

All recurrent constituent skills can be described as the application of cognitive rules and can be analyzed into if-then rules (Anderson, 1993). There are, however, many different analysis methods that take advantage of specific characteristics of the skill under consideration to simplify the analysis process (for an overview of methods, see Jonassen, Hannum, & Tessmer, 1989; Kennedy, Esquire, & Novak, 1983). *Behavioral task analysis*, for instance, is particularly useful if the majority of conditions and actions specified in the rules are observable or "overt" (cf. Figure 10.1 showing a procedure for changing the page orientation of a document). *Cognitive task analysis* is more powerful because it can also deal with skills for which the conditions and actions are not observable or "covert". This chapter discusses two popular methods for cognitive task analysis. Rule-based analysis is a highly flexible method suitable for analyzing recurrent skills that lack a temporal order of steps. Information-processing analysis is somewhat simpler to perform, but is only useful for analyzing recurrent skills characterized by a temporal ordering of steps into a procedure (e.g., adding digits, repairing a flat tire).

Rule-Based Analysis

Rule-based analysis is used if most of the steps involved in performing a task do not show a temporal order. Examples are handling a keyboard or control panel, typing or editing text, and operating a software program. Rules specify under which conditions the task performer should take particular actions. They have a condition part, which is called the if-side, and an action part, which is called the then-side:

If condition(s)
Then action(s).

The if-side specifies the conditions in terms of 'states,' which either represent objects from the outside world or particular mental states in the process of performing the task. The then-side specifies the actions to be taken when the rule applies. When this occurs, the rule is said to "fire". Actions can change either objects in the outside world or mental states. Rules, thus, reflect cognitive contingencies: If a certain condition is met then certain actions are taken. The performance of a task can be modeled by a set of rules; rules from this set fire by turns in a so-called *recognize-act cycle*. One rule from the set recognizes a particular state because its if-side matches; it acts by changing the state according to the actions specified in its then-side; another rule recognizes this new state because it matches its if-side; it acts by changing this state; yet another rule recognizes this new state and changes it, and so on until the task is completed.

The working of rule-based analysis will be illustrated with a simple set of rules. The rules describe the recurrent skill of stacking buckets, in such a way that smaller buckets are always placed into larger ones. The first if-then rule specifies when the task is finished:

1.
If   there is only one visible bucket
Then   the task is finished.

Another if-then rule specifies what should be done to reach this goal:

2.
If   there are at least two buckets
Then   use the two leftmost buckets and put the smaller one into the larger one.

In this rule, the term bucket might refer to either a single bucket or a stack of buckets. As shown in the upper part of Figure 11.1 these two rules already describe the performance of this task for a great deal of all possible situations. However, the middle part shows a situation in which yet another rule is needed. Here, an impasse occurs because a larger bucket has been placed on a smaller bucket. The following rule may help to overcome this impasse:

3.
If   a smaller bucket blocks a larger bucket
Then   put the larger bucket to the leftmost side and put the smallest bucket to the leftmost side.

As shown in the bottom part of Figure 11.1, this additional rule helps to overcome the impasse. The three identified if-then rules are actually sufficient to stack up buckets for all situations one might think of. Moreover, the rules are independent of one another, meaning that their order is of no importance. This makes it possible to add or delete if-then rules without perturbing the behavior of the whole set of rules. For example, stacking up buckets can be made more efficient by adding the following rule:

4.
If   the largest and the smallest bucket are both at the leftmost side
Then   put the smallest bucket to the rightmost side.

If you try out the rule set with this new rule, it becomes clear that in many situations fewer cycles are necessary to stack up the buckets. Moreover, this has been reached by simply adding one rule to the set, without having to bother about the position of this new rule in the whole set.

It should be noted that the performance of a specific task may not only be a function of the identified rules, but also of the way those rules are handled by so-called higher-order rules. For instance, it may be the case that more than one rule has an if-side that matches the given state (actually, this is also the case for rules 2, 3, & 4!). In this situation, a conflict must be solved by selecting precisely one rule from among the candidates. This process is called *conflict resolution*.

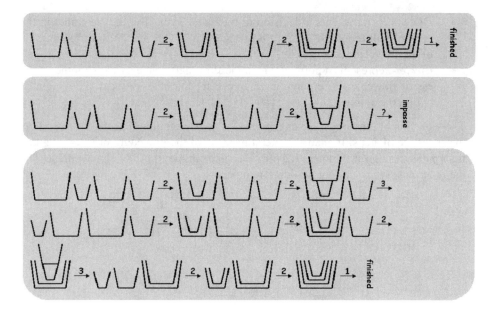

Figure 11.1   Working of a set of if-then rules describing the task of stacking buckets.

Common approaches to conflict resolution are to give more specific rules precedence over more general rules (e.g., give rule 3 precedence over rule 2), to give
rules that match more recent states precedence over rules that match older states
(e.g., give rules 3 & 4 precedence over rule 2), and give a rule that has not been
selected in the previous cycle precedence above a rule that has been selected. For
different approaches to conflict resolution, the interested reader might read the literature on specific forms of rule-based analysis such as Factor Transfer Analysis
(Reigeluth & Merrill, 1984), production system analysis (Klahr, Langley, &
Neches, 1987), FlexForm analysis (Scandura, 2001), and GOMS analysis (Goals-
Operators-Methods-Selection rules; Kieras, 1988). What these analysis methods
have in common is their focus on highly domain-specific if-then rules that algorithmically describe correct task performance.

Information-Processing Analysis

Information-processing analysis can be used if the steps involved in performing
a task show a temporal order (P. Merrill, 1980, 1987). The ordered sequence of
steps is called a *procedure*. Examples are procedures for doing multiplication, starting up a machine, and traversing a fault tree when troubleshooting a device. Information-processing analysis focuses on the overt and/or covert decisions and actions
made by the task performer and yields a procedure that is typically represented as a
flowchart. A typical flowchart uses the following symbols:

- *Box* - represents an action to be taken. In most flowcharts, this will be the
  most frequently used symbol.

- *Diamond* - represents a decision to be made. Typically, the statement in the symbol will require a *yes* or a *no* response and will branch to different parts of the flowchart accordingly.
- *Circle* - represents a point at which the flowchart connects with another process or flowchart. The name or reference for the other process should appear within the symbol.

The inclusion of diamonds makes it possible to pay attention to decisions that affect the sequence of steps. It enables reiterating parts of the procedure or following distinct paths through it. Figure 11.2 provides an example of a flowchart representing the recurrent skill of adding two-digit numbers.

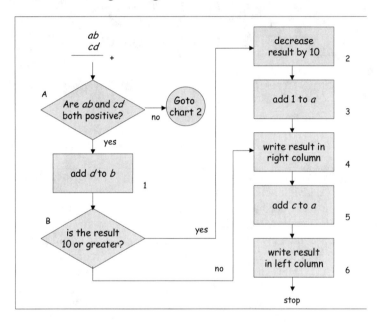

Figure 11.2   Flowchart resulting from an information-processing analysis on adding two-digit numbers.

In this flowchart, some actions are covert (e.g., add, decrease) and some are overt (e.g., write result). To make it easier to refer to the different elements in the flowchart, the actions have been indicated with the numbers 1 to 6 and the decisions have been indicated with the letters A and B.

Before ending the analysis process, the flowchart should be validated and verified in order to make sure that all (mental) actions and decisions, as well as all possible branches from decisions, have been included. Professional task performers and instructors with experience in teaching the task can both furnish important information on the quality and completeness of a flowchart. Furthermore, learners from the target group should be asked to perform the task based on a given flowchart. This should be done for all versions of the task requiring the learner to follow different paths through it. If learners have difficulties performing the task, it might be necessary to specify the steps further because they are not yet formulated at the entry level of the target group.

Specification at the Entry Level of the Target Group

As indicated before, the description of task performance in a rule-based or information-processing analysis is highly specific and algorithmic. Thus, using the applicable rules, making the specified decisions, and performing the actions in the given order should guarantee that all learners perform the task correctly. This raises the question "At which level of detail should the prescriptions be given?" Theoretically, the analysis might be continued to a level of mental operations, such as recalling an item from long-term memory or temporarily storing an item in short-term memory, or perceptual-motor operations, such as directing attention to a particular object or moving specific fingers. This, however, would clearly yield a cumbersome analysis.

Therefore, the question of how specific the prescriptions should be is answered *relative* to the entry level of the target group. That is, the analysis is continued until a level where the lowest-ability learner masters the steps. One severe risk is to stop this reiterative process too early; analysts often overestimate learners' prior knowledge. Therefore, the analyst may consider reiterating the process one or two levels beyond the expected entry-level of the target group. This analysis of the recurrent skill is complemented with the analysis of the prior knowledge of the target group by repeatedly asking the question "Will my lowest-ability learners be able to perform this step correctly, assuming that the prerequisite knowledge (i.e., concepts used in the step) is already known by them?" This ensures that the developed instruction is at the right grain size: It pays no attention to steps already mastered by the learners, but is specific enough to be correctly performed by all of them.

The specificity of the steps clearly distinguishes flowcharts that result from an information-processing analysis from SAP-charts (cf. Figures 7.1 & 8.1). A SAP-analysis leads to the description of a systematic approach that is general in nature. It merely provides a description of the goals that must be reached, and the heuristics that may be helpful for obtaining those goals. It can never assure that the problem will be solved because the goals are not at the entry level of the target group and the heuristics are only rules-of-thumb that may help reach these goals. Learners instructed according to the SAP are provided with "direction" in problem solving and this might shorten the long and arduous process of arriving at this general plan themselves; but it does not necessarily do so. In summary, SAPs serve as a heuristic guide to the problem-solving process while if-then rules and flowcharts resulting from an information-processing analysis yield an algorithmic prescription for performing the task correctly.

11.2   Analyzing Typical Errors and Malrules

The Ten Steps focus on a rational analysis of correct if-then rules and procedures. This provides the basis for telling learners how the recurrent aspects of the task *should* be performed. In addition, an empirical analysis can and should be performed to find out which typical errors learners tend to make when applying particular rules or performing particular procedural steps and which malrules they apply at the start of a training program - either intuitively or based upon their prior experiences. Table 11.1 provides some examples of typical errors and malrules.

Table 11.1   Examples of typical errors and malrules.

Typical error / malrule	Correct rule
If you want to switch the values of variables A and B, then state A=B and B=A	If you want to switch the values of variables A and B, then state C=A, A=B, and B=C
If you want to switch off the computer, then press the power button	If you want to shut down the computer, then click <Start>, and then click <Shut Down>
If you want to expand the expression $(x+y)^2$, then just square each term (x^2+y^2)	If you want to expand the expression $(x+y)^2$, then multiply x+y by x+y $(x^2+2xy+y^2)$

In contrast to malrules, which provide an incorrect alternative to correct rules, typical errors often reflect the intention to apply the correct rules but still having things go wrong. *Errors* relate to rules or procedural steps that are difficult to apply, dangerous to perform, or easily omitted by the learners in the target-group. For instance, for the rule "if you want to highlight a word, then place the cursor on it and double-click the mouse" it is important to stress that the two clicks quickly follow each other, because especially young children and elderly learners have difficulties with rapid double-clicking. For the rule "if you need to release the fishing net, cut the cord moving the knife away from you" it is important to stress the movement of the knife because of the risk of injuries. And for the step "decrease the left column by 1", which is part of the procedure for subtracting two-digit numbers with borrowing, it is important to stress this step because novice learners who borrowed 10 often omit it.

11.3   Using Cognitive Rules to make Design Decisions

Step 8 will only be performed if information on rules and procedures is not yet available in existing instructional materials. If the step is performed, the results of the analysis provide the basis for a number of different activities, namely providing input for the analysis of prerequisite knowledge, providing input for the design of an important part of the procedural information and, when applicable, input for part-task practice. Furthermore, the identification of malrules and typical errors might affect design decisions.

Analyzing Prerequisite Knowledge

The analysis of cognitive rules focuses exclusively on *how* recurrent aspects of tasks are performed. Consequently, information on knowledge prerequisite to learning to perform the tasks is missing. Here, the central question is "What knowledge enables learners to carry out the task for which the correct performance is specified in the rules and/or procedures?" For instance, the learners can only correctly perform the rule "if you want to highlight a word, then place the cursor on it and double-click the mouse" if concepts such as 'cursor' and 'mouse' are familiar to them. If they are not, these concepts should be taught to them because they are "prerequisites" and enable correct use of the rule. Note that there is a *unidirectional relationship* between rules and their prerequisite knowledge. By definition, prerequisite knowledge enables the correct use of the rules but the reverse does not make sense (this is different from the bi-directional relationship between cognitive strategies and mental models). For this reason, one should start with the analysis of cognitive rules and only then continue with the analysis of prerequisite knowledge. The analysis of prerequisite knowledge is also called instructional analysis, or when performed in direct combination with the analysis of cognitive rules, combination analysis (Dick & Carey, 1996). These will be further discussed in Chapter 12. Together, the analysis results for cognitive rules and for prerequisite knowledge provide the main input for the design of procedural information (Chapter 10).

Designing Procedural Information

In a psychological sense, recurrent constituent skills are analyzed *as if* they were automatic psychological processes. This is done because instructional methods for the design of procedural information and part-task practice must directly foster compilation (see Box 4 in Chapter 10) and, for skills that need to be developed to a very high level of automaticity, subsequent strengthening of identified cognitive rules (see Box 5 in Chapter 13). Compilation is facilitated by explicitly presenting the applicable rules or procedures precisely when learners need them as part of JIT information-displays. Well-designed displays are self-contained units that spell out the rule or procedure at the level of the lowest-ability learner, use simple language, and physically integrate the display with the task environment to prevent split attention (see Chapter 10.1). Then, identified rules and procedures help develop demonstrations that give learners concrete application examples. These demonstrations point out that correct application of the rules or procedural steps always yields the desired solution: Due to its algorithmic nature, applying the rules or performing the steps simply *is* the desired solution (see Chapter 10.2). Finally, identified rules and procedures can help provide corrective feedback to learners. If a learner makes an error, the feedback should point out that there is an error, explain its cause, and give a hint as to how to reach the correct goal. The hint will often have the form of a reference to the relevant information display and/or a demonstration (see Chapter 10.4).

Designing Part-Task Practice

Part-task practice is designed for one or more recurrent constituent skills only if those skills need to be developed to a very high level of automaticity, through a learning process called strengthening (see Box 5 in Chapter 13). Part-task practice increases the fluency of final whole-task performance and helps learners pay more attention to the problem-solving and reasoning aspects of learning tasks. Providing many practice items that require learners to repeatedly apply the identified rules or perform the procedures facilitates strengthening. For highly complex algorithms, the identified rule-sets or procedures are used to sequence practice items from simple to complex, using part-whole techniques. The identified rules and procedures are then used to determine suitable methods for drill and overlearning. The design of part-task practice is further discussed in Chapter 13, which concerns the last activity of the Ten Steps.

Dealing with Typical Errors and Malrules

The identification of malrules and typical errors may affect decision making for the design activities discussed. Regarding the design of procedural information, the existence of malrules or typical errors may be a reason to apply particular instructional methods (see Chapter 10.3). First, students' attention should be focused on those rules or procedural steps that are prone to errors or mistakes. Unsolicited information presentation, relatively slow fading of presented information, and the use of many divergent demonstrations for rules and steps that are error prone may help here. Second, learners should be stimulated to compare and contrast correct rules and procedural steps with their buggy counterparts. Finally, error recovery information might be included in the information displays presented. This information helps learners undo or repair the undesired consequences of errors once they have been made.

11.4   Summary of Guidelines

- If you analyze cognitive rules, then observe thinking-aloud task performers to identify if-then rules and/or procedures that algorithmically specify correct task performance.
- If you conduct a rule-based analysis for recurrent skills that do not show a temporal order, then specify at the level of the lowest-ability learner a set of if-then rules that describe desired task performance. Higher-order rules may describe how to select among several applicable rules.
- If you conduct an information-processing analysis for recurrent skills that show a temporal order, then specify at the level of the lowest-ability learner a procedure that describes desired task performance. The procedure may be presented as a flowchart with actions (in boxes) and decisions (in diamonds).
- If you analyze malrules or typical errors, then focus on behaviors shown by naive learners as well as steps that are difficult, dangerous, or easily omitted.

- If you use rules and procedures to analyze prerequisite knowledge, then answer for each rule or each procedural step the question what knowledge is needed to correctly apply this rule or perform this step.
- If you use rules and procedures to design procedural information, then include them in JIT information-displays, to develop useful demonstrations, and to provide corrective feedback on performance.
- If you use rules and procedures to design part-task practice, then use them to specify practice items, to sequence practice items for highly complex algorithms, and to select methods for drill and overlearning.
- If you use malrules and typical errors to design procedural information, then focus the learners' attention on rules and steps that are liable to errors, ask them to compare and contrast correct rules with incorrect ones, and include related error-recovery information in JIT information-displays.

12
STEP 9: ANALYZE PREREQUISITE KNOWLEDGE

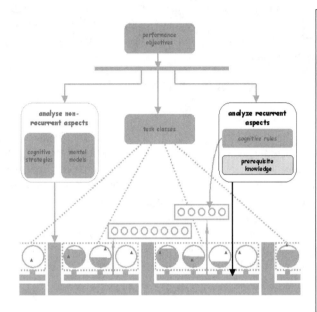

Necessity

The analysis of pre-requisite knowledge provides the basis for the design of procedural informa-tion. This step should only be per-formed if the proce-dural information is not yet specified in existing instruc-tional materials and if you have already analyzed cognitive rules in the previous Step 8.

Prerequisite knowledge enables a learner to apply if-then rules or to carry out pro-cedural steps correctly. Prerequisite knowledge is the knowledge that must be ac-quired in *order to be able to perform* recurrent aspects of a complex task. Learning indicates here that the knowledge becomes part of the cognitive rules that a learner develops. This chapter focuses on the analysis of prerequisite knowledge in the form of concepts, plans, and principles, which may be further analyzed into facts and physical models. Sometimes, relevant if-then rules, procedures and associated prerequisite knowledge are already available in existing job aids, instructional ma-terials, or other documents. If this is the case, then there is no need to analyze pre-requisite knowledge. In all other cases, an analysis of cognitive rules should be un-dertaken first (Step 8), followed by an analysis of prerequisite knowledge (this Step). The analysis of prerequisite knowledge is typically known as instructional analysis (Hoffman & Medsker, 1983), or when performed in direct combination with an analysis of rules or procedures, as combination analysis (Dick & Carey, 1996). The results of the analysis of cognitive rules, together with the analysis of prerequisite knowledge provides the basis for the design of procedural information.

The structure of this chapter is as follows. First, the specification of prerequisite knowledge is discussed, including identification of concepts, plans, and principles as well as their further analysis into facts and, if applicable, physical models. This analysis is hierarchical in nature and is reiterated until the prerequisite knowledge is specified at the level of the target group's lowest-ability learner. Second, the empirical analysis of misconceptions is briefly discussed because their existence may interfere with the acquisition of prerequisite knowledge. Third, the use of prerequisite knowledge for the design process is discussed. Together with the analysis results of cognitive rules, the analysis of prerequisite knowledge yields the input for the design of procedural information. The existence of misconceptions may affect the selection of instructional methods for presenting this information. The chapter concludes with a summary of main guidelines.

12.1   Specify Concepts, Facts, and Physical Models

Conceptual knowledge can be described at different levels (see Figure 12.1). At the highest levels, conceptual knowledge is described in terms of domain models that offer rich descriptions of how the world is organized in a particular domain; these models use concepts, plans, and principles as their building blocks. Step 6 dealt with the analysis of mental models into such domain models and made a distinction between conceptual models (what is this?), structural models (how is this built or organized?), and causal models (how does this work?). Domain models allow for reasoning and problem solving in a task domain and are less relevant to the performance of recurrent aspects of a skill, which can be algorithmically described in terms of the application of rules and procedures.

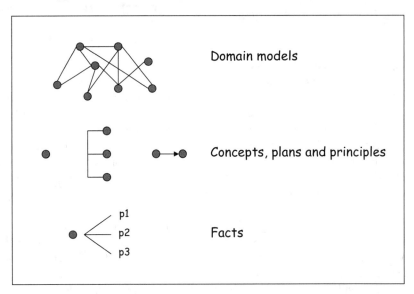

Figure 12.1   Three levels to describe conceptual knowledge.

This chapter is primarily concerned with the two lowest levels of Figure 12.1. It deals first with the level of concepts, plans (that relate two or more concepts by location-in-time or location-in-space relationships), and principles (that relate two or more concepts by cause-effect or natural-process relationships). Concepts are the basic building blocks at this level and may be further analyzed into facts and, especially for concrete concepts referring to tools and objects, physical models.

The analysis of prerequisite knowledge starts from the if-then rules and procedural steps that were identified in the analysis of cognitive rules (Chapter 11). Thus, the analysis of cognitive rules (Step 8) must always precede the analysis of prerequisite knowledge (Step 9). The analysis of if-then rules and procedures focuses on the question how a task is performed. Consequently, after Step 8 it is still not known what knowledge is prerequisite to learning to carry out the learning task. The basic question for the analysis of prerequisite knowledge and that must be asked for each identified rule and each identified procedural step, is "Which concepts, plans, and/or principles does the learner need to know in order to learn to correctly apply the rule or perform the procedural step?" It is precisely this knowledge that the learner needs to embed in to-be-developed cognitive rules, in a learning process called knowledge compilation (see Box 4 in Chapter 10). It should be noted that the answers to the basic question might introduce yet other concepts that are not yet known by the learners; thus, the analysis is hierarchical in nature and should be reiterated until a level is reached where the learners are familiar with all of the concepts used. At the lowest level, these concepts may be defined by stating the facts or propositions that apply to them. Such propositions are typically seen as the smallest building blocks of cognition, so that a further analysis is not possible.

Identify Concepts, Plans, and Principles

Concepts allow for the description and classification of objects, events, and processes (Tennyson & Cocchiarella, 1986). They enable us to give the same name to different *instances* that share some common characteristics (e.g., poodles, terriers, and dachshunds are all dogs). Concepts are important for all kinds of tasks, because they allow task performers to talk about a domain using the appropriate terminology, and to classify the things that have to be dealt with in this domain. For the analysis of prerequisite knowledge, the relevant question is "are there any concepts that are not yet mastered by the learners, but which are necessary for them to master in order to correctly apply a particular rule, or to correctly perform a particular procedural step?" For instance, in the domain of photography, a procedural step for repairing cameras might be "remove the lens from the camera". Presenting the concept "lens" might be prerequisite for the correct application of this step. If this really is the case depends on the prior knowledge of the learners. It is only prerequisite if the lowest-ability learner does not yet know what a lens is. Another example in the domain of database management is the rule: "if you want to permanently delete a field, then choose Clear Field from the Edit Menu". Here, the concept "field" might be unfamiliar for the learners, and thus could be prerequisite to a correct use of the rule.

Plans relate concepts to each other in space to form *templates* or *building blocks*, or in time to form *scripts*. Plans are often important prerequisite knowledge for tasks involving the understanding, design and repair of artifacts such as texts, electronic circuits, machinery, and so forth. For analyzing prerequisite knowledge the relevant question is "Are there any plans that are not yet mastered by the learners, but which are yet necessary for them to master in order to correctly apply a particular rule, or to correctly perform a particular procedural step?" A rule in the domain of statistics, for example, might state "if you present descriptive statistics for normally distributed data sets, then report means and standard deviations". A simple template prerequisite to the correct application of this rule may describe how means and standard deviations are typically presented in a scientific text, namely as "M = x.xx; SD = y.yy", where x.xx is the computed mean and y.yy is the computed standard deviation. As another example, a rule in the domain of text processing might be "If you want to change a text from a Roman typeface to *italic*, then open the Context Menu, click Style, and click Italic". (see Figure 12.2). A simple script that is prerequisite to the correct application of this rule may describe that for the formatting of text first the text that needs to be formatted is selected, and only after having done this can the desired formatting option be selected from the toolbar or keyed in. The reader should note that this script might also contain one or more new concepts that are not yet known by the learners. For instance, the concept "Context Menu" might be new to them and thus require further analysis.

Italic

Makes the selected text italic. If the cursor is in a word, the entire word is made italic. If the selection or word is already italic, the formatting is removed.

If the cursor is not inside a word, and no text is selected, then the font style is applied to the text that you type.

Figure 12.2   Example of a display presenting the procedure for making text italic (taken from OpenOffice.org Writer).

Principles relate concepts to each other with cause-effect or natural-process relationships. Principles describe how changes in one thing are related to changes in another. Principles are often important prerequisite knowledge for tasks involving giving explanations and making predictions. They help learners understand *why* particular rules are applied or *why* particular procedural steps are performed. For the analysis of prerequisite knowledge, the relevant question is "Are there any principles that are not yet mastered by the learners, but which are yet necessary for them to master in order to correctly apply a particular rule, or correctly perform a particular procedural step? For instance, the steps related to borrowing in the procedure for subtracting two-digit numbers from each other in the form *ab* are "decrease *a* by 1" and "add 10 to *b*". A principle that may help perform these steps correctly is "each column to the left indicates a tenfold of the column directly to its right". This principle indicates that the rightmost column denotes units, the column left of that column denotes tens, the next column to the left denotes hundreds, and so forth. It provides an explanation for why particular steps are performed and is thus important to their effective application. To a certain degree, the provision of such principles distinguishes rote learning of a procedure from learning it with understanding. The principles allow the learner to understand why particular steps are performed or why particular rules are applied. Be that as it may, principles at best yield some *limited comprehension* or *understanding* (thus, shallow) because deep understanding requires far more elaborated mental models. Furthermore, it should be noted that identified principles might contain new concepts that are not yet known by the learners. For instance, the concept "column" in the identified principle may be new to the learners and require further analysis.

Identify Facts in Feature Lists

Plans and principles may be analyzed into their constituting concepts, and concepts, in turn, may be further analyzed into facts and/or physical models that apply to instances of the concept. One common way to specify a concept is to list all facts that apply to its instances in a *feature list*. The features or facts that apply to instances of the concept take the form of *propositions*. A proposition consists of a predicate or relationship, and at least one argument. Examples of propositions or facts that characterize the concept "column" are, for instance:

- A column is elongated - This is a proposition with one argument (column, which is the subject) and the predicate "elongated".
- A column organizes items - This is a proposition with two arguments (column, which is the subject; items, which are the objects) and the predicate "organize".
- A text processor may construct columns using the table function - This is a proposition with three arguments (text processor, which is the subject; column, which is the object; and table function, which is the tool connected with the predicate "construct").

As indicated in Figure 12.3, propositions can be represented graphically. The basic format is simple. From a *propositional node*, one link points to the predicate and one or more links point to the argument(s). If desired, the links can be labeled as subject, object, and so on. Propositions are typically seen as the smallest building blocks of cognition. There are no facts that enable the learning of other facts. The factual relationship conveys meaningless, arbitrary links (A predicates B). In a sense, facts or propositions cannot be understood but can only be memorized by learners. This is not to say that learners must actually learn all facts identified as prerequisite knowledge by heart. On the contrary, well-designed instruction ensures that knowledge prerequisite to the performance of particular procedural steps or to the application of particular rules is repeatedly presented precisely when it is needed to perform those steps or apply those rules. Then, the prerequisite knowledge is available in the learners' working memory at the right time so that it can be embedded in cognitive rules that develop as a function of practice.

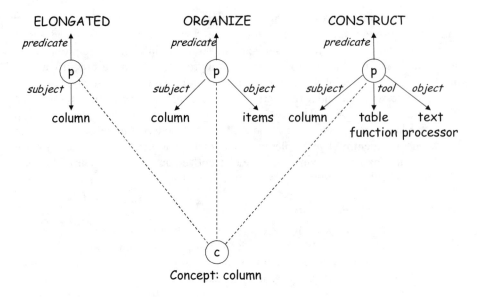

Figure 12.3   Three propositions connected to a conceptual node.

Propositions can be linked to one concept node and so make up a feature list for this concept. In Figure 12.3, the three propositions are linked to the concept node "column" because they are part of a feature list that can be used to define this concept. The most salient features are usually included in a textual definition of the concept. For instance, a column may be defined as "one of the elongated sections of a vertically divided page, used to organize a set of similar items". In the graphical representation, multiple concept nodes may be interrelated to each other to form higher-level conceptual models that allow for problem solving and reasoning in a domain (see top of Figure 12.1 & Chapter 9).

Identify Physical Models

For concrete concepts, that is, concepts referring to tangible and visible things, the acquisition of concepts may not only require learning their features but also learning their physical images. The identification of physical models, for example, is often important for those objects and tools that have been specified as being part of performance objectives (Step 3). Physical models describe the appearance or "external stimulus pattern" of a tool or object and its parts in pictures, drawings, graphics, schematic diagrams, and so forth (Figure 12.4 provides an example of a physical model of a resistor). They help learners to develop mental images that enable them to look at the world with "expert eyes", and to act according to this different view. In general, it is best to develop a physical model of the complete tool or object first. Then, the model may be detailed by adding those parts and sub parts that are necessary to perform particular procedural steps or to apply particular if-then rules. Exploded views and 3D-models may help to show these relevant parts (and sub parts) of the object or tool, the location of those parts in relation to each other (i.e., the topology) and, if necessary, their appearance by sound, smell, or other senses. The model should not contain details that are irrelevant for performing identified procedural steps and if-then rules. Thus, there should be a one-to-one mapping between the analysis of rules and procedures and the analysis of their related physical models.

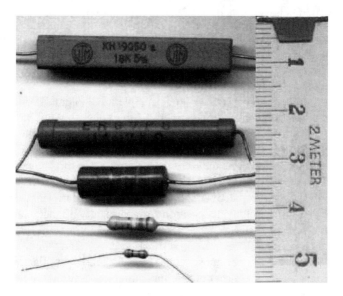

Figure 12.4   Physical models of resistors.

In conclusion, the analysis of prerequisite knowledge yields feature lists and definitions that characterize concepts (and plans and principles made up of those concepts) and, if appropriate, physical models that may help to classify things as belonging to the concept. Thus, the concept "resistor" would specify the main attributes of a resistor in some kind of feature list (it opposes the flow of electrical current, it looks like a rod with colored stripes, etc.), thereby enabling a task performer to classify something as being either a resistor or not. In addition, a physical model might be identified (see Figure 12.4), helping a task performer to recognize something as being a resistor or not. This example may also be used to illustrate the difference between the analysis of prerequisite knowledge and the analysis of mental models into domain models. In the analysis of mental models, a conceptual model of "resistors" (cf. top of Figure 12.1) would not only focus on the resistor itself, but would also include comparisons with other electronic components (e.g., transistors, capacitors, etc.); their function in relation to voltage, current, and resistance (including Ohm's law); a description of different kinds (e.g., thermistors, metal oxide varistors, rheostats) and parts of resistors, and so on. The physical model would not only depict one isolated resistor, but be replaced by a functional model illustrating the working of resistors in larger electronic circuits.

Specification at the Entry Level of the Target Group

Both the analysis of cognitive rules (Step 8) and the analysis of prerequisite knowledge are hierarchical in nature, meaning that the analysis is reiterated until it reaches a level where the prerequisite knowledge is already available prior to the instruction by the lowest-ability learners in the target group. An example of this hierarchical approach was already introduced in the previous examples:

- Starting from the procedural steps for subtracting two-digit numbers (e.g., "decrease *a* by 1", "add 10 to *b*"), the analyst might identify the following principle as prerequisite knowledge: "each column to the left indicates a tenfold of the column directly to its right",
- Newly introduced concepts in this principle are "column", "left", "tenfold", and "right". The analyst might identify the concepts "left", "tenfold", and "right" as already familiar to the lowest-ability learner in the target group, indicating that a further analysis of these concepts is unnecessary. The concept "column", however, may *not* yet be familiar to the learners and thus require further analysis.
- An analysis of the concept "column" in its main features may yield the definition: "one of the elongated sections of a vertically divided page, used to organize a set of similar items". Newly introduced concepts in this definition are, among others, "section", "vertical", "page" and "item". The analyst might identify some of those concepts as already familiar to the lowest-ability learners in the target group, indicating that a further analysis is unnecessary. Again here, one or more concepts (e.g., "vertical") may not yet be familiar to the learners and thus require a further analysis.
- An analysis of the concept "vertical" in its main features yields again a definition that may contain both familiar and unfamiliar concepts. This process is reiterated until *all* identified concepts are at the entry level of the target group.

The analyst should be aware not to stop this reiterative, hierarchical process too early. It is common that the prior knowledge of learners is overestimated by professionals in the task domain and, to a lesser degree, by their teachers. This is because experienced task performers are very familiar in the domain, which makes it difficult to put themselves in the position of novices. Therefore, the analysis process should typically go one or two levels beyond the entry-level as indicated by proficient task performers or teachers.

12.2   Analyzing Misconceptions

In addition to a rational analysis of the knowledge prerequisite to learning to perform particular rules or procedural steps, an empirical analysis may be performed to identify misconceptions that may hinder the acquisition of prerequisite knowledge. The term misconception is often used in a broad sense, referring not only to erroneous concepts but also to naive or buggy plans (for knowledge of plans) and misunderstandings (for knowledge of principles). Quite often, misconceptions arise from differences in linguistic usage. For instance, whereas the same language is spoken in the United Strates and Great Britain, some words have other meanings. In the United States, the concept "tip" refers to what one adds to a restaurant bill for good service whereas in Great Britain it refers to a place where garbage is dumped. For a designer, the concept "elegant" refers to how attractive something is while for a programmer "elegant" refers to how parsimonious the program is (i.e., how few lines were needed for the program). In teaching, one should be aware of such differences to prevent misconceptions hindering learning.

With regard to plans, an example of a common naive plan in scientific writing concerns the misuse of "and others" for all citations in the body text with more than two authors. For three, four, or five authors, the correct plan (according to the Publication Manual of the American Psychological Association, 5th edition) is to cite all authors the first time the reference occurs and to include only the surname of the first authors followed by "et al.". (not underlined or italic and with a period after "al") in subsequent citations. For six or more authors, the correct plan is to cite only the surname of the first author followed by "et al". from the very first time that the reference occurs.

With regard to principles, an example of a common misunderstanding (often referred to as a misconception) is that heavy objects fall faster than light objects. This misunderstanding might easily interfere with the correct application of the procedures for computing forces, masses, and acceleration. Actually, in the absence of air resistance all objects fall at the same rate of acceleration, regardless of their mass. The analysis of misconceptions best starts from a description of all prerequisite knowledge for one particular recurrent task aspect. Then, the question to ask for each concept, plan, or principle is "Are there any misconceptions or misunderstandings for my target group that may interfere with the acquisition of this concept, plan, or principle?" Experienced teachers are often the best source of information to answer this question.

12.3   Using Prerequisite Knowledge to Make Design Decisions

Step 9 will only be performed if prerequisite knowledge is not yet available in existing instructional materials, job aids, or help systems and, must always be carried out after Step 8 has been performed. The results of this analysis provide the basis for the design of an important part of the procedural information. The identification of misconceptions and misunderstandings may affect design decisions.

Designing Procedural Information

The results of the analysis of prerequisite knowledge, together with the description of if-then rules and procedures from Step 8, yield the main input for designing procedural information. Procedural information may be presented to learners while they are carrying out their learning tasks (Step 1), where it is only relevant to the recurrent task aspects, and when they perform part-task practice (Step 10) where it is relevant to the entire recurrent task that is practiced. Because of the analysis previously sketched, this information is organized in small units according to the rules and procedural steps that describe the correct performance of recurrent task aspects. Thus, all concepts, plans, and principles that are prerequisite for learning to applying one particular rule, or to performing one particular procedural step, are connected to this rule or step. This is an optimal form of organization because so-called just-in-time (JIT) information-displays are best presented precisely at the moment that learners have to apply a new rule, or have to carry out a new procedural step. Then, at the level of the least-experienced learner, the displays present the necessary rule or step (i.e., *how-to* information) together with the information that is prerequisite to correctly performing this rule or step. As learners acquire more expertise, the JIT information-displays quickly fade. This type of information presentation facilitates knowledge compilation (see Box 4 in Chapter 10) because it helps learners embed presented prerequisite knowledge in to-be-learned cognitive rules.

Dealing with Misconceptions

The identification of misconceptions may affect decision-making when designing procedural information. First, it is important to focus the learners' attention on those concepts, plans, and principles for which misconceptions may occur. Unsolicited information presentation, relatively slow fading of presented information, and the use of many instances that give concrete examples of concepts, plans, and principles prone to misconceptions may help. Second, when dealing with a misconception it may be helpful to use multiple representations. In addition to the presentation of feature lists and verbal definitions of concepts, presenting images of physical models and instances may help learners to develop an accurate cognitive schema that builds on both

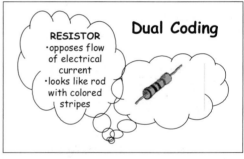

verbal and visual encodings (i.e., *dual coding*; Paivio, 1986). Finally, learners should be stimulated to compare and contrast prerequisite concepts, plans, and principles with their ineffective counterparts, that is, with misconceptions, buggy plans, and misunderstandings.

12.4 Summary of Guidelines

- If you analyze prerequisite knowledge, then start from if-then rules or procedural steps that describe correct task performance and ask which concepts, plans, and/or principles the learner needs to know in order to - learn - to correctly apply these rules or perform these steps.
- If you identify prerequisite plans, then describe the constituting concepts and the location-in-time or location-in-space relations that interrelate those concepts.

- If you identify prerequisite principles, then describe the constituting concepts and the cause-effect or natural-process relations that interrelate those concepts.
- If you identify prerequisite concepts, then describe the facts or propositions that characterize the concept in a feature list and/or concept definition.
- If you identify prerequisite concepts and a concept refers to a tool or object necessary for task performance, then depict it as a physical model.
- If you identify prerequisite concepts, plans, or principles, then be aware that their descriptions may yet introduce other concepts unfamiliar for your target group and thus reiterate the analysis in a hierarchical fashion until all identified concepts are already mastered by the lowest-ability learner.
- If you analyze misconceptions, including buggy plans and misunderstandings, then ask experienced teachers for any common misconceptions within the target group that may interfere with the acquisition of prerequisite knowledge.
- If you design procedural information, then include a description of prerequisite knowledge in JIT information-displays so that the learner has it available when the connected rule or procedural step needs to be applied.
- If there are known misconceptions when you design procedural information, then focus the learners' attention on those concepts that are liable to the misconceptions, use multiple representations (verbal and visual), and stimulate learners to compare and contrast the misconceptions with more accurate conceptions.

13
STEP 10: DESIGN PART-TASK PRACTICE

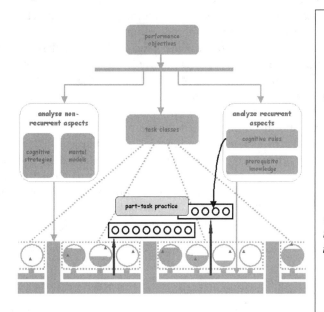

Necessity

Part-task practice is one of the four design components. The other three design components are always necessary but part-task practice is not. You should only perform this step if additional practice of recurrent task aspects is strictly necessary to reach a very high level of automation.

Suppose that you were taking a course in Semi-micro Qualitative Analysis, a chemistry course where the goal is to start from an unknown solution and through a series of steps "discover", or better said "determine" what the solution actually is. To achieve its goals the course was designed according to the Ten Steps where you worked on meaningful whole tasks arranged in task classes with all of the trimmings. Within this course, you also have to carry out titrations that involve adding the reagent to the solution by turning a valve to let the reagent drip into the solution (or releasing your finger from the top of a tube); a critical process requiring a great deal of manual dexterity that only can be achieved by a lot of practice. Unfortunately each determination takes anywhere from 15 minutes to two hours so that there is not much room for receiving the amount of practice needed to properly learn to titer. Also, if you do it wrong (adding too much reagent for example) the analysis fails and you've "wasted" two hours. Enter part-task practice to save the day.

This chapter presents guidelines for the design of such part-task practice. In general, an over-reliance on part-task practice is not helpful for complex learning. On top of this, part-task practice is often pointless because the learning tasks themselves provide sufficient opportunity to practice both the non-recurrent and the recurrent aspects of a complex skill. After all, good information presentation can often take care of the different nature of underlying learning processes for recurrent and non-recurrent constituent skills. Presenting procedural information aims at automating cognitive rules through compilation whereas presenting supportive information aims at the construction and reconstruction of schemas through elaboration. However, if a very high level of automaticity of particular recurrent aspects is required, the total number of learning tasks may be too small to provide the necessary repetition. *Only then*, is it necessary to include additional part-task practice for one or more selected recurrent aspects in the training program.

The structure of this chapter is as follows. First, practice items are described as the building blocks for part-task practice. Different types of practice items provide different levels of support, and the whole set of practice items should be so divergent that they cover all variants of the procedure taught. Then, several methods of sequencing practice items from easy to difficult are presented. Third, special characteristics of procedural information presented during part-task practice are discussed including techniques for demonstrating complex procedures, realizing contingent tutoring, and providing corrective feedback through model tracing. Fourth, instructional techniques explicitly aimed at "overlearning" such as changing performance criteria, compressing simulated time, and distributing practice sessions over time are described. Finally, the positioning of part-task practice in the training blueprint is discussed. The chapter concludes with a brief summary of guidelines.

13.1   Practice Items

Part-task practice requires extensive amounts of practice items. Well-known examples of part-task practice are drilling addition, subtraction and multiplication tables, practicing musical scales, or practicing a tennis serve - all of which are skills requiring speed and accuracy. In training design, part-task practice also is often applied for recurrent constituent skills that are critical to safety, because their incorrect per-
formance may cause danger to life, cause loss of materials, or damage to equipment. For instance, part-task practice may be given for re-animating patients or for executing emergency shutdown procedures in a chemical factory. Moreover, if instructional time allows, part-task practice may also be used for recurrent constituent skills with relations in the skills hierarchy indicating that they:

- enable performing many other skills higher in a skills hierarchy. Additional practice with the order of letters in the alphabet with elementary school children could be enacted, because this skill enables search skills such as using dictionaries, telephone books, and other alphabetically ordered materials.
- are performed simultaneously with other coordinate skills in the hierarchy. Detection of dangerous situations on a radar screen in air-traffic control is the object of additional practice because it is performed simultaneously with communicating with pilots and labeling new aircraft entering the airspace.

Types of Practice Items

Compared to the specification of learning tasks, the specification of practice items for part-task practice is a very straightforward process. The criterion for specifying practice items for part-task practice is that there is only one relevant recurrent constituent skill whose effective performance can algorithmically be described as a procedure or set of if-then rules. A distinction between a problem-solving process and a solution, or between task support and problem-solving guidance is not relevant because correctly performing the procedure or applying the if-then rules (cf. the problem-solving process) simply *is* the solution. For this reason, some people do not call it problem solving; but it is equally justified to call it the most effective type of problem solving one can think of.

Practice items should invite learners to perform the recurrent constituent skill repeatedly; performing the procedural steps or applying the if-then rules repeatedly. The saying "practice makes perfect" is actually true for part-task practice because extensive amounts of practice items will lead to routines that can be performed fast, accurately, and without conscious effort. Unlike learning tasks, part-task practice will typically not be performed in a real or simulated high-fidelity task environment, but in a simplified environment such as a "skills lab" or a drill-and-practice computer program (e.g., a batting cage and a computer multiplication program respectively). A conventional practice item, which is sometimes called a *produce item* (Gropper, 1983), confronts the learner with a given situation and a goal and requires the learner to execute a procedure (see top row in Table 13.1; the algorithm has been explained in Chapter 11, Figure 11.2). For instance, a practice item may ask the learner to compute the product of 3 times 4, label a situation as dangerous or safe by observing aircraft on a radar screen, or play a musical scale.

For part-task practice, the general recommendation is to use conventional practice items as quickly as possible. Special practice items should only be considered if (a) particular procedural steps or if-then rules leave learners error-prone, (b) procedures are long and multi-branched or the set of if-then rules is very large, or (c) learners have difficulties recognizing which procedural step or if-then rule to use because there are different alternatives for highly similar situations or highly similar alternatives for different situations. Table 13.1 includes two special types of practice items for learning to add two-digit numbers, namely, edit items and recognize items. *Edit practice items* asks learners to correct an incorrect solution by identifying the faulty step(s) or if-then rule(s) and providing the correct ones. They are especially useful to practice error-prone procedures, when "typical errors" are introduced that need to be detected and corrected by the learners.

The example given in Table 13.1 illustrates the typical error that learners forget to carry the 10 during addition. *Recognize practice items* requires learners to select a correct procedure from a set of options. Such items are especially useful if it is difficult to recognize which procedure or which if-then rules need to be used for a particular situation or goal. Pairing similar procedures may also focus the learners' attention on the conditions underlying the application of each of the procedures.

Table 13.1   Examples of conventional, edit, and recognize practice items for adding two-digit numbers.

Practice Item	Solution or procedure	Example Task Description
Produce/conventional item	?execute	*Compute 43+29 = ?*
Edit practice item	?edit	Step 1: add 9 to 3 = 12
		Step 2: decrease 12 by 10 = 2
		Step 3: add 1 to 4 = 5
		Step 4: write 2 in right column
		Step 5[a]: add 2 to 4 = 6
		Step 6: write 6 in left column
		Which step is incorrect and why?
Recognize practice item	?name	a. Addition without carrying
		Step 1: add 9 to 3 = 12
		Step 2: write 12 in right column
		Step 3: add 2 to 4 = 6
		Step 4: write 6 in left column
		b. Addition with carrying
		Step 1: add 9 to 3 = 12
		Step 2: decrease 12 by 10 = 2
		Step 3: add 1 to 4 = 5
		Step 4: write 2 in right column
		Step 5: add 2 to 5 = 7
		Step 6: write 7 in left column
		Which of the two procedures is correct and why?

[a]   This step is incorrect because the carried 1 is neglected.

Fading Support and Training Wheels

Edit practice items and recognize practice items both provide learners with task support (refer back to Figure 4.1), because they give them - a part of - the solution. If part-task practice cannot immediately start with conventional items because they are too difficult for the learner, the best option is to start with items that provide high support and work as quickly as possible toward items without support. A well-known fading strategy is the recognize-edit-produce sequence (Gropper, 1983), which starts with items that require learners to recognize which steps or if-then rules to apply, continues with items where learners have to edit incorrect steps or if-then rules, and ends with conventional items for which learners have to apply the steps or rules independently in order to produce the solution.

Problem-solving guidance is irrelevant for practice items, because performing the procedure correctly always yields the right solution. This process is algorithmic rather than heuristic, so that there is no need for the learner to try out mental operations to find an acceptable solution. This makes providing modeling examples, process worksheets, or other heuristic aids superfluous. For part-task practice, the procedural information should specify a straightforward way to perform the procedure or apply the rules (see Section 13.3 hereafter). Performance constraints, however, may be useful to support the learner who is performing complex procedures because such constraints impede or prevent the use of ineffective behaviors. Performance constraints for part-task practice often take the form of *training wheels interfaces* (Carroll & Carrithers, 1984; Carroll, Smith-Kerker, Ford, & Mazur-Rimetz, 1988), a term indicating the resemblance with the use of training wheels on a child's bicycle. In the beginning of the training, the wheels are on the same plane as the rear wheel, which makes the bicycle very stable and prevents it from falling over. As the child's sense of balance increases, the wheels are moved up above the plane so that the bicycle still cannot fall over, but if the child is in balance, then the wheels will not touch the ground. The child is actually riding on two wheels, except during the negotiation of curves where the child has to slow down, tends to lose balance and would be prone to falling. Ultimately, the child can ride the bicycle and the training wheels are removed, often replaced by a parent running behind the child to insure that she or he does not fall.

Figure 13.1   A skydiving instructor providing training wheels to his student.

Thus, the basic idea behind the use of training-wheel interfaces is to ensure that actions that are related to ineffective procedural steps or rules are unreachable for learners. For instance, a training wheels interface in a word processing course would first present only the minimum number of toolbars and menu options necessary for creating a document. All other options and toolbars would be unavailable to the learner. New options and toolbars (e.g., for advanced formatting, drawing, making tables) only become available to the learners after they have mastered using the previous ones. Another example is provided in a touch-type course where it is common to cover the typewriter keys so that the learner cannot see the key symbols. The ineffective or even detrimental behavior of "looking at the keys" in order to find and use the correct one is blocked. The key covers are removed later in the training program. A final example may be found in the teaching of motor skills, where an instructor may be holding or steering the learner in such a way (see Figure 13.1) that the learner is forced to make a particular body movement. Again, holding the learner prevents the making of ineffective, undesired, or even dangerous body movements.

Divergence of Practice Items

To conclude this section, it is important to note that the whole set of practice items used in part-task practice should be *divergent*, meaning that the items used are representative for *all* situations relevant to the procedure or if-then rules. Divergence is necessary to develop a broad set of cognitive rules that allow for optimal rule-based transfer (see Chapter 2.5) to new problem situations. For instance, part-task practice for addition of two-digit numbers should include both practice items with carrying the 10 and practice items without carrying the 10, and part-task practice for spelling words should include a broad set of practice items (i.e., words) requiring the learner to use all different letters from the alphabet. Divergence of practice items is somewhat similar to variability of learning tasks, but divergence of practice items only claims that practice items must be representative for all situations that can be handled by the procedure or by the set of if-then rules. The divergent items never go beyond those rules. Variability of practice, in contrast, claims that learning tasks must be representative for all situations that may be encountered in the real world, including unfamiliar situations for which no known approaches are available.

13.2 Part-Task Sequencing for Part-Task Practice

Thus far, we have only discussed practice items that require the learner to perform the "whole" recurrent constituent skill. For highly complex procedures or large sets of rules, however, it may be necessary to decompose the procedures into parts. Learners are then extensively trained in separately carrying out parts of the procedure or set of rules before they begin to practice the complete recurrent skill. Under highly exceptional circumstances, part-task sequencing is also applied to learning tasks (see Chapter 5.3). An important difference here is that part-task sequencing for learning tasks preferably uses a *backward-chaining* approach, so that the learners are confronted with useful examples and models right from the beginning of the training program. In contrast to this, *forward-chaining* approaches are more effective for part-task practice, because the performance of each step or the application of each rule then creates the conditions that prompt the next step or action. Thus, rule automation is facilitated because learners must repeatedly perform a step or action under the appropriate conditions.

Table 13.2 presents three sequencing techniques that are suitable for part-task practice, namely *segmentation*, *simplification*, and *fractionation* (Wightman

& Lintern, 1985). These techniques often use a forward-chaining approach based on a natural process or simple-to-complex order. If instructional time is severely limited, you may decide to train the parts only in a separate fashion. However, if it is possible, it is better to use a form of part-whole forward chaining such as the snowballing approach. For training a task consisting of the parts A, B, and C, practice items would then first practice A, then A plus B, and finally A plus B plus C.

Table 13.2   Techniques for sequencing practice items for highly complex procedures (Wightman & Lintern, 1985).

Sequencing technique	Description	Example	Easy to use for
Segmentation	Break the procedure down in distinct temporal or spatial parts.	For repairing a flat tire, first give practice items to remove the tire, then to repair the puncture, and finally to replace the tire.	Linear order of steps resulting from a behavioral task analysis.
Simplification	Break the procedure down in parts that represent increasingly more complex versions of the procedure.	For subtracting numbers, first give practice items without borrowing, then with borrowing, and finally with multiple borrowing.	Branched order of steps and decisions (a flow chart) resulting from an information processing analysis.
Fractionation	Break the procedure down in different functional parts.	For touch-typing, first give practice items for the index fingers, then for the middle fingers, and so on.	Set of if-then rules resulting from a rule-based analysis.

The forward-chaining approaches listed in Table 13.2 all result in a *low* contextual interference of practice items: Practice items are grouped or "blocked" for one part of the task so that learners practice only one set of - more-or-less - similar practice items at the same time. In contrast, learning tasks are best ordered in a random fashion, yielding a *high* contextual interference. Then, each learning task differs from its surrounding learning tasks on dimensions that also differ in the real world, which is believed to facilitate the construction of mental models and cognitive strategies. Thus, each practice item is similar to its surrounding items and the repeated practice of the same things is believed to facilitate the desired automation of cognitive rules (Jelsma, van Merriënboer, & Bijlstra, 1990; Salisbury, 1990; Salisbury, Richards, & Klein, 1985).

To conclude, sequencing techniques for highly complex procedures can obviously be combined with fading support strategies. Suppose that a complex procedure is practiced in its parts A, B, and C. Then, practice items for part A can proceed through a recognize-edit-produce sequence before starting practice on part B. For part B (or, in a snowballing approach parts A plus B), again, a recognize-edit-produce sequence can be used. And so on until conventional items are provided for the whole procedure, that is, parts A plus B plus C. Such complicated sequencing techniques are only required for the teaching of extremely complex procedures.

13.3   Procedural Information for Part-Task Practice

Step 7 discussed the design of procedural information, with a focus on its presentation during the learners' performance of the whole learning task. For whole tasks, it only pertains to the recurrent aspects of those tasks. Obviously, procedural information is also relevant to part-task practice, where only the recurrent aspects are practiced and where all of the information given to the learner pertains to the recurrent skill being practiced. The same principles for the design of procedural information apply, basically, to both situations, namely presenting rules and procedures in small information units, using simple and active language at the level of the lowest-ability learner, and preventing split attention effects (see Chapter 10). However, due to the nature of part-task practice there are also some shifts in the emphasized techniques, namely:

- demonstrations of complex procedures may be isolated from the whole task;
- contingent tutoring is easier to realize, and
- a model-tracing paradigm may be used to generate immediate feedback on errors.

Demonstrating Complex Procedures

If learners work on whole learning-tasks, procedural information is best demonstrated in the context of those whole tasks. For instance, if student hairstylists learn to cut curly hair, how the scissors should be held (i.e., a recurrent aspect of the task) is best demonstrated in the context of the whole haircutting task. During part-task practice, however, demonstrations of the part-task will often be isolated from the whole task. This may be especially helpful for teaching recurrent constituent skills that are characterized by long or complex procedures or large sets of rules. For instance, a particular emergency procedure may be demonstrated to student pilots apart from their normal task of flying an airplane from one airport to another. Such demonstrations should clearly indicate the given situation, the desired goal or outcome, the materials and equipment need to be manipulated, and the actual execution of the procedures using the materials and equipment (Merrill, 1983). Needless to say, a good instructional design should then allow the learners to integrate the part-task behaviors into the whole task. This is typically realized by introducing the part-task only after introducing the whole task (i.e., there is a fruitful cognitive context) and by "intermixing" part-task practice with whole-task practice.

For complex procedures, it is often advisable to pay special attention to rules or procedural steps that are difficult or even dangerous for learners when incorrectly applied. Often, such rules are associated with typical errors resulting from malrules or buggy rules, and/or with misconceptions identified during an empirical analysis (see Chapters 11.2 & 12.2). Table 13.3 presents four instructional methods that can help learners deal with difficult aspects of a recurrent constituent skill.

Table 13.3   Four techniques for dealing with complex procedures.

Technique	Description	Example
Subgoaling	Ask the learner to specify the goal or sub goal that is reached by a particular procedure or rule.	Partly demonstrate a procedure and ask the learners what the next sub goal is (also called *milestone practice*; Halff, 1993).
Attention focusing	Focus the learners' attention on those procedural steps or rules that are difficult or dangerous.	Present a graphical demonstration of a complex procedure and color-code the dangerous steps in red.
Multiple representations	Use multiple representation formats, such as texts and visuals, for presenting difficult procedures or rules.	Present a demonstration both in real-life and as a simulated animation that can be controlled by the learner.
Matching	Compare and contrast correct demonstrations of procedures or rules with their incorrect counterparts.	Demonstrate the procedure for addition with (correct) and without carrying (incorrect) and use the contrast to explain why carrying is necessary.

Subgoaling forces learners to identify the goals and sub goals that are reached by particular procedural steps or rules. *Attention-focusing* ensures that learners pay more attention to the difficult aspects than to the easy aspects. Using *multiple representations* helps learners process the given information in more than one way. *Matching* allows learners to critically compare and contrast correct task-performance with incorrect task-performance. In this case, it is extremely important to clearly point out which of the two demonstrations is incorrect and why.

Contingent Tutoring

Contingent tutoring requires an instructor or computer system to closely monitor and interpret the learner's performance, and present procedural information precisely at the moment that the learner needs it. Contingent tutoring may be realized for whole learning tasks by one-on-one tutoring (i.e., the Assistant Looking Over Your Shoulder), but this is very hard to realize if no human tutor is available. Therefore, the Ten Steps prescribed another type of unsolicited information presentation as a default strategy, namely *system-initiated help* where JIT information-displays are connected to the first learning task(s) for which they are relevant. For part-task practice, in contrast, contingent tutoring is the preferred and default strategy for presenting procedural information.

Contingent tutoring during part-task practice may be realized by a human tutor or by a computer system. Because only one single recurrent skill is involved, it is relatively easy to trace the learner's actions back to particular procedural steps or rules. Landa (1983) recommends a step-by-step approach in which a specific action to be taken and its related prerequisite knowledge are presented to the learner exactly at the moment that the step has to be performed. The instruction may be spoken by a tutor, or may be presented in a visual or graphical fashion. A complex procedure, for example, may be presented graphically where the relevant next step is highlighted at the exact moment that it needs to be carried out. Relevant prerequisite knowledge could be included in, or connected to, this highlighted part (for an example, refer back to Figure 10.1).

Model Tracing and Corrective Feedback

Like contingent tutoring, providing immediate corrective feedback requires an instructor or computer system to monitor and interpret the learner's performance. If learners work on whole tasks, a human tutor may give immediate corrective feedback, but this too is hard to realize by other means. If learners work on part-tasks, however, it becomes easier to provide immediate feedback because the learner's behavior can be traced either step-by-step or rule-by-rule. To achieve this, the if-then rules or procedural steps identified in the analysis of cognitive rules (Step 8) are used as diagnostic tools in a *model-tracing* paradigm (Corbett & Anderson, 1995). Model-tracing is often applied in drill-and-practice computer programs and Intelligent Tutoring Systems and entails the following steps:

1   Each learner-action is traced back to a specific if-then rule or procedural step that describes or models the recurrent constituent skill taught.

2a   As long as the tracing process succeeds and observed behavior is consistent with the rules or steps, the learner is on track and no feedback needs to be given.

2b   If the tracing process fails and the observed behavior cannot be explained by the rules or steps, a deviation from the model trace must have appeared and the following feedback is given:

- The learner is told that an error has occurred.
- If possible, an explanation (*why* there is an error) is provided for the deviation from the model trace. This may be based on available malrules or misconceptions that were identified in an empirical analysis of the recurrent skill under consideration (see Chapters 11.2 & 12.2).
- The learner is told how to recover from the results of the error and is given a hint for the next step or action to be taken.

Suppose that a learner is writing a computer program in which the values of two variables need to be exchanged and she makes a typical error, namely, first stating

A=B and then stating B=A to exchange the values. This typical error can be traced back to a malrule for switching the values of two variables (refer back to Table 11.1). Consequently, corrective feedback may take the following form:

Deviation from correct path:
  You made an error.
Malrule that may explain the deviation:
  It seems that you tried to switch the values of A and B by first stating that A=B and then stating that B=A.
Explanation why malrule does not work:
  This does not work. Suppose that the value of A is 3 and the value of B is 5. If you state A=B, A will get the value 5; if you subsequently state B=A, B will *also* get the value 5. Thus, both variables end up with the same value.
Hint for how to continue:
  Try to switch the values of the variables by using a third variable.

13.4 Overlearning

The instructional methods discussed in the previous sections are sufficient to teach a recurrent skill to a level where the learner can accurately perform it. However, part-task practice is typically not aimed at accurate performance, but at very high level of automaticity for which accurate performance is only a very first step. *Overlearning* with extensive amounts of conventional practice items that are divergent and that are representative for all situations that can be handled by the procedure or rules is necessary to fully automate a recurrent skill. The very slow learning process underlying overlearning is strengthening (see Box 5). Three instructional strategies that explicitly aim at strengthening through overlearning are changing performance criteria, compressing simulated time, and spaced or distributed practice.

Box 5 - Strengthening and Part-Task Practice

Well-designed part-task practice makes it possible for learners to perform a recurrent or routine aspect of a complex skill after it has been separately trained, at a very high level of automaticity. Part-task practice should provide the repetition needed to reach this. Together with knowledge compilation (see Box 4), which always precedes strengthening; it is a major learning process responsible for rule automation.

Accumulating Strength
It is usually assumed that each cognitive rule has a strength associated with it that determines the chance that it applies under the conditions specified after the "IF", as well as how rapidly it then applies. While knowledge compilation leads to domain-specific rules that are assumed to underlie accurate performance of the skill, those rules still have a weak strength. Thus, performance is not fully stable because weak rules may simply fail to apply.

Moreover, while it is fairly fast in comparison with weak-method or even schema-based problem solving, it could still benefit from large improvements in speed. Strengthening is a straightforward learning mechanism. It is simply assumed that rules accumulate strength each time they are successfully applied. Only after further practice might the skill become fully automatic.

The Power Law of Practice

The improvement that results from strengthening requires long periods of training. The Power Law of Practice (Newell & Rosenbloom, 1981; Snoddy, 1926) characterizes strengthening and the development of automaticity. This law predicts that the log of the time to complete a response will be a linear function of the log of the number of successful executions of that particular response. For instance, the Power Law predicts that if the time needed to add two digits decreased from 3 seconds to 2 seconds over the first 100 practice items, it will take 1.6 seconds after 1000 items, 1.3 seconds after 10,000 items, and about 1 second to add two digits after 100,000 trials! In addition to adding digits, the Power Law has been found to be a good predictor for a variety of tasks such as editing texts, playing card games, performing choice reaction tasks, detecting letter targets, and rolling cigars.

Compilation Versus Strengthening

Both knowledge compilation and strengthening are elementary cognitive processes that are not subject to strategic control, but are mainly a function of the quantity and quality of practice. The Power Law makes clear that the time it takes to compile a rule (which may even be a one-trial process) is very modest in comparison to the time needed to reach full skill automaticity. Strengthening may account for the continued improvement of a skill long after the point where it can be accurately performed. In an old study, Crossman (1959) reported on the development of skill in rolling cigars. While it typically takes only a few hundred trials to reach accurate performance of this skill, his participants showed improvement after three million trials and two years. It should thus be clear that ample amounts of overlearning are necessary to reach full automaticity.

Further Reading

Crossman, E. R. F. W. (1959). A theory of the acquisition of speed skill. *Ergonomics, 2,* 53–166.

Newell, A., & Rosenbloom, P. S. (1981). Mechanisms of skill acquisition and the law of practice. In J. R. Anderson (Ed.), *Cognitive skills and their acquisition* (p. 1–55), Hillsdale, NJ: awrence Erlbaum Associates.

Palmeri, T. J. (1999). Theories of automaticity and the power law of practice. *Journal of Experimental Psychology: Learning, Memory, and Cognition, 25,* 543–551.

Snoddy, G. S. (1926). Learning and stability. *Journal of Applied Psychology, 10,* 1–36.

Change Performance Criteria

Performance objectives for a recurrent constituent skill specify the standards for its acceptable performance (Chapter 6), and often include criteria related to accuracy, speed, and timesharing (i.e., performing the skill simultaneously to other skills). For most to-be-automated recurrent skills, the ultimate goal is not to reach highest possible accuracy, but to obtain satisfactory accuracy, combined with high speed as well as the ability to perform the skill together with other skills and, ultimately, in the context of the whole task. Three phases of overtraining that involve changing performance criteria lead to this goal:

1. In the first phase, which is typically completed before overtraining starts, the skill is trained to an acceptable level of accuracy.
2. In the second phase, the skill is trained under - moderate - speed stress while maintaining the accuracy criterion. Speed stress makes it impossible for learners to follow the steps in a procedure consciously and, thus, forces them to automate the skill.
3. In the third phase, the skill is trained together with an increasing number of other skills, while maintaining the accuracy and speed criteria. This continues until the skill can be performed at a very high level of automaticity in the context of the whole task.

Compress Simulated Time

Thousands of practice items may be necessary to reach full automaticity of recurrent skills. For slow processes such as weather prediction and other natural processes, or steering large sea-vessels and other slowly responding systems, the time required for practicing the skill under normal conditions becomes enormous. Compressing simulated time with a factor of 10–100 can drastically reduce the necessary training time and at the same time facilitate automation due to increased speed stress and latency time of feedback.

Schneider (1985) provides an example in the field of air traffic control. Making judgments about where an aircraft should turn and seeing the results of this decision normally takes about five minutes, but the simulated time for this maneuver was compressed with a factor 100 so that a practice item could be completed in a few seconds. Consequently, it becomes possible to practice more items on one day than in one year of normal training, and the associated speed stress promotes overlearning.

Distribute Practice over Time

Relatively short periods of part-task practice distributed over time (spaced practice) give better results than long, concentrated periods of drill (massed practice). In an old study carried out by Bray (1948), participants had to practice using Morse code either for four hours a day or seven hours a day. No difference between practice schedules was found. The learners in the seven-hours-a-day group were thus wasting the additional three hours of practice. Other studies (see Dempster, 1988) indicate that the longer the spacing between practice sessions, and the more they are alternated with other learning activities, the more effective the practice is. This suggests that part-task training sessions are best mixed with practicing whole learning tasks, and that the sessions end when the learner reaches the standards of the part-task.

13.5 Part-Task Practice in the Training Blueprint

Two guidelines help connect part-task practice to the training blueprint. First, part-task practice should always be provided in a fruitful cognitive context, meaning that learners must already be able to relate and integrate it to required whole-task performance (Schneider & Detweiler, 1988). This could be reached by first presenting modeling examples or other learning tasks that allow learners to understand how the part-task fits into the whole task. Part-task practice without an appropriate cognitive context, such as extensive part-task practice in advance to whole-task training, or drill courses prior to the actual training program, are likely to be ineffective. This principle is clearly illustrated in a study by Carlson, Khoo, and Elliot (1990) who found no positive effect of 8,000 items for Boolean functions that were practiced *before* the whole task of troubleshooting logical circuits, but the practice items for Boolean functions did have a positive effect on the fluency of whole-task performance when they were practiced *after* exposure to a simple version of the whole task.

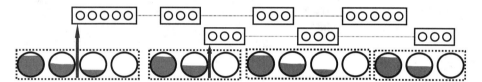

Figure 13.2   Intermixing practice on learning tasks and part-task practice for two selected recurrent task aspects.

Second, part-task training is best distributed over time in sessions that are alternated with learners working on learning tasks (see Figure 13.2). Further, if part-task practice is provided for more than one recurrent aspect of the whole skill, both different part-task practice sessions and working on the whole learning tasks are *intermixed* to promote integration (Schneider, 1985). Intermixed training might also be useful for the training of double classified skills (refer back to Chapter 6.3). In this case, extensive part-task practice is provided even though it is known that the developed routines are not powerful enough to cope with all situations the learner might encounter. The learning tasks are then used to create occasional impasses which confront the learners with situations where the routines do not work and which train them to switch from an automatic to a problem-solving mode.

To conclude this chapter, Table 13.4 presents one of the task classes from a training blueprint for the moderately complex skill "searching for research literature" (you may refer back to Table 5.2 for a description of the other task classes). A specification of part-task practice has been added to this task class, indicating that part-task practice in the use of Boolean operators starts parallel to a learning task for which it is relevant. Part-task practice continues until learners reach the standards for acceptable performance. See Appendix 2 for the complete training blueprint.

Table 13.4   A preliminary training blueprint for the moderately complex skill "searching for relevant research literature". For one task class, a specification of part-task practice has been added to the blueprint.

Task Class 3
Learners are confronted with situations where the concepts in the to-be-searched domain are not clearly defined. Identical terms are used for different concepts, and identical concepts are described with different terms. A large number of articles are written about the subject and articles are written in several fields of research. Therefore, next to searching on titles of articles, the search also needs to be performed on abstracts and texts. In addition, databases from different fields of research have to be searched. Many search terms need to be interconnected with Boolean operators to make sure that all relevant articles (using different terminology) are found and that irrelevant articles (using the same terminology as relevant ones) are excluded.

Supportive Information: *Presentation of cognitive strategies*
• SAP for determining the number of databases to search and whether to also search on abstracts and full texts.

Supportive Information: *Presentation of mental models*
• Structural model of search query templates describing Boolean combinations of search terms that can be used to search for articles about ill-defined subjects.
• Conceptual model of different types of databases for different fields of study, describing structure, special search requirements, etc.

Learning Task 3.1: *Completion + Reverse* Learners receive a research question and an elaborate search query. They have to predict which databases should be used and then perform the query. They then have to refine the query and select relevant articles.	**Procedural information** • Procedures for searching specific databases	**Part-task Practice** Applying Boolean operators
Learning Task 3.2: *Conventional* Learners receive a research question and have to perform a literature search for the 10 most relevant articles.	**Procedural information** • Procedures for searching specific databases (fading)	

Supportive Information: *Cognitive feedback*
• Learners receive feedback on their approach to solve the problem in Learning Task 3.2.

13.6 Summary of Guidelines

- Provide only part-task practice for selected recurrent aspects of a complex skill if a high level of automaticity is required, and if the recurrent skill is critical, enables the performance of many other skills, or if it is simultaneously performed with many other skills.
- Part-task practice should aim as quickly as possible at the use of conventional practice items in a process of overlearning.
- Consider the use of edit items, recognize items, and training wheels for error-prone, multi-branched or easily mixed up procedures; in these cases, first provide support through recognize or edit items and/or through training wheels and then quickly fade the support as learners acquire more expertise.
- Ensure that the whole set of practice items used in part-task practice is divergent. The items must be representative for all situations that can be handled with the procedure or the set of if-then rules.
- Apply part-task sequencing techniques such as segmentation, simplification and fractionation for highly complex procedures or large sets of rules; these techniques apply a forward-chaining approach and yield low contextual interference.
- The procedural information presented during part-task practice should (a) provide demonstrations that focus the learners' attention on difficult or dangerous actions, (b) apply contingent, step-by-step tutoring, and (c) use a model-tracing paradigm to give immediate corrective feedback.
- In order to promote overlearning, change performance criteria from accuracy, via accuracy plus speed, to accuracy plus speed plus timesharing; compress simulated time with a factor 10–100, and distribute practice sessions over time.
- Intermix part-task practice for a selected recurrent skill with the work on whole learning tasks and, if applicable, with part-task practice on other recurrent skills.

PART III

APPLICATIONS

14
USE OF MEDIA

À l'École

Application of the Ten Steps results in a detailed blueprint for an educational program aimed at complex learning. In the terminology of Instructional Systems Design, such a blueprint marks the transition from the design phase to the development or production phase (see Chapter 3.4). In the design phase, a series of decisions need to be made as to the media that can best be used to implement the instructional design. Media selection is a gradual process in which media choices are narrowed down as the design process continues. This chapter is only concerned with the *preliminary* selection of media, based on the premise that particular media are better suited to enabling or sustaining particular learning processes than others are. Because each of the four blueprint components aims at a different basic learning process, it might be expected that different media are better suited to supporting each of the components (i.e., learning tasks, supportive information, procedural information, and part-task practice; Van Merriënboer & Kester, 2005). Figure 14.1 indicates the relationships between learning processes, blueprint components, and media.

It should be stressed that the Ten Steps do *not* provide guidelines for the final selection and the production of media. The final selection is influenced not only by the instructional goals, but also by factors such as constraints (e.g., available personnel, equipment, time, money), task requirements (e.g., media attributes necessary for carrying out learning tasks and the required response options for learners), and target group characteristics (group size, computer literacy, handicaps). Specialized models for media selection that consider those factors are necessary to make a final selection of one or more media (e.g., Romizowski, 1988) and many hand-books and reviews have been written about education and media (e.g., Mayer, 2005; Salomon, 1979; van Merriënboer, 1994; van Merriënboer & Brand-Gruwel, 2005). Furthermore, guidelines for development and production are highly media-specific and, thus, fall beyond the scope of the Ten Steps. Development guidelines for written texts are, for instance, very different from guidelines for developing dynamic visualizations (Khalil, Paas, Johnson, & Payer, 2005a, 2005b), computer simulations, or instructor-led sessions.

Learning Processes		Blueprint components	Media
Schema construction	Induction (Box 2)	Learning tasks	Real or simulated task environments
	Elaboration (Box 3)	Supportive information	Hyper- & multi-media systems
Schema automation	Compilation (Box 4)	Procedural information	EPSS, on-line help systems
	Strengthening (Box 5)	Part-task practice	Drill & practice CBT

Figure 14.1   Relationships among basic learning processes, blueprint components, and media.

The structure of this chapter is as follows. First, media that allow learners to work on the learning tasks are discussed. These may be either "real" or "simulated" task environments, including computer-based simulations. Second, media that allow for the dynamic selection of learning tasks are discussed. Dynamic task selection makes it possible to offer individual learners a sequence of learning tasks that is optimally adapted to their individual learning needs. Third, so-called *secondary media* for presenting supportive information, procedural information, and part-task practice are discussed. The chapter ends with a brief summary of main points.

14.1   Media for Learning Tasks

According to the Ten Steps, learning tasks are the backbone of an educational pro-gram. For this reason, the medium that allows learners to work on those learning tasks is called the *primary medium*. Often, the primary medium is simply the "real" task environment with its tools and objects in which regular task perform-ance takes place. There may, however, be reasons to practice the learning tasks in a simulated environment, including computer-based forms of simulation. If this is the case, then an important design decision concerns the level of fidelity of the simulation, which is defined as the degree of similarity between the simulated and the real task environment.

Task Environments

The primary goal of learning tasks is to help learners inductively construct cognitive schemas from concrete experiences. Thus, the primary educational medium must allow learners to work on learning tasks offering those concrete experiences and will usually take the form of a real or simulated task environment. In many cases, the real task environment is a suitable setting for the learners to perform their learning tasks. Nevertheless, especially in the earlier phases of the learning process (i.e., task classes in the beginning of the educational program), simulated task environments may offer more favorable opportunities for learning than real task environments. Table 14.1 lists reasons for the use of simulation. Examples of simulated task environments are simulated offices and workshops, physical simulators (see Figure 14.2), virtual companies, role-plays management games, and computer-simulated task environments.

Figure 14.2   British wooden mechanical horse simulator, taken before 1915.

Table 14.1   Reasons to practice learning tasks in simulated task environments.

Reason for using a simulated rather than real task environment	Example
Gaining control over the sequence of learning tasks offered to learners.	Giving learners increasingly more demanding clients (i.e., tasks) in a simulated shopping store rather than being dependent on the arbitrary clients walking into a real store.
Better opportunity to add support and guidance to learning tasks (i.e., change their format).	Giving learners tasks to make strategy decisions in a management game, with the opportunity to consult experts and peers, rather than making these decisions in the boardroom of a real company.
Prevent unsafe and dangerous situations while performing the learning tasks.	Giving medical students tasks to perform surgical operations on corpses rather than on real patients.
Speed up or slow down the process of performing the learning tasks.	Giving learners tasks to steer a large vessel in a time-compressed simulator rather than to steer a real vessel in open sea.
Reduce costs of performing the learning tasks.	Giving learners tasks to shut down a simulated nuclear power plant rather than letting them shut down a real plant.
Create learning tasks that rarely occur in the real world.	Giving pilot trainees tasks to deal with emergency situations in an aircraft simulator rather than waiting for these situations to happen in a real aircraft.
Create learning tasks that would otherwise be impossible due to limited materials or resources.	Giving student dentists tasks to fill holes in porcelain molars rather than to fill holes in the teeth of real patients.

Computer-Simulated Task Environments

In multimedia learning, the heart of the learning environment will typically consist of a computer simulation. According to the Ten Steps, the learning tasks to be performed in the environment are developed based on authentic, real-life tasks. On one hand, this always yields a high *psychological fidelity* because performing the learning tasks is more or less similar to performing the real-life tasks. In other words, there is a clear correspondence between the cognitive processes involved in carrying out the task. On the other hand, this allows the tasks to be performed in a range of environments from those environments where there has not really been an attempt to mimic the real task environment (i.e., simulation with low *physical fidelity*) to environments that are very close to the real task environment (i.e., simulation with high physical fidelity; see Figure 14.3). Learning tasks that train psychotherapists to make diagnoses, for example, may take the form of textual case descriptions of clients presented in a web-based course (low-fidelity simulation) or they may take the form of lifelike simulated characters (avatars) that can be interviewed in a virtual reality environment (high-fidelity simulation). A step further is the type of simulation found in first aid courses or advanced medical courses where role-playing actors simulate real accident victims or patients. For an in-depth discussion of the different aspects of authenticity, the reader is referred to Gulikers, Bastiaens, and Kirschner (2004).

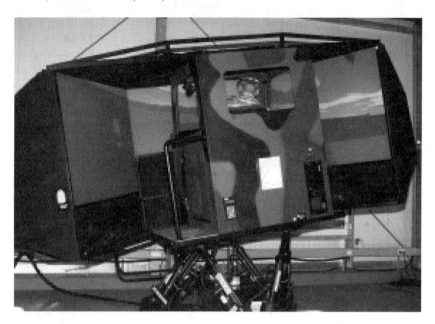

Figure 14.3   High-fidelity heavy-wheeled-vehicle driver simulator.

According to the Ten Steps, it could be desirable to start training with task classes in which the learning tasks are performed in an environment with low physical fidelity, and then gradually increase fidelity as learners' expertise increases (see Table 14.2). A low-fidelity environment only represents those aspects of the real environment that are strictly necessary to perform the learning tasks. It does not contain any details or features that are irrelevant in the current stage of the learning process, but that may nevertheless attract learners' attention and so disrupt learning. This design principle is in agreement with the finding that the exclusion of irrelevant or *seductive details* from a training program has positive effects on learning outcomes and transfer (Harp & Mayer, 1998; Mayer, Heiser, & Lonn, 2001; Moreno & Mayer, 2000). In later task classes and with increasingly advanced learners, more and more details of the real task environment become relevant, making it necessary to perform the learning tasks in a high-fidelity simulation or in the real task environment (Gulikers, Bastiaens, & Martens, 2005; Maran & Glavin, 2003).

Table 14.2   Examples of computer-simulated task environments ordered from low to high physical fidelity.

	Low fidelity	Medium fidelity	High fidelity
Making diagnoses in psychotherapy	In a web-based course, clients are represented by textual descriptions of their characteristics and psychological complaints.	In a web-based course, clients are represented by video recordings showing them in different therapeutic sessions.	In a virtual reality environment, clients are represented by lifelike simulated characters that may be interviewed by the learners.
Repairing complex technical systems	The complex system is represented by a non-interactive figure on the computer screen combined with a list of its major malfunctions.	The complex system is represented by an interactive figure, allowing the learner to perform tests and to make changes by clicking the mouse.	The complex system is represented by 3D Virtual Reality, allowing the learner to perform tests and make changes to objects with regular tools.
Designing instruction	In a web-based course, a textual case study is presented to students, illustrating a performance problem that needs to be solved.	In a multimedia learning environment, students can interview different stakeholders and consult different resources in order to analyze a performance problem.	In a virtual company, students participate in a (distributed) project team working on a performance problem that has been brought in by a real client.

In general, even if learning tasks are not performed in the real task environment from the start of the educational program, they will eventually be performed in the real environment at the end of the program. Thus, medical students will treat real patients in a hospital, learners in a pilot training program will fly real aircraft, and trainees in accountancy will deal with real clients and carry out real financial audits. The simple reason is that even high-fidelity simulation cannot compete with the real world. An exception may be made for training tasks that almost never occur in the real world (e.g., disaster management, dealing with failures in complex technical systems) and tasks that are associated with very high costs (e.g., launching a space shuttle, shutting down a large plant). For these kinds of tasks, high-fidelity simulation using Virtual Reality with advanced input-output facilities (VR helmets, data gloves; see Figure 14.4) and complex software models running in the background may help to limit the gap between the real world and simulations of it.

Figure 14.4   Virtual Reality (VR) parachute trainer.

14.2   Dynamic Task Selection

Some media, including computer-based simulated task environments, allow for the dynamic selection of learning tasks. Rather than offering one-and-the-same educational program to all learners, *dynamic task selection* makes it possible to offer a unique educational program to each individual learner. This section first discusses *adaptive learning* as one approach to the dynamic selection of learning tasks. Then efficiency is discussed as an alternative to learner's performance as the main factor to base the selection of learning tasks on. To conclude, problems with regard to diagnosis and feedback in computer-based training are discussed.

Adaptive Learning

In traditional, non-adaptive educational programs, the same sequence of learning tasks is presented to all learners. In adaptive programs, learning tasks are dynamically selected based on the characteristics and needs of each individual learner (Camp, Paas, Rikers, & van Merriënboer, 2001). Adaptive educational programs typically yield higher learning outcomes and better transfer performance than their non-adaptive counterparts (for an overview, see Salden, Paas, & van Merriënboer, 2006). In other words adaptive training programs are more effective than non-adaptive programs. In an adaptive program, a high-ability student may quickly proceed from simple learning tasks to difficult ones and work mainly on tasks with little support, while a low-ability learner can make use of many learning tasks, progress slowly from simple tasks to difficult ones, and work mainly on tasks with a great deal of support. The Ten Steps provide a good starting point for the design of adaptive educational programs. For each individual student, it is possible at any

215

given point in time to select the best task class to work on (i.e., the optimal difficulty of the next task), and to select a learning task from within this task class with
an optimal level of support and guidance. Three applicable rules correspond with
the principles of task classes, support and guidance, and variability of practice:

1   Task classes.
    a   If performance on unsupported learning tasks meets the standards for all
        relevant performance objectives, then let the learner proceed to the next
        task class and present a more difficult task with a high level of support
        and/or guidance.
    b   If performance on unsupported learning tasks does not yet meet the stan-
        dards for one or more relevant objectives, then give the learner, at the
        current difficulty level, either another unsupported learning task or a task
        with specific support and/or guidance.
2   Support and guidance.
    a   If performance on supported learning tasks meets the standards for all
        relevant objectives, then decrease support and/or guidance for the next
        learning task.
    b   If performance on supported learning tasks does not yet meet the stan-
        dards for one or more relevant objectives, then give the learner either a
        learning task with the same level of support and/or guidance or a task
        with a higher level of specific support and/or guidance.
3   Variability.
    Choose next learning tasks in such a way that the whole set of presented
    learning tasks varies on all dimensions that also vary in the real world.

Dynamic selection of learning tasks requires continuous assessment of the progress
of individual learners (see Figure 14.5). Such assessment takes place on the basis of
the performance objectives for the educational program (Step 3) and, in particular,
the *standards* (criteria, values, attitudes) that are defined for all constituent skills
relevant for the learning tasks under consideration. In general, a scoring rubric will
be used to assess the learners' different aspects of performance on all relevant standards (Chapter 6.4; see also Table 6.2). As indicated earlier, learning tasks without
support will typically be used to make decisions on progress to more-difficult tasks
(i.e., a next task class). If the learner meets the standards for all constituent skills
involved, he or she may proceed to the next task class. If desired, performance assessment on unsupported learning tasks may be used as a form of summative assessment. In this case, the tasks can better be seen as *test* tasks, meaning that they
provide a basis for grading, pass/fail decisions, and certification. If the learner has
not yet reached the standards for all constituent skills involved, additional learning
tasks at the same level of difficulty can be provided. If only additional practice is
necessary, these will again be learning tasks without support. If, however, learners
have difficulties with particular aspects of performance, these will be learning tasks
with specific additional support and guidance to help the learners to improve their
performance on precisely those aspects.

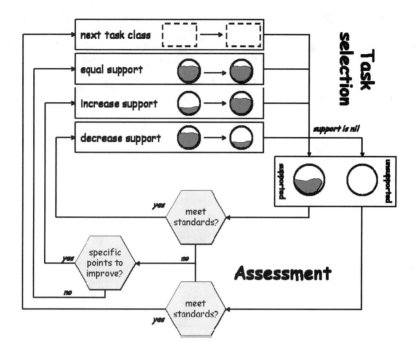

Figure 14.5   The cycle for dynamic task selection based on continuous assessment of learning tasks.

Assessment of learning tasks *with* support and guidance will typically be used to make decisions about adjusting the level of support and/or guidance for the following tasks. Performance assessment on supported learning tasks is only used for *formative assessment*, meaning that its goal is to improve the quality of the learning process. If the learner meets the standards for all constituent skills involved, he or she will next receive a learning task with less support and less guidance and, eventually, a learning task with no support at all. If the learner has not yet reached the standards for all constituent skills involved, additional learning tasks with support will be provided. If only additional practice is necessary, these will again be learning tasks with roughly the same level of support. If, however, learners have difficulties with particular aspects of performance, these will be learning tasks with specific additional support and guidance directed at improving performance on precisely those aspects.

Efficiency as a Combination of Mental Effort and Performance

Models for adaptive learning are typically based on the assessment of a learner's task performance. Adaptation, however, might also be based on a combination of performance and mental effort invested to obtain this performance (Kalyuga & Sweller, 2005; Salden, Paas, Broers, & van Merriënboer, 2004; Tuovinen & Paas, 2004). Paas and van Merriënboer (1993) developed a computational approach to combine measures of mental effort with measures of performance to compare the *mental efficiency* associated with instructional conditions. The assumption underlying this is that learner behavior in a particular condition is more efficient if performance is higher than might be expected based on invested mental effort or, equivalently, if invested mental effort is lower than might be expected based on performance. Using this approach, high task performance associated with low effort is called high mental efficiency, whereas low task performance with high effort is called low mental efficiency (see Figure 14.6).

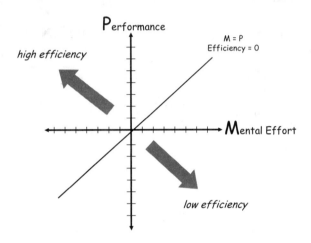

Figure 14.6   Efficiency in relation to performance and invested mental effort.

Efficiency yields important information that is not necessarily reflected in performance measures, because the learners' voluntary investment of cognitive resources is now taken into account. For instance, it is quite feasible for two learners to attain the same performance levels with one student working through a very laborious process to arrive at the correct solution (i.e., low efficiency), whereas the other student reaches the same solution with a minimum of effort (i.e., high efficiency). Whereas both learners demonstrate identical performance, the efficiency for the student who exerts substantial effort is lower than for the student who performs the task with minimal effort. In this case, the optimal next learning task for the first learner is likely to be less difficult, and/or contain more support, than the optimal next task for the second learner. Thus, efficiency might be a better basis for the selection of learning tasks than performance alone.

Diagnosis and Feedback

Continuous assessment, based on performance objectives and standards as reflected in a scoring rubric (see Chapter 6.4), is critical to the dynamic selection of learning tasks. For all relevant aspects of performance, it repeatedly determines if the learner has reached the standards that were set. Both the difficulty and the level of support and guidance of the next learning task(s) are adjusted to the assessment results. If the standards for particular aspects of performance (i.e., there are points for improvement) have not yet been met, subsequent support and guidance might be directed precisely toward those aspects.

Assessment should, however, not be confused with *diagnosis*. Assessment only determines whether performance objectives have been met. If this is not the case for particular aspects of performance, assessment cannot identify possible misconceptions, malrules, naive mental models, or intuitive strategies that provide an explanation for this shortcoming. Thus, assessment alone is often not enough for providing learners with effective corrective and cognitive feedback. Assessment needs to be complemented by in-depth diagnosis as described in previous chapters. For the recurrent, routine aspects of performance, the diagnosis might be based on an analysis of the typical errors that learners make, as well as misconceptions that may negatively affect task performance (see Chapters 11.2 and 12.2). In computer-based systems, *model tracing* provides a technique to diagnose errors and give corrective feedback to learners (see Chapter 13.3). Remember, in model tracing, the learners' behavior is traced rule-by-rule. No feedback is provided as long as the learners' behavior can be explained by correct rules; corrective feedback is provided only if the learners' behavior can be explained by so-called malrules that represent typical errors.

For the non-recurrent, problem solving and reasoning aspects of performance, the diagnosis might be based on an analysis of the intuitive problem-solving strategies that learners apply as well as the naive mental models they possess (see Chapters 8.2 and 9.2). Outside of the artificial-intelligence laboratory, computer-based systems are not yet able to perform an in-depth analysis of sub optimal problem-solving and reasoning processes to provide cognitive feedback. Thus, the teacher or instructor will typically provide this type of cognitive feedback, or the learners will be invited to critically compare and contrast their own problem-solving and reasoning processes with those of others - including expert task performers. Along the same lines, learners could be involved in the assessment of their own performance (i.e., self-assessment), or the performance of other learners (i.e., peer-assessment) as will be further described in Chapter 15.

14.3 Secondary Media

In educational programs developed with the Ten Steps, the primary medium is always a real or simulated task environment. The psychological fidelity of the learning tasks is high right from the start, although the physical fidelity of the environment in which those tasks are performed might change from low to high. All other media used in the environment are referred to as secondary media. According to the Ten Steps, they refer to the presentation of supportive information, procedural information, and part-task practice.

Supportive Information: Hyper- and Multimedia Systems

Supportive information helps learners construct cognitive schemas in a process of elaboration; connecting new information to prior knowledge already available in memory. Traditional media for teaching supportive information are textbooks, teachers, and realia (i.e., "real" things). Textbooks contain a description of the "theory;" the domain models that characterize a field of study and, alas, often in a lesser degree the Systematic Approaches to Problem-Solving (SAPs) that can help learners solve problems and perform non-trivial tasks in the domain. Teachers typically discuss the highlights in the theory (lectures), demonstrate or provide expert models of SAPs, and provide cognitive feedback on learner performance. Realia or descriptions of real entities are used to illustrate the theory.

Computer-based hypermedia and multimedia systems may take over some or even all of those functions. These systems present theoretical models and concrete cases that illustrate the models and cases in a highly interactive way, and explain problem-solving approaches and illustrate those approaches by showing, for example, expert models on video or animated lifelike avatars. Computer-based simulations of conceptual domains are a special category of multimedia in that they offer a highly interactive approach to the presentation of case studies where learners can change the settings of particular variables and study the effects of those changes on other variables. In other words, the learner can explore relationships that exist in a domain (de Jong & van Joolingen, 1998). The main goal of such *microworlds* is not to help learners practice a complex skill (as is the case in simulated task environments), but to help them construct, through active exploration and experimentation, mental models of how the world is organized.

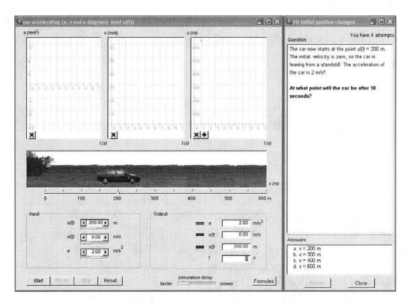

Figure 14.7   Computer-based SimQuest simulation of a theoretical domain: moving objects.

Microworlds help learners construct conceptual models, structural models, causal models, or combinations of the three. To support the learning of *conceptual models*, for example, a microworld of the animal kingdom might present a taxonomy of different species (e.g., mammals, birds, reptiles, fish, insects, etc.) to the learner, offering definitions along with the opportunity for studying examples of members of the different species (e.g., by looking at pictures or watching video clips). To support the learning of *structural models*, artificially designed objects might be represented as a set of building blocks or plans enabling learners to experiment with designing and composing solutions from different building blocks, and observe the effects of changing a particular design. For example, such a simulation might present a set of building blocks to the learner for designing integrated circuits, factories, and plants, or even roller coasters (as in RollerCoaster Tycoon®). Finally, to support the learning of *causal models*, processes might be represented in such a way that they enable learners to change the settings of particular variables and observe the effects of these changes on other variables. Such process simulations might be relatively simple, such as a simulation of moving objects to illustrate the Newtonian laws of motion (as in a simulation of accelerating cars developed in SimQuest; see Figure 14.7), but also extremely complex, such as a simulation of an advanced production process in chemical industry or a delta ecosystem.

It is critical that students elaborate and deeply process the information presented in hyper- and multimedia systems. Microworlds try to encourage this by inviting learners to explore the simulated processes and run the experiments. Hypermedia may also help reach this goal because their structure, to a certain extent, reflects the way human knowledge is organized in elements (called "nodes") and non-arbitrary, meaningful relationships between those elements (called "links"). Therefore, hypermedia environments allow learners to explore information by traversing from one information element (i.e., node) to another, related element, and so forth. It is, however, of utmost importance to provoke deep processing by asking leading questions, to stimulate reflection by giving prompts, and to promote discussion. Some relevant principles in this respect are the redundancy, self-explanation, and self-pacing principles (see Table 14.3 for examples).

The *redundancy principle* indicates that the presentation of redundant information typically has a negative impact on learning (for an overview of studies, see Sweller, van Merriënboer, & Paas, 1998). It is a counter-intuitive principle, because most people think that the presentation of the same information, in a somewhat different way, will have a neutral or even positive effect on learning. However, learners must first process the information to determine that the information from the different sources is actually redundant. This cognitively demanding process does not contribute to meaningful learning.

The *self-explanation* principle relates to what Salomon (1984) called *easy learning* in learning from educational television: television is "easy" and print is "tough" because of a differential investment of mental effort in learning as a function of perceptions and attributions and what he called the *butterfly defect* (Salomon, 1998) in hypermedia learning. Multimedia may act as or be perceived as an opportunity to relax (cf. watching television) - while for meaningful learning to occur the presented information should be associated with deep processing and invite learners to "self-explain" the information. Renkl (1997) introduced the self-explanation principle in the context of learning from worked examples. The degree to which learners self-explain the solution steps in worked examples is a good predictor for their learning outcomes, and direct elicitation of self-explanation by prompting the learners has beneficial effects on transfer of learning.

Table 14.3   Some principles for learning with hypermedia.

Principle	Example
Redundancy principle	For students in econometrics who learn to explain periods of economic growth, first present a qualitative model (which allows them to predict if there will be any growth) and only then present a more encompassing quantitative model (laws that may help them to compute the amount of growth) - but without repeating the qualitative information as such.
Self-explanation principle	For medical students who learn to diagnose malfunctions in the human cardiovascular system, present an animation of how the heart works and provide prompts that provoke them to explain the underlying mechanisms to themselves or to their peers.
Self-pacing principle	For students in psychotherapy who learn to conduct intake conversations with depressed clients, show video-examples of real-life intake conversations and give them the opportunity to stop/replay the recording after each segment in order to reflect on this particular segment.

Finally, the *self-pacing principle* indicates that giving learners control over the pace of the presentation may also facilitate elaboration and deep processing of information. Elaboration is an effortful, time-consuming process and "streaming" or transient information (e.g., video, dynamic animation, etc.) may not allow learners sufficient time for the necessary processing. In the Ten Steps, "streaming" information will often refer to case studies (e.g., an animation illustrating a particular dynamic domain model) and modeling examples (e.g., a video of an expert modeling a particular problem-solving process or SAP). For this type of multimedia information presentation, it is important to give learners control over the pace in which the information is presented to them. This means allowing learners to pause the stream, stop the stream, replay the stream, and so forth. The self-pacing principle allows them to pause and better reflect on the new information in order to couple it to already existing cognitive structures.

Procedural Information: EPSS and Online Help Systems

Procedural information helps learners automate their cognitive schemas via knowledge compilation. The traditional media for presenting procedural information are the teacher and all kinds of job aids and learning aids. The teacher's role is to walk through the classroom, laboratory, or workplace, peer over the learner's shoulder (the teacher's name is *Aloys* - the Assistant Looking Over Your Shoulder), and give directions for performing the routine aspects of learning tasks (e.g., "no - you should hold that instrument like this…", "watch, you should now select this option…"). Job aids may be the posters with frequently used software commands that are hung on the walls of computer classes, quick reference guides adjacent to a piece of machinery, or booklets with instructions on the house-style for interns at a company.

In computer-based environments, the presentation of procedural information is being taken over by Electronic Performance Support Systems (EPSSs) such as online job aids and help systems, wizards, and (intelligent) pedagogical agents (Bastiaens, 1999). Such systems provide procedural information at the request of the learner (on demand) or do this at their own initiative (e.g., pedagogical agents). This information is preferably presented precisely when the learners need it for their work on the learning tasks. Mobile devices such as Personal Digital Assistants and mobile telephones are quickly becoming important tools for the presentation of procedural information (see Figure 14.8). Such devices are particularly useful for presenting small displays of information during task performance that tell learners what to do in order to perform the recurrent aspects of the task at hand correctly.

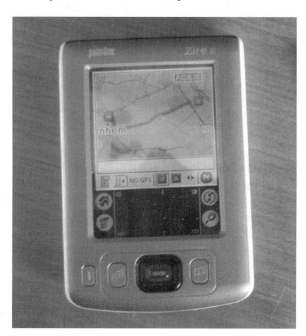

Figure 14.8   Example of a PDA giving information on a travel optimal route.

It is critical that the procedural information is readily available for the learners when they need it and that it is presented in small, self-contained information units. Some relevant principles in this respect are the *temporal* and *spatial split attention principles*, the *signaling principle*, and the *modality principle* (see Table 14.4 for examples).

Table 14.4   Some Principles for learning from EPSSs and online help systems.

Principle	Example
Temporal split-attention principle	For students in web design who learn to develop web pages in a new software environment, a pedagogical agent tells them how to use the different functions of the software environment precisely when they need them to implement particular aspect of their design - instead of discussing all available functions beforehand.
Spatial split-attention principle	For social science students who learn to conduct statistical analyses on their data files with SPSS, present procedural information describing how to conduct a particular analysis or enter specific data and variables on the computer screen and not in a separate manual.
Signaling principle	For students in automotive engineering who learn to disassemble an engine block, animate the disassembling process in a step-by-step fashion and always put a spotlight on those parts that are loosened and removed.
Modality principle	For students in instructional design who learn to develop training blueprints by studying a sequence of more and more detailed blueprints, explain the blueprints with narration or spoken text instead of visual (on-screen) text.

The *temporal split-attention principle* originally indicated that learning from mutually referring information sources is facilitated if these sources are not separated from each other in time but, rather, are presented simultaneously. Thus, how-to instructions for performing the routine aspects of the learning task are best presented just in time, precisely when the learner needs them. The related *spatial split-attention principle* refers to the research finding that higher learning outcomes are reached when mutually referring information sources are physically integrated with each other in space. Thus, procedural information should be presented in such a way that it is optimally integrated with the learning tasks and the task environment.

The attention focusing or *signaling principle* indicates that learning may be improved if the learner's attention is focused on the critical aspects of the learning task or the presented information. It reduces the need for visual search and so frees up cognitive resources that may then be devoted to processing the procedural information. For instance, if a teacher instructs a learner how to operate a piece of machinery, it is useful to point a finger at those parts that must be controlled, or if a video-based example is used to demonstrate particular routine aspects of performance, it is helpful to focus the learners' attention through signaling (e.g., by spotlighting hand movements) on precisely those aspects.

Finally, the *modality principle* indicates that dual-mode presentation techniques that use auditory text or narration to explain visual diagrams, animations, or demonstrations, result in better learning than equivalent, single-mode presentations that only use visual information (Tabbers, Martens, & van Merriënboer, 2004). The positive effect of dual-mode presentation is typically attributed to an expansion of effective working-memory capacity, because for dual-mode presentations both the auditory and visual subsystems of working memory can be used rather than either subsystem alone. Consequently, procedural information that specifies how to perform routine aspects of learning tasks just-in-time can better be spoken by a teacher or other pedagogical agent than visually presented.

Part-Task Practice: Drill & Practice CBT

Part-task practice helps learners automate the cognitive schemas that drive routine aspects of behavior through a process of strengthening. Traditional media include paper-and-pencil for doing small exercises (e.g., simple addition, conjugate verbs), skills labs for practicing perceptual-motor skills (e.g., operate machinery, give intravenous injections), and the real task environment (e.g., marching on the street, taking penalty kicks on the soccer field). The main reason for applying part-task practice is the *component-fluency hypothesis*, which indicates that drill-and-practice on one or more routine aspects of a task may have positive effects on learning and performing the whole task. A very high level of automaticity for routine aspects frees up cognitive capacity for other processes because these automated aspects no longer require resources for conscious processing. As a result, all available cognitive capacity can be allocated to the non-recurrent, problem solving and reasoning aspects of whole-task performance.

For part-task practice, the computer has proved its worth in the last decades. Drill-and-practice Computer Based Training (CBT) is without doubt the most successful type of educational software produced. The computer is sometimes abused for its use of drill, but most critiques seem to miss the point. They contrast drill-and-practice CBT with educational software that focuses on rich, authentic learning tasks. According to the Ten Steps, however, part-task practice *never* replaces meaningful whole-task practice. It merely complements work on rich learning tasks and is applied only when the learning tasks themselves cannot provide enough practice to reach the desired level of automaticity for selected routine aspects. If such part-task practice is necessary, the computer is a highly suitable medium because it can make drill effective and appealing through the presentation of procedural support, by compressing simulated time so that more exercises can be done than in real time, by giving knowledge of results and immediate feedback on errors, and using multiple representations, gaming elements, sound effects, and so forth.

14.4 Summary

- According to the Ten Steps, the primary medium is always a real or simulated task environment allowing learners to perform the learning tasks.

- Whereas the psychological fidelity of learning tasks should always be as high as possible, the physical fidelity of the environment in which the tasks are performed may change from low to high in order to limit the amount of irrelevant details for the learners.
- In an adaptive training program, continuous assessment of learner progress is the basis for the selection of each next learning task in such a way that it provides (a) an optimal level of difficulty (i.e., positioning in the best task class), (b) an optimal level of support and guidance, and (c) sufficient variability in the whole set of presented tasks.
- Continuous assessment might not only be based on learners' performance but on a combination of performance and invested mental effort, or, efficiency. This makes it possible to make a distinction between two learners who reach the same performance, but one reaches this performance with minimum effort and the other reaches it through a laborious process.
- Hyper- and multimedia systems are useful to present supportive information because they might help students to elaborate and deeply process the presented information.
- Electronic Performance Support Systems (EPSS) and on-line help systems are useful to present procedural information because they present how-to information in small units, precisely when learners need it (just in time).
- Drill-and-practice computer-based training programs are useful to provide part-task practice because they allow students to practice recurrent aspects of a task repeatedly, which eventually increases the fluency of whole-task performance.

15
SELF-DIRECTED LEARNING

The Ten Steps help to develop training blueprints for educational programs. These programs are often more or less the same for the whole target group, especially when this group is rather homogeneous as is often the case in many training situations. However, this is not and need not necessarily be the case. Through the dynamic selection of learning tasks, the program could also be made highly flexible with each learner receiving a unique sequence of learning tasks adapted to her or his individual needs, progress, and preferences (see Chapter 14.2). Thus, within the limits of the developed blueprint, the Ten Steps allow for highly adaptive and flexible types of learning. *Self-directed learning* is one way to implement adaptive education. In such a system (see Figure 15.1), individual learners are responsible for orienting themselves to learning opportunities, planning of their own learning tasks, and monitoring, adjusting, and assessing their own performance (Bolhuis, 1996; Garrison, 1997). The learner, rather than some other intelligent agent such as a teacher or an e-learning application, is responsible for assessing performance and selecting learning tasks.

This chapter discusses how the Ten Steps may be used to sustain self-directed learning. Readers interested in self-directed learning itself should consult other sources (e.g., Gray, 2003) for an in-depth analysis of self-directed learning including the skills that the learner needs to possess, namely orienting skills (Which opportunities for learning arise? What could I learn from this task?), planning skills

(Which tasks should I perform? How much time and effort would I need to invest in this task?), monitoring skills (Did I learn enough to stop working on this task? Am I sensitive to contextual changes?), adjusting skills (Do I need to change my learning style? Should I ask for help?), and assessment skills (Did I reach all standards for acceptable performance? Which are my main points for improvement?).

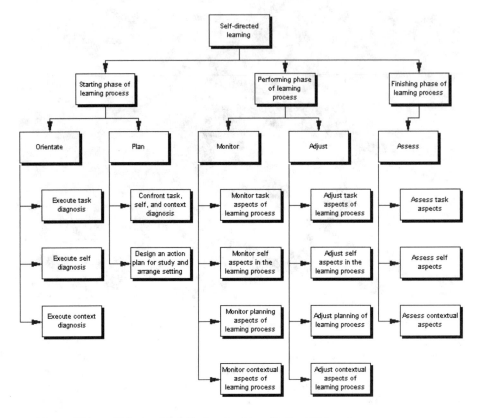

Figure 15.1   Higher-order skills involved in self-directed learning.

According to the Ten Steps, the last set of skills - those relating to assessment - is critical to the selection of suitable learning tasks. At one extreme, the system (i.e., the teacher or the e-learning application) assesses learner progress and selects the next learning task for students to work on. At the other extreme, self-directed learners continuously assess their own progress and select the next learning task from all available tasks. In a well-developed system of self-directed learning, learning-task selection is a shared responsibility of both system and learners, where the learners' responsibility increases as they further develop their self-directed learning skills.

The structure of this chapter is as follows. First, a distinction is made between three levels of self-directed learning. At the lowest level, learners have control over part-task practice; at the intermediate level, they have control over supportive information, and at the highest level they choose their own learning tasks. After this, assessment is discussed as the key to the highest level of self-directed learning because learners must know where they stand and where they want to go in order to select learning tasks properly. Protocol portfolio scoring is discussed as a way to gather, store, and interpret assessment results in a systematic fashion. Finally, support and guidance for self-directed learning is discussed. Based on their portfolio with assessment results, students learn to select suitable learning tasks for themselves. In the beginning of the learning process, they might choose learning tasks from a small - pre-selected - set of available tasks and receive detailed advice from their coach or teacher; at the end of the learning process, they select tasks from all available tasks without additional advice. The chapter ends with a summary of its main points.

15.1   Levels of Self-Directed Learning

Different levels of self-directed learning may be coupled to the four blueprint-components of the Ten Steps. The lowest level of self-directed learning concerns on-demand presentation of procedural information (i.e., the opposite of unsolicited information presentation; see Chapter 10.3). In the context of working on either learning tasks or part-task practice items, the learner decides which information displays will be consulted because these displays are expected to help learners perform routine aspects of the tasks. Increasingly higher levels of self-directed learning allow the learners also to decide on part-task practice, supportive information, and the learning tasks to be performed.

Independent Part-Task Practice

With *independent part-task practice*, the learner decides which routine aspects of the learning tasks will receive additional practice and when they will be practiced. In general, a learner's initiative to carry out additional part-task practice is triggered by a desire to improve performance on whole learning-tasks. Economics students, for example, working on learning tasks dealing with financial analysis may feel the need to become more proficient in working with spreadsheet programs and, thus, decide to take an online course on how to use a specific spreadsheet application. Medicine students working in a hospital may feel the need to improve their life-saving skills (e.g., mouth-to-mouth resuscitation, intubation, external cardiac massage) and, thus, enroll in a workshop on this. Finally, schoolchildren writing in a foreign language may feel the need to improve certain language skills and use a drill-and-practice computer program to conjugating irregular verbs. Independent part-task practice is relatively easy to implement because it:

- concerns only one well-defined recurrent skill or routine, with no need to organize the contents of the program for each individual learner;
- often takes the form of individual practice, with no need to form groups of learners on the fly, and
- can often be supported with drill-and-practice computer programs, with no need to schedule teachers or instructors.

Just-In-Time Open Learning

With *just-in-time open learning* (JITOL; Goodyear & Steeples, 1992), the learner not only decides to consult procedural information and practice part-task items, but also chooses to study supportive information to improve performance on problem-solving and reasoning aspects of the learning tasks. JITOL is a form of resource-based learning because educational resources (i.e., books, films, videos, software programs, manuals, help systems, experts who may be consulted, etc.) are made available to the learners. The learner decides which resources to consult and when to consult them; thus, all resources must be available on demand and just in time. As for independent part-task practice, the work that the learners are carrying out on the learning tasks generally triggers them to consult particular educational resources. Architecture students who are required to design an office building, for example, may feel the need to interview experts (i.e., working architects) on their preferred approaches and rules-of-thumb that they use. Students in aircraft maintenance dealing with tasks on troubleshooting electrical systems might decide to consult the technical manuals of different aircraft systems. Finally, student teachers who want to improve their motivational skills may decide to watch different children's television shows to study the techniques used there. In general, the implementation of JITOL is more difficult than the implementation of independent part-task practice because it might be necessary to organize learning content and form groups of learners on an ad-hoc basis, and because teachers and/or other experts often play an important role for the presentation of supportive information, especially in modeling systematic approaches to problem solving and providing cognitive feedback.

On-Demand Education

In the most far-reaching form of on-demand education, learners not only decide on the educational resources to be consulted, but also decide on which learning tasks to perform and when to perform them. This is a form of dynamic task selection where the learner rather than the teacher or some intelligent, computer-based agent selects subsequent learning tasks. In line with both the Ten Steps and with our basic model for dynamic task selection (see Chapter 14.2), learners should preferably select learning tasks in such a way that they:

1 are at an appropriate level of *difficulty*. The learner should choose more difficult learning tasks, coming from a next task class, only if all standards for acceptable performance have been reached for unsupported tasks at the current level of difficulty.

2 provide an optimal level of *support and guidance*. The learner should choose learning tasks with less support and guidance only after all standards for acceptable performance have been reached for supported tasks; should choose learning tasks with the same level of support and guidance if all standards have not yet been reached, and should choose tasks with specific support and guidance if difficulties occur with particular aspects of performance.

3   provide enough *variability* of practice. Subsequent learning tasks should preferably be chosen such that the tasks in the selected set eventually vary on all dimensions that also vary in the real world.

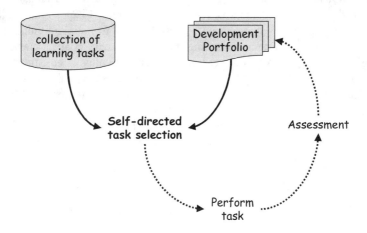

Figure 15.2   A cyclical model for self-directed task selection.

Figure 15.2 depicts a cyclical process of self-directed task selection. Learners select a task from a database with descriptions of all available learning tasks. Each task is characterized by *metadata* related to (a) the difficulty of the task, which is a description of the task class it belongs to, (b) its level of support and/or guidance, such as task format (e.g., worked example, completion task, conventional task) and/or available support (e.g., available process worksheets, performance constraints), and (c) its other features, such as all dimensions on which tasks also differ in the real word. After a task has been selected, the learner performs it, and uses available feedback to monitor her or his performance (Butler & Winne, 1995; Van den Boom, Paas, van Merriënboer, & van Gog, 2004), and eventually judges the quality of her or his own performance, either by self-assessment or by asking others such as peers, teacher, employers, and so forth (Sluijsmans & Moerkerke, 1999) to assess it. The assessment results are added to a development portfolio, which contains an overview of all learning tasks performed and their assessment results. Given the information in the portfolio, a next learning task is selected and so further. The next section discusses the protocol portfolio scoring, which is a systematic approach to gather assessment results, store them, and use them for task selection.

15.2   Protocol Portfolio Scoring

Performance assessment is fully integrated in the Ten Steps. In Step 3, setting performance objectives, standards for acceptable performance (i.e., criteria, values, & attitudes) are formulated for all different aspects of performance, including both non-recurrent (i.e., problem-solving & reasoning) and recurrent constituent skills (i.e., routines). A scoring rubric (see Chapter 6.4) is developed to assess performance on learning tasks, where learning tasks without support and guidance can be seen as "test tasks". In addition, continuous assessments can be used as a basis for dynamic task selection and adaptive learning (see Chapter 14.2), so that all learners receive a - sequence of - learning tasks fully tailored to their individual learning needs. In essence, self-directed learning aims at the same goal, namely, learners working on learning tasks that are tailored to their individual needs, though it now concerns *self-selected* learning tasks. In order to sustain such self-directed learning, assessment results are gathered in a development portfolio. An approach fully compatible with the Ten Steps is the *protocol portfolio scoring* (Straetmans, Sluijsmans, Bolhuis, & van Merriënboer, 2003) which uses a constant set of standards, stores assessment results from a mix of methods, and allows for vertical and horizontal assessments.

Constant Set of Standards

The standards for acceptable behavior are part of the performance objectives (Hambleton, Jaeger, Plake, & Mills, 2000), which correspond with all constituent skills that make up the complex skill or professional competency the educational program is aiming to achieve. These standards remain constant throughout the whole program! Thus, in the beginning of the first task class, the learner tries to reach the relevant standards, but only for the simplest versions of the task and with ample support and guidance. At the end of the first task class, the learner should be able to perform the simplest versions of the unsupported tasks at the relevant standards. This continues until in the beginning of the final task class where the learner tries to reach the same standards for the most difficult versions of the task and with ample support and guidance, and at the end of the final task class, the most difficult versions of unsupported tasks up to those standards. Thus, it is neither the standards nor the level of the standards that changes throughout the educational program but, in contrast, the difficulty of the learning tasks and the support and guidance provided to learners for carrying out those tasks.

Whereas there is a constant set of standards for the entire educational program, this does *not* imply that each separate learning task is assessed with exactly the same set of standards. First, not all standards are relevant for all tasks. For instance, constituent skills of the complex skill "searching for research literature" include "selecting appropriate databases", "formulating search queries", "performing searches", and "selecting results" (cf. Figure 2.2). Each of those constituent skills has its own performance objectives and its own standards. However, for the first task class, learners may perform searches in only one particular database. In this case, the standards for "selecting appropriate databases" are not relevant for the learning tasks in this task class for the simple reason that there is nothing to choose. In general, more and more standards will become relevant as learners progress through the program.

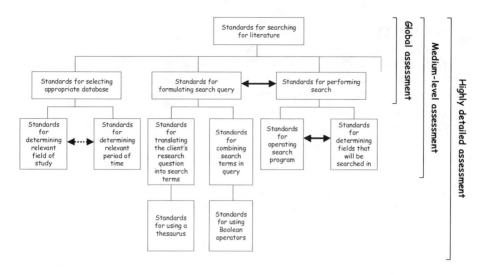

Figure 15.3   Level of detail of assessments related to the hierarchy of constituent skills, with their corresponding performance objectives and standards.

In addition, standards are hierarchically ordered, making it possible to vary the level of detail of the assessments. Figure 15.3, for example, depicts the standards for "searching for relevant research literature" ordered according to its corresponding skill hierarchy. The use of standards associated with constituent skills high in the hierarchy will assess performance at a global level; the added use of standards lower in the hierarchy will assess performance at an intermediate level, and the added use of standards at the lowest level of the hierarchy will assess performance at a highly detailed level. For example, only the standards at the level of the constituent skills "selecting appropriate databases", "formulating search queries", "performing searches", and "selecting results" are taken into account for global assessment. For intermediate-level assessment, standards that are part of the performance objectives for constituent skills lower in the hierarchy are also taken into account: In addition to standards for "formulating the search query", for instance, standards for "combining search terms in the query" and "translating the client's research question into relevant search terms" are also taken into account (e.g., pleasant communication [value]; only use search terms listed in thesauri [criterion]; check relevance of search terms using normal working procedures [value], and complete task within five working days [criterion]). For a highly detailed assessment, standards that are part of the performance objectives at the lowest level of the hierarchy are also taken into account: In addition to standards for "combining search terms in the query", for example, standards for "using Boolean operators" are taken into account (e.g., use of Boolean operators is faultless and very fast [criterion]). In general, highly detailed assessments will be limited to those constituent skills not yet mastered or for which learners still have to improve their performance.

Mix of Assessment Methods

There are many, many methods to assess task performance. Open answer questions (both short answer and essay) or multiple-choice questions can be used to assess learner understanding of a case study or worked example. Situational judgment tests describe work-related situations and require learners to choose a course of action by responding to questions (e.g., What would you do first or what is the most important action to take?). Work sample tests require learners to perform tasks similar to those performed on the job, while performance-on-the-job assessments observe learner's task performance under regular working conditions. There are many other assessment methods, but a full discussion of them falls beyond the scope of this book. The point is that all assessment methods have their own advantages and disadvantages (Baartman, Bastiaens, Kirschner, & van der Vleuten, 2006). Assessment methods with a high reliability (e.g., multiple choice tests) have, in general, a relatively low external validity and, vice versa, assessment methods with a high external validity (e.g., on the job performance) have a relatively low reliability. Therefore, the Ten Steps recommend using a rich mix of assessment methods. Baartman et al. (2006) call this a competency assessment program. In this way, the disadvantages of one particular assessment method are counterbalanced by the strengths of other assessment methods.

Along with a mix of assessment methods, a mix of assessors should also be used. In a system of self-directed learning, the most important assessor is the learner herself who self-assesses the quality of her own performance. In addition, peer assessments may be used to gather input from fellow learners or colleagues (Prins, Sluijsmans, Kirschner, & Strijbos, 2005; Sluijsmans, Brand-Gruwel, & van Merriënboer, 2002; Sluijsmans, Moerkerke, van Merriënboer, & Dochy, 2001). Finally, important assessors include teachers, instructors and other experts in the task domain; clients, customers and other people served by the learners, as well as employers and other responsible managers. The whole group of assessors is able to provide *360-degree assessments*, taking different perspectives on the learner's performance. Mixing both methods and assessors, creates a strong basis for decision-making (e.g., What are important points for improvement? Which tasks to do next?). In an ultimate system of self-directed learning, the learner independently decides on the mix of methods and assessors used. In other words, to get a complete picture of the level of performance, it is best to use a rich mix of both methods and assessors.

Vertical and Horizontal Assessment

Protocol portfolio scoring allows for both vertical and horizontal assessment of performance. Vertical assessments indicate the degree to which standards for *one particular aspect* of performance have been met, as assessed on a range of learning tasks by various assessment methods. They reflect the learner's mastery of distinct aspects of the complex skill. Horizontal assessments indicate the degree to which standards for *overall* performance have been met; it reflects the student's mastery of the entire complex skill. Table 15.1 provides an example of protocol portfolio scoring. Each row corresponds to one learning task. The first four columns present the task class number, the task number, the format of the task assessment (i.e., the task and how it is assessed), and the assessor. Abbreviations of the task and how it is assessed include a worked-out example with a multiple-choice test (WOE-MCT), a completion assignment with a situational judgment test (COM-SJT), a worked-out example with a work-sample test (WOE-WST), a conventional task with a performance on-the-job assessment (CON-POJ), a completion assignment with a work-sample test (COM-WST), and a worked-out example plus process support with a multiple-choice test (WOP-MCT). Abbreviations of the assessor include self-assessments (SA), peer assessments (PA), and assessments by others.

The next eight columns relate to eight aspects on which performance is vertically assessed. This constant set of standards may refer to criteria, values, and attitudes for both routine and problem-solving aspects of behavior. In the example, vertical standards are set to 4.7 for the first aspect, 3.5 for the second aspect, 2.5 for the third aspect, and so forth on a 6-point scale. The performance on each learning task is assessed on all aspects relevant for this task. Table 15.1 indicates, for example, that assessor HK judges the first aspect for performance on the first learning task with a score of 3; well below the vertical standard of 4.7. This yields a negative decision meaning that this aspect remains a point for improvement for following tasks. The learner self-assesses the first aspect for the second learning task with a score of 5, yielding an average score over the first two learning tasks of 4.0. This moving average is still below the standard of 4.7, and thus the first aspect continues to be a point for improvement. Assessor GS judges the first aspect for performance on the third learning task with a score of 6, yielding an average score over the first three learning tasks of 4.7. This moving average is now equal to the standard, meaning that there is no longer a need to consider this aspect a point for improvement. The other seven aspects of performance are assessed in the same way. Vertical assessment results chiefly indicate which aspects of performance should be emphasized or de-emphasized in following learning tasks.

The final three columns in Table 15.1 concern the horizontal assessments. The horizontal standard is the mean of the measured vertical standards; the mean horizontal score is the mean of all measured vertical scores. In the example, the overall assessment score of assessor HK for the first learning task is 3.0 (sum of 15.0 divided by 5 measured aspects), which is below the horizontal standard of 3.74 (also computed over five measured aspects).

Table **Error! No text of specified style in document..1**   Example of a fictitious protocol portfolio scoring.

				Vertical Standards (for 8 aspects)							Horizontal Standards (over scored aspects)		
				Score per Aspect (Maximum score = 6 for each aspect)							Horizontal Standard	Mean Score	Decision
Class	Task	Format	Assessor	4.7	3.5	2.5	3.5	3.5	4.0	4.5			
1	1.1	woe-mct	HK	3		3		4		3			
			average	3.0	3.0	3.0	4.0	4.0	3.0	3.0	3.74	3.0	-
			decision	-	+	+	+	+	-	-			
1	1.2	com-sit	SA	5	2	1	3	4	2				
			average	4.0	2.0	2.0	3.0	3.5	2.0	3.0	3.71	2.8	-
			decision	-	-	-	-	+	-	-			
1	1.3	woe-wst	GS	6	5	5	5	5	6	5			
			average	4.7	3.5	3.0	3.0	4.0	4.0	4.0	3.71	3.8	+
			decision	+	+	+	-	+	+	-			
1	1.4	con-poj	PA	3	4	2	2	4	3	4			
			average	4.3	3.7	3.0	2.5	4.0	3.7	4.0	3.71	3.7	-
			decision	-	+	+	-	+	-	-			
1	1.5	com-wst	HK	5	5	4	5	6	6	5			
			average	4.3	4.0	3.3	3.3	4.4	4.3	4.3	3.71	4.0	+
			decision	-	+	+	-	+	+	-			
1	1.6	con-poj	AH	5	6	6	6	5	6	6			
			average	4.4	3.8	3.8	4.0	4.5	4.6	4.6	3.71	4.3	+
			decision	-	+	+	+	+	+	+			
2	2.1	wop-mct	PA	2	5	3	3	3	5	4			
			average	2.0	5.0	3.0	3.0	3.0	5.0	4.0	3.9	3.7	-
			decision	-	+	-	-	-	-	-			

Etcetera

This yields a negative decision, meaning that the next task again includes learner support. The learner self-assesses the second learning task with a score of 2.8, which is still below the horizontal standard of 3.71 (now computed over all eight aspects). Performance is degrading so that the next task will provide additional support: it will be a worked-out example instead of a completion assignment. Assessor GS gives an overall assessment score for the third learning task of 3.8, which is above the horizontal standard. Therefore, the next learning task will be a conventional task without support or guidance. A peer gives an overall assessment score for the fourth, unsupported task of 3.7, which is yet a little below the horizontal standard. Therefore, the next task will again provide support and guidance. Assessor HK gives an overall assessment score for the fifth task of 4.0, which is above the horizontal standard. Consequently, the next task is a conventional task without support. Assessor AH gives an overall assessment of the sixth, unsupported task of 4.3, which is well above the horizontal standard. Consequently, the next learning task will be more difficult, that is, will be part of a second task class. This example shows that horizontal assessments are critical for selecting learning tasks. Support decreases when horizontal assessment results improve; support increases when horizontal assessment results degrade, and support is stopped when horizontal assessment results are above the standard. With regard to the desired level of difficulty, horizontal assessment of unsupported tasks is critical: The learner progresses to a next task class or difficulty level only when assessment results for unsupported tasks are above the horizontal standard. This process repeats itself until the learner successfully performs the conventional, unsupported tasks in the most difficult task class.

15.3   Support and Guidance for Self-Directed Learning

When complex skills are taught according to the Ten Steps, learner support and guidance should be high at the beginning of the educational program and should smoothly decrease in a process of scaffolding until learners are able to perform the skills without support or guidance. This same principle applies to the teaching of higher-order skills such as self-directed learning. Two ways to provide support and guidance are limiting the number of learning tasks the learner can choose from, and giving learners advice on the process of task selection, including the use of a portfolio. Both approaches will be discussed and illustrated with a practical example.

Setting the Number of Tasks from which the Learner can Choose

In a flexible educational system, some intelligent agent other than the learner might perform dynamic task-selection. This intelligent agent, for example, could be a teacher or a sophisticated e-learning application (see Chapter 14.2). Such a "system-controlled" model of task selection, however, does *not* allow for self-directed learning. It should be replaced by a "learner-controlled" model in which the learner takes responsibility for the task-selection process. However, two opposing tendencies must be taken into account with regard to learner control. On the positive side, learner control makes it possible to develop self-directed learning skills and has a positive effect on the learner's motivation to learn (see Corbalan, Kester, & van Merriënboer, 2006; Paas, Tuovinen, van Merriënboer, & Darabi, 2005). On the negative side, unlimited learner control and too much freedom of choice may lead to stress, high mental effort, and demotivation (Iyengar & Lepper, 2000; Schwartz, 2004), which is especially true for low-ability learners. Kirschner, Martens, and Strijbos (2004) add to this that learners often do not have or do not know how to utilize appropriate strategies when they are left to themselves to manage their learning. Therefore, the optimal number of tasks the learner may choose from should be neither too low nor too high. Furthermore, this optimum should increase as the learner's self-directed learning skills develop.

A shared-responsibility model in which an intelligent agent makes a preselection of suitable learning tasks from all available tasks, followed by the learner who makes a final selection of one task from this subset, meets the objections of both the system-controlled and learner-controlled model. In such a *mixed model*, there is partial system-control (i.e., selecting the subset) and partial learner-control (i.e., selecting the final task from this subset). Furthermore, the shared-responsibility model allows for a gradual transfer of responsibility for task selection from the system to the learner, as his or her self-directed learning skills develop. A system-controlled model for dynamic task-selection could be used to make a pre-selection of suitable learning tasks (cf. Figure 14.5). Three possible phases in an educational program that gives increasing control to learners are:

1 Pre-selection of tasks of suitable difficulty and with a suitable level of support - The learner's final selection is based on other task features (i.e., features on which learning tasks differ because those features also differ in the real world).

2 Pre-selection of tasks of suitable difficulty - The learner's final selection is based on the given level of support (e.g., study a worked example, finish a completion assignment, work on a conventional problem, etc.) and other task features.

3 Pre-selection of a highly varied set of tasks - The learner's final selection is based on difficulty, level of support, and other task features.

Giving Learners Advice on Task Selection

Even when the number of learning tasks from which the learner can choose is limited, task selection is still a difficult higher-order skill to learn. Giving learners advice on the process of task selection (cf. giving them support and guidance for first-order skills), and diminishing the frequency and level of detail of this advice as they develop their self-directed learning skills, is an approach consistent with the Ten Steps. Here, a distinction can be made between procedural and strategic advisory models. *Procedural advisory models* provide students with the same rules that would be applied to implement system control over dynamic task selection. The procedure presented in Figure 14.5 provides a good example: Given their assessment results, learners may use this algorithm to decide on the difficulty, level of support, and other features of the next learning task to choose. Procedural models provide straightforward advice and may, for instance, be used in the same way as product comparison sheets for consumers which provide basic data to help advise consumers on a particular purchase (e.g., maximum price, preference for a particular brand, minimum requirements, etc.). In our case, learners have to specify - vertical and horizontal - assessment results for previous learning tasks, as well as the metadata of those learning tasks (difficulty, support, other features), to enable a comparison of all learning tasks from which the next task may be chosen.

Strategic advisory models explicitly help students apply cognitive strategies for assessing their own performance and recording the scores, for interpreting horizontal and vertical assessment results from a development portfolio, for matching assessment results with the qualities of available learning tasks, for making an informed selection from those tasks, for planning their own work on those learning tasks, and so forth. These models provide SAPs and rules-of-thumb helpful for developing self-directed learning skills. Often, a coach or tutor will have regular meetings with individual learners to give them this type of advice. In such coaching meetings, reflection on previous learning tasks takes place, the overall level of the learner's performance is assessed, specific points for improvement are identified, and future learning tasks are planned (Van der Klink, Gielen, & Nauta, 2001). Information from a portfolio provides important input for these coaching meetings. *Digital development portfolios* are particularly useful because they release the learner from many administrative and arithmetic duties.

Figure 15.4 presents a screenshot of a digital development portfolio used for student hairstylists (Kicken, Brand-Gruwel, & van Merriënboer, 2005). The portfolio sustains self-directed learning in full on-demand education based on the Ten Steps. After each learning task, which will typically take the form of styling a client's or a lifelike model's hair, the learner can update his personal portfolio, using a computer available at the school or in the salon. If preferred, the portfolio can also be updated after performing a number of tasks. Each completed learning task is characterized in terms of its difficulty (i.e., the task class it belongs to) and its support, for example an independently performed task, a task performed partly by the employer or trainer and partly by the learner, or even a task performed by a more experienced peer student or trainer and only observed by the learner (i.e., a modeling example). The learner can also upload a digital photograph of the client's hairstyle before and after the treatment. The learner then indicates who will perform the assessment: the learner, a peer student, the employer, or another stakeholder.

To assess performance on the previous learning task(s), the assessor - usually the learner - selects the constituent skills relevant for the performed task from the left side of the screen (see left part of Figure 15.4).

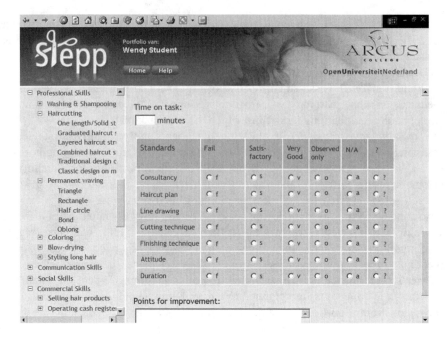

Figure 15.4   Screenshot of a digital portfolio for student hair stylists.

The constituent skills of the complex skill "styling hair" are hierarchically ordered and include, for example, washing and shampooing, haircutting, permanent waving, coloring, communicating with clients, selling hair-treatment products, and so forth. Clicking the right mouse button shows the performance objective for the selected constituent skill, including the standards for acceptable performance (i.e., criteria, values, attitudes). The learner selects a relevant aspect at the desired level of detail by clicking the left mouse button revealing a scoring rubric for this aspect at the right side of the screen. The learner fills out the scoring rubric, the time spent to this aspect of performance and, in a separate text box, points for improvement. This process is repeated for all aspects relevant for the learning task being assessed, and if more than one task is assessed, it is repeated for all tasks.

One of the main advantages of a digital portfolio is that it takes over the administrative and computational tasks of the protocol portfolio scoring. With regard to vertical assessments, an overview can be given for each aspect of performance, including an overview of all learning tasks for which this particular aspect has been assessed, its development over time, points for improvement, and so forth. With regard to horizontal assessments, an overview can be given of overall progress over learning tasks and task classes, considering available support. Furthermore, a digital portfolio allows comparing different assessment methods and different assessors. For instance, it might turn out that a particular group of assessors systematically judges a learner's performance lower or higher than another group.

To conclude, learners can use the digital portfolio to plan future learning tasks in a systematic fashion. They can create descriptions of learning tasks in terms of difficulty and/or task classes, support and guidance available, other task features expected to remediate weak aspects of performance (i.e., offer points for improvement), and improve overall performance. The overviews generated by the portfolio as well as the plans for future learning tasks provide helpful information for regular meetings with a coach or supervisor. The main aim of such meetings is to reflect on the work on previous learning tasks and identify future opportunities for performance improvement. If a learner, for example, made good progress in overall hair-styling performance on a basic difficulty level (e.g., a task class including only washing and cutting), but still has specific difficulties cutting curly hair, it might be decided to provide the learner with as many clients (or models) as possible with curly hair, because this provides additional practice for this particular aspect of performance, as well as clients who want their hair dyed, because this is a new aspect not practiced before.

15.4 Summary

- Three increasingly higher levels of self-directed learning distinguish learner control over part-task practice (independent part-task practice), learner control over supportive information (just-in-time open learning), and learner control over learning tasks (on-demand education).
- In on-demand education, learners select their own learning tasks based on assessment of their own performance as well as metadata of tasks from which they may choose (i.e., difficulty, available support and guidance, other task features).
- A development portfolio gathers and stores assessment results in such a way that it provides a good basis for dynamic task selection by the learner (or by any other intelligent agent).
- The protocol portfolio scoring prescribes to apply a constant set of standards throughout the entire educational program, to use a mix of assessors and assessment methods, and to assess performance both vertically (per aspect/constituent skill) and horizontally (overall performance).
- Limiting the number of learning tasks from which to choose may support learners develop their self-directed learning skills; the number of tasks increases as learners' skills develop.
- A coach who provides strategic advice on how to assess one's own performance and plan opportunities for future learning provides guidance to learners who develop their self-directed learning skills; the frequency and level of detail of the given advice decreases as the learners' skills develop.
- In on-demand education, a digital development portfolio is useful to generate overviews of assessment results and provides valuable input for regular meetings with a coach or supervisor.

16
CLOSING REMARKS

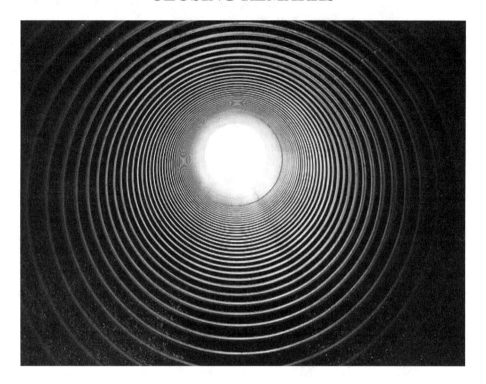

This chapter concludes the description of the Ten Steps to Complex Learning. The introductory Chapters 1–3 discussed the main aims of the model, the four blueprint components, and the Ten Steps to develop educational blueprints based on the four components. Chapters 4–13 discussed each of the steps in detail. The two application Chapters focused on the questions how to combine the Ten Steps with different media and how to use them to stimulate the development of self-directed learning. This final chapter briefly discusses the position of the Ten Steps in the current field of instructional design and sketches some directions for the model's further development.

16.1 Positioning the Ten Steps

The Ten Steps shares its focus on complex learning and its use of real-life tasks or problems as the basis for the design of learning tasks with several recent models for instructional design, such as learning by doing (Schank, Berman, & MacPerson, 1999), cognitive apprenticeship learning (Collins, Brown, & Newman, 1989), and constructivist and powerful learning environments (Jonassen, 1999; De Corte, Verschaffel, Entwistle, & van Merriënboer, 2003). In an influential review article,

Merrill (2002a) carefully analyzed and compared a representative set of recent instructional design models, including the aforementioned models, the Ten Steps, and several other models. According to his analysis, five prescriptive principles (he called them the "first principles of instruction") are central to effective instructional design, noting that learning is promoted when:

1 learners are engaged in performing real-life tasks or solving real-world problems;
2 existing knowledge is activated as a foundation for new knowledge;
3 new knowledge is demonstrated to the learner;
4 new knowledge is applied by the learner; and
5 new knowledge is integrated into the learner's world.

It is interesting to note that different models, including the Ten Steps, share these five fundamental principles although they are based on different theoretical assumptions and make use of different conceptual descriptions and practical methods. More important, there is increasing empirical evidence that the five principles help improve transfer of learning, that is, the ability to apply what has been learned in real-life contexts. With regard to the Ten Steps, empirical evidence for increased transfer in the domains of computer programming, fault diagnosis, and statistical analysis is discussed in the book Training Complex Cognitive Skills (van Merriënboer, 1997). Positive effects on transfer of learning have also been found for other domains and other models that use whole, meaningful tasks as the backbone of the training program. Van Merriënboer and Kester (in press; see also Kirschner, Carr, & van Merriënboer, 2002; Spector & Anderson, 2000) provide a recent review of such whole-task models and their effects on transfer of learning.

Compared to traditional models for instructional design (e.g., Reigeluth, 1983a, 1987a), recent models involve new roles for both designers and teachers. For designers, three interrelated changes involve learning objectives, analysis methods, and design approach. The traditional focus on separate and specific objectives has been replaced by a focus on integrated objectives that allow for transfer of learning. Traditional analysis methods that decompose a learning domain into small pieces which can subsequently be "transmitted" to the learners have been replaced by analysis methods that merely help identify learning opportunities and tasks that learners should be confronted with. Finally, the design approach reflects a *toppling* where practice tasks are no longer coupled to the information presented but, in contrast, where helpful information is coupled to learning tasks (see Figure 16.1). Together, these changes reflect a - moderate - constructivist view of learning and instruction because the learning tasks are primarily meant to drive a process of active knowledge construction by the learner, but based upon instructional principles.

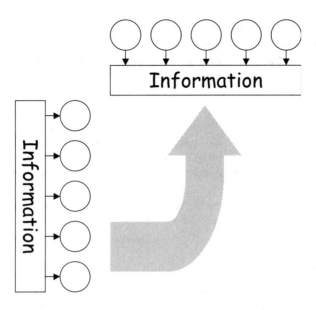

Figure 16.1   Toppling of the design approach.

For teachers, their traditional role of presenting and explaining new information is augmented by several new roles. With regard to learning tasks, teachers become designers of those tasks, often in cooperation with practitioners in the relevant professional field (Hoogveld, Paas, & Jochems, 2005; Hoogveld, Paas, Jochems, & van Merriënboer, 2001, 2002) and, in environments for self-directed learning, in cooperation with their students (Könings, Brand-Gruwel, & van Merriënboer, 2005). With regard to supportive information, teachers will stick to their traditional role of explaining how a learning domain is organized, but they will also increasingly fulfill the role of model, demonstrating how to approach real-life tasks systematically and explaining which rules-of-thumb may help overcome difficulties (van Gog, Paas, & van Merriënboer, 2004, 2005). With regard to procedural information, teachers will sometimes act as an instructor or "assistant looking over your shoulder", to present information on routine aspects of learning tasks or to present information on part-task practice (Kester, Kirschner, van Merriënboer, & Baumer, 2001). Finally, because of a possible switch to a flexible system of self-directed learning, teachers will fulfill the role of coach, advising learners on the planning of their learning trajectory, including the selection of new learning tasks (Kicken, Brand-Gruwel, & van Merriënboer, 2005). Obviously, these new roles pose new requirements to the form and content of future teacher training programs, with a more intensive use of new technologies (Kirschner & Davis, 2003; Kirschner & Selinger, 2003) and knowledge communities that allow for the exchange of learning experiences (Kirschner & Wopereis, 2003).

16.2 Future Directions

The Ten Steps to Complex Learning are based on the four-component instructional design model (4C/ID-model; van Merriënboer, 1997; see also Janssen-Noordman & van Merriënboer, 2002; van Merriënboer, Clark, & de Croock, 2002; van Merriënboer & Dijkstra, 1997; van Merriënboer, Jelsma, & Paas, 1992), which can be seen as its immediate forerunner. Whereas the 4C/ID-model focused on the four blueprint components and their basis in cognitive learning theory, the Ten Steps provide a systematic and systemic approach to the design of training blueprints. Future developments will aim at improving the usability of this design model for complex learning, including the creation of visual design languages and computer-based tools to support the Ten-Steps design process, the development of methods for mass customization in the context of e-learning, and the expansion of the Ten Steps to integrate the teaching of first-order and higher-order skills.

Design Languages and Tools

Most design sciences such as software engineering, mechanical engineering, or civil engineering have their own, dedicated design languages. Such languages allow designers to unambiguously express their ideas and communicate easily. The field of instructional design uses, in contrast, almost no dedicated design languages. If design languages are used at all, they are general-purpose languages such as flow-charts and concept maps that are not really focused on the specific requirements of instructional design. The further development of dedicated languages will help instructional designers to communicate about their designs both with each other and with their stakeholders (e.g., teachers, programmers, multimedia specialists, etc.; Gibbons & Brewer, 2004). The Ten Steps introduced a simple yet unambiguous visual design language, using basic forms representing learning tasks (circles), supportive information (L-shapes), procedural information (arrows), and part-task practice (boxed series of circles). Furthermore, Ten-Steps training blueprints can be expressed in IMS-LD, a formalism based on the Educational Modeling Language (EML; Koper & Manderveld, 2004). The further development of such design languages is critical to the future development of systematic instructional design approaches.

Another future direction which would be facilitated by the availability of powerful design languages is the development of computer-based instructional design tools (for an overview of tools, see van Merriënboer & Martens, 2002). The ADAPT[IT] Blueprint Designer®, for example, is a commercially available tool that supports the application of the Ten Steps (De Croock, Paas, Schlanbusch, & van Merriënboer, 2002; see also http://www.enovateas.com). Blueprint Designer® supports designers in a highly flexible way, allowing for zigzag design approaches. Its main function is to support the management of all the intermediate and final products constructed during the analysis and design process (e.g., skill hierarchies, task classes, learning tasks, different types of information, etc.). First, the Blueprint Designer provides functions for entering, editing, storing, maintaining, and re-using analysis and design products. This is achieved by providing templates for easily entering information in a way consistent with the Ten Steps. Second, it provides functions for examining the products from multiple perspectives. The designer can filter out undesired information, specify different textual and graphical views on products (e.g., zoom in on supportive information for a selected task class, list procedural information for all learning tasks, examine differences between task classes, etc.), and use printing-on-demand functions to export the training blueprint in any desired format. Third, Blueprint Designer® provides functions to check whether the analysis and design products are complete, internally consistent, and in line with the Ten Steps.

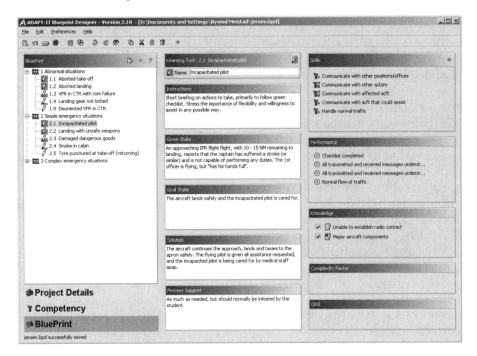

Figure 16.2   The Blueprint Designer® (http://www.enovateas.com).

Figure 16.2 shows an overview of the Blueprint Designer's® main interface. The screen is divided into three different regions. In the left column is the project browser which displays all elements of the training project in a hierarchical way. In addition, the project browser gives the designer access to other training projects and, if applicable, to other files with relevant information that can be imported into a Ten-Steps project. To the right of the project browser, in the middle column, is the blueprint browser. This browser provides access to diagram editors for the four blueprint components, that is, (a) learning tasks and task classes, (b) supportive information, (c) procedural information, and (d) part-task practice. These editors allow the designer to construct and specify the whole blueprint for the educational program. In the right column is the analysis browser. This browser provides access to diagram editors for (a) the skill hierarchy, (b) performance objectives, and (c) mental models, cognitive strategies, cognitive rules and procedures, and prerequisite information.

Mass Customization

Modern society is characterized by a diminishing half-life of knowledge and skills and thus a growing importance of lifelong learning. Quick technological changes make existing jobs obsolete and introduce new jobs. Moreover, the population in many countries is becoming increasingly multicultural and pluralistic. Consequently, there is an increasing need for highly flexible educational programs that can serve heterogeneous target groups, with learners who greatly differ in age, prior knowledge, and cultural background. For instance, such programs should make it possible to use different instructional methods for young learners and elderly learners, who suffer from a decrease in working-memory capacity (Van Gerven, Paas, van Merriënboer, & Schmidt, 2000, 2002, 2004; Van Gerven, Paas, van Merriënboer, Hendriks, & Schmidt, 2003). The Ten Steps allow for developing such flexible programs. On one hand, e-learning systems offer good opportunities for adaptive instruction, including the dynamic selection of learning tasks (Stoyanov & Kirschner, 2004; see also Chapter 14.2). On the other hand, self-directed learning can be sustained in such a way that maximum flexibility is offered to individual learners (see Chapter 15.3). A drawback of both approaches, however, is that they are often not cost-effective. This is because an expensive intelligent agent is needed either to steer the process of assessment and task selection or to guide and advise the individual learner in doing this.

Making flexible educational systems more cost-effective requires a combination of computer-based intelligent agents and large target groups. This combination is typical for *mass customization* or mass individualization which replaces a product-oriented approach with a service-oriented approach (Schellekens, Paas, & van Merriënboer, 2003). In the field of instructional design, web-based training (Jochems, van Merriënboer, & Koper, 2004; Kirschner, 2001) provides the best opportunities for a service-oriented approach. Web-based training makes it both relatively easy to include intelligent agents and reach a large target group because instruction can be offered in a way that is independent of place and time. In the field of learning and instruction, two levels of customization can be distinguished. On the "consumer level", mass customization makes it possible to offer each individual student the instruction desired. On this level there is a clear correspondence between the learner and the client who uses the "car configuration" on the website of a car manufacturer to design his or her new car (choosing type and size of engine, available optional equipment, color, etc.). After configuration, this unique car is built and delivered according to the client's specifications. The learner-as-consumer metaphor, however, falls short because the learner should also - learn to - take responsibility for his or her own learning processes. On the "learning-to-learn level", mass customization should also make it possible to provide learners with a level of control they can handle and, preferably, help them become better learners. Therefore, an important line for future research is the development of approaches to mass customization that give learners control over those aspects of the learning environment they can already handle, give them advice on dealing with those aspects they cannot fully handle yet, and give them no control over aspects beyond their capabilities.

Integrating Higher-Order Skills

If one word were chosen to characterize the essence of the Ten Steps, it would be *integration*. In terms of what is taught, learning tasks are always whole, meaningful tasks that stimulate learners to integrate knowledge, skills, and attitudes important for the complex cognitive skill or professional competency to be mastered at the end of the training program. In this way, the Ten Steps try to solve the problem of compartmentalization by simultaneously supporting different learning processes. In terms of how complex skills are taught, learning tasks provide one undivided backbone for the educational program, to which supportive information, procedural information, and part-task practice are subordinated. In this way, the Ten Steps try to solve the problem of fragmentation by the construction of an "integrated curriculum".

A future challenge is to aim at a third level of integration, namely, integrating learning first-order skills which are bound to a domain or profession, with learning higher-order skills, which are largely independent of a particular domain. One example was provided in Chapter 15 on self-directed learning. This higher-order skill can be taught in training programs designed according to the Ten Steps, provided the program offers the necessary flexibility to individual learners. In order to reach integration at this level, tasks for monitoring and assessing one's own performance should be fully integrated with the learning tasks, and tasks for planning one's own learning should be directed toward an informed selection of future learning tasks. In addition, the main guidelines for teaching first-order skills also apply to teaching higher-order skills. There will, for example, be an increase in difficulty (e.g., selecting own learning tasks from an increasingly larger set of available tasks) and a decrease in support and guidance (e.g., less advice is given by a coach or teacher as the learner progresses throughout the program). Future research should also aim at integrating other higher-order skills that are important in modern society, such as information problem solving skills (Brand-Gruwel, Wopereis, & Vermetten, 2005; Lazonder, Biemans, & Wopereis, 2000) and scientific discovery skills (de Jong & van Joolingen, 1998).

16.3   A Final Word

In April 2000, the magazine *Training* expressed a growing discontent with instructional systems design in a cover story with the title *Is ISD R.I.P.?* (Gordon & Zemke, 2000). A panel of instructional design experts addressed the question of whether instructional design was dead and argued that mainstream instructional design was moribund because it cannot deal with the highly complex skills needed in modern society, is not based on sound learning and performance theory, and uses a cookbook approach that forces designers in an unproductive straitjacket. Whether the arguments for writing off instructional design were completely valid or not, these are precisely the issues raised by the Ten Steps: a focus on complex learning, a strong basis in learning theory, and a highly flexible design approach. It is our hope that the Ten Steps, as well as other models for whole-task design, will contribute to a revival of the field of instructional design. In our view, such a revival is a condition to cope with the educational requirements of a fast-changing knowledge society.

APPENDIX 1

OVERVIEW OF THE TEN STEPS

1. Design Learning Tasks	Design learning tasks or whole-task problems which require the learners to perform (almost) all constituent skills in a coordinated fashion. Take care of a high variability between learning tasks: They must differ from each other on all those dimensions that also differ in the real world. Start with learning tasks with high built-in learner support and slowly decrease learner support to zero. Specify product-oriented learner support (e.g., case studies, completion problems) to exemplify criteria and templates for good solutions to problems, and process-oriented learner support (e.g., modeling examples, process worksheets) to exemplify effective approaches to problem solving.
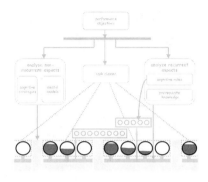	
2. Sequence Task Classes	Organize learning tasks in simple-to-complex task classes, in order to develop a global outline of the training program. Each task class describes a category of learning tasks that learners will work on during the training. If it is not possible to create one single task class sequence because even the simplest task class that can be defined is still too complex to start the training with, it may be necessary to first partition the training blueprint in skill clusters. These skill clusters may be seen as parts of the complex cognitive skill; they contain a fairly large, meaningful set of interrelated constituent skills, and they are best sequence in a backward chaining approach with snowballing.
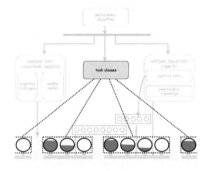	
3. Set Performance Objectives	Performance objectives are set for all constituent skills involved in whole-task performance. Their interrelationships are represented in a skill hierarchy or other type of structural representation. Performance objectives always describe the starting situation for a constituent skill, the conditions under which the constituent skill needs to be performed, and the standards and criteria for acceptable performance. Constituent skills are classified as either recurrent, nonrecurrent, or, in exceptional situations, both. For recurrent constituent skills, a further specification refers to regular recurrent constituent skills and to-be-automated recurrent constituent skills.
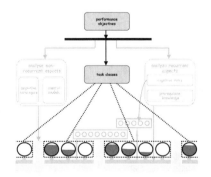	

4. Design Supportive Information 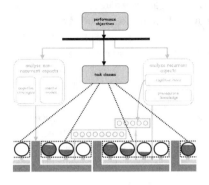	Supportive information presents and exemplifies at the beginning and parallel to each task class, generally applicable information describing cognitive strategies (Systematic Approaches to Problem solving or SAPs) and mental models (conceptual, causal and structural). By default, use an inductive-expository strategy: Design modeling examples and/or case studies and then design the SAPs and general models as exemplified in these modeling examples and/or case studies. Alternatively, select an inductive-inquisitory strategy if a deep level of understanding is necessary or a deductive-expository strategy if training time is severely limited. Finally, design cognitive feedback.
5. Analyze Cognitive Strategies 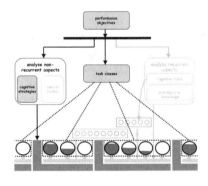	Analyze the cognitive strategies that guide experts' problem solving behavior. The analysis results typically take the form of SAPs, which describe the successive phases and (sub)phases in the problem solving process and represent them in a linear sequence or in a SAP chart. Specify heuristics or rules of thumb that might be helpful to successfully complete each (sub)phase and specify the criteria for successful completion of each (sub)phase. SAPs may pertain to the whole complex cognitive skill or to its non-recurrent constituent skills.
6. Analyze Mental Models 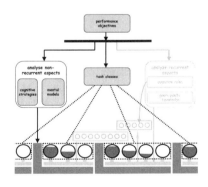	Analyze the mental models that experts use to reason about their tasks. Mental models are representations of how the world is organized for a particular domain; they might be helpful in performing non-recurrent constituent skills. The analysis results typically take the form of conceptual models (What is this?), structural models (How is this organized?), and causal models (How does this work?). The different types of models can also be combined when necessary. Make a (graphic) representation of each model by identifying and describing propositions (i.e., facts), simple schemas (i.e., concepts, plans, and principles), and how these relate to each other.

7. Design Procedural Information

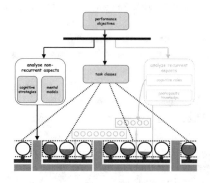

Design procedural information for each learning task, specifying how to perform the recurrent aspects practiced for this task. Give complete information at first, and then fade. Teach at the level of the least experienced learner. Do not require memorization, instead, have the procedure available as it is being learned. Provide all steps in the procedure, and all facts, concepts and principles necessary to perform it. Give demonstrations of a procedure, instances of facts/concepts/et cetera. coinciding with case study. Give immediate, corrective feedback about what is wrong, why, and corrective hint. Finally, ask for remedial practice that includes correction.

8. Analyze Cognitive Rules

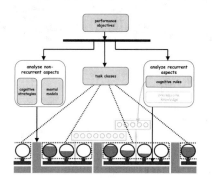

Analyze expert task performance to identify cognitive rules or procedures that algorithmically describe correct performance of recurrent constituent skills. A cognitive rule describes the exact condition under which a certain action has to be performed. A procedure is a set of steps and decisions that are always applied in a prescribed order. Perform a procedural analysis (e.g., information processing analysis) for recurrent skills that show a temporal order of steps. Perform a rule-based analysis for recurrent skills that show no temporal order of steps.

9. Analyze Prerequisite Knowledge

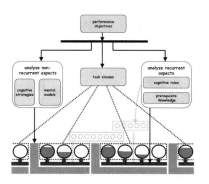

Further analyze the results of the procedural or rule-based analysis from Step 8 and specify for each cognitive rule the knowledge that enables the correct performance of this rule, or for each procedural step or decision the knowledge that enables performing the step or making the decision. The question to ask is: What must the learner know in order to be able to apply this rule, or to perform this procedural step, correctly? Represent the knowledge as simple facts, concepts, principles, or plans.

10. Design Part-task Practice

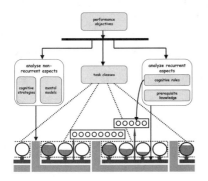

Design part-task practice for recurrent constituent skills that need a very high level of automaticity after the training, and for which learning tasks cannot provide enough practice to reach this. For highly complex procedures, work from simple to complex tasks. For less complex procedures simply repeat until mastered. Use divergent examples that are representative of the span of situations where the skill will be used. Practice first for accuracy, next for speed, and finally for speed and accuracy under high workload. Practice on distributed, not massed, training schedule. Intermix with learning tasks.

APPENDIX 2

EXAMPLE OF A TRAINING BLUEPRINT

Task Class 1:
Learners are confronted with situations where the concepts in the—to be searched—domain are clearly defined. Only a few articles are written about the subject and articles are only written in one research field. Thus, the search needs only to be performed on titles of articles in one database from the particular field of research. There are only a few search terms needed to perform the search and the search will yield a limited amount of articles.

Supportive Information: *Modeling example*
Learners watch an expert performing a literature search explaining his/her actions while doing so.

Supportive Information: *Presentation of cognitive strategies*
• SAP of the four phases in performing a literature search: (a) selecting an appropriate database, (b) formulating a search query, (c) performing a search, (d) selecting results. • SAPs for quickly scanning the relevance of scientific articles.

Supportive Information: *Presentation of mental models*
• Conceptual model of literature search concepts. • Structural model of how databases are organized and can be used. • Conceptual model of different types of scientific articles and how they are organized.

Learning Task 1.1: *Case study* Learners receive three worked-out (good) examples of literature searches. Each example describes a different research questions in the same subject matter domain, the search query and the produced list of articles. The learners have to study the examples and explain why the different search queries produced the desired results.		
Learning Task 1.2: *Completion* Learners receive a research question and an incomplete search query that produces a list containing irrelevant items. They must refine the search query using additional search terms, perform the search and select the relevant articles.	**Procedural information** • Procedures for operating the search program • Procedures for using a thesaurus	
Learning Task 1.3: *Conventional* Learners receive a research question. They have to perform a literature search for the 10 most relevant articles.	**Procedural information** • Procedures for operating the search program (fading) • Procedures for using a thesaurus (fading)	

Task Class 2:
Learners are confronted with situations where the concepts in the to-be-searched domain are clearly defined. A large amount of articles are written about the subject, but only in one field of research. Therefore, the search needs only to be performed on titles of articles in one database from the particular field of research. However, many search terms need to be interconnected with Boolean operators to limit the otherwise large amount of articles the search can yield.

Supportive Information: *Case study*
Learners receive three worked-out (good) examples of literature searches. Each example contains an elaborate search query in which Boolean operators are used.

Supportive Information: *Inquiry for mental models*
- Learners are asked to identify templates of search queries describing Boolean combinations of search terms that can be used to make search queries more specific.

Learning Task 2.1: *Imitation + constraint* Learners have a worked-out example of a research question available, a list of articles and an elaborate Boolean search query to produce the list of articles. They receive a similar research question, and a goal to produce a list with a limited amount of relevant articles. By imitating the given example they must formulate the search query, perform the search and select relevant articles. They can only perform the search after the search query is approved.	**Procedural information** - Syntax for specifying Boolean search queries	**Part-task Practice** / Applying Boolean operators
Learning Task 2.2: *Completion* Learners receive a research question and a list of search terms. They have to formulate a search query by combining the given search terms using Boolean operators.	**Procedural information** - Syntax for specifying Boolean search queries (fading)	
Learning Task 2.3: *Conventional* Learners receive a research question. They have to perform a literature search for the 10 most relevant articles.	**Procedural information** - Syntax for specifying Boolean search queries (fading)	

Supportive Information: *Cognitive feedback*
Learners receive feedback on their approach to solve the problem in Learning Task 2.3.

Task Class 3:

Learners are confronted with situations where the concepts in the to-be-searched domain are not clearly defined. Identical terms are used for different concepts, and identical concepts are described with different terms. A large amount of articles are written about the subject and articles are written in several fields of research. Therefore, next to searching on titles of articles, the search also needs to be performed on abstracts and texts. Also, databases from different fields of research have to be searched. Many search terms need to be interconnected with Boolean operators to make sure that all relevant articles (using different terminology) are found and that irrelevant articles (using the same terminology as relevant ones) are excluded.

Supportive Information: *Presentation of cognitive strategies*
* SAP for determining the number of databases to search and whether to also search on abstracts and full texts.

Supportive Information: *Presentation of mental models*
* Structural model of templates of search queries describing Boolean combinations of search terms that can be used to search for articles about ill-defined subjects.
* Conceptual model of different types of databases for different fields of study, describing structure, special search requirements, etc.

		Part-task Practice · Applying Boolean operators
Learning Task 3.1: *Completion + Reverse* Learners receive a research question and an elaborate search query. They have to predict which databases should be used and then perform the query. They then have to refine the query and select relevant articles.	**Procedural information** • Procedures for searching specific databases	
Learning Task 3.2: *Conventional* Learners receive a research question. They have to perform a literature search for the 10 most relevant articles.	**Procedural information** • Procedures for searching specific databases (fading)	

Supportive Information: *Cognitive feedback*

Learners receive feedback on their approach to solve the problem in Learning Task 3.2.

REFERENCES

Achtenhagen, F. (2001). Criteria for the development of complex teaching-learning environments. *Instructional Science, 29*, 361–380.

Aleven, V., Stahl, E., Schworm, S., Fischer, F., & Wallace, R. (2003). Help seeking and help design in interactive learning environments. *Review of Educational Research, 73*, 277–320.

Allen, W. J. (2001) *Working together for environmental management: the role of information sharing and collaborative learning.* Unpublished PhD thesis, Massey University, New Zealand.

Alred, G. J., Brusaw, C. T., & Oliu, W. E. (2003). *The business writer's handbook* (7th ed.). Boston, MA: Bedford St. Martins.

Anderson, J. R. (1983). *The architecture of cognition.* Cambridge, MA: Harvard University Press.

Anderson, J. R. (1987). Skill acquisition: Compilation of weak-method problem solutions. *Psychological Review, 94*, 192–210.

Anderson, J. R. (1993). *Rules of the mind.* Hillsdale, NJ: Lawrence Erlbaum.

Anderson, J. R., & Lebière, C. J. (1998). *The atomic components of thought.* Mahwah, NJ: Lawrence Erlbaum Associates.

Andre, T. (1997). Selected micro-instructional methods to facilitate knowledge construction: Implications for instructional design. In R. D. Tennyson, F. Schott, N. Seel, & S. Dijkstra (Eds.), *Instructional design - International perspectives: Theory, research, and models* (Vol. 1) (pp. 243–267). Mahwah, NJ: Lawrence Erlbaum Associates.

Annett, J., & Sparrow, J. (1985). Transfer of training: A review of research and practical implications. *Programmed Learning and Educational Technology, 22*, 116–124.

Argyris, C., & Schön, D. (1978) *Organizational learning: A theory of action perspective.* Reading, MA: Addison Wesley.

Ausubel, D. P. (1960). The use of advance organizers in the learning and retention of meaningful verbal material. *Journal of Educational Psychology, 51*, 267–272.

Ausubel, D. P. (1968). *Educational psychology: A cognitive view.* New York: Holt, Rinehart, and Winston.

Ayres, P. L. (1993). Why goal-free problems can facilitate learning. *Contemporary Educational Psychology, 18*, 376–381.

Baartman, L. K. J., Bastiaens, Th. J., Kirscher, P. A., & van der Vleuten, C. P. M. (2006). The wheel of competency assessment: Presenting quality criteria for competency assessment programs. *Studies in Educational Evaluation, 32*, 153–170.

Balzer, W. K., Doherty, M. E., & O'Connor, R. (1989). Effects of cognitive feedback on performance. *Psychological Bulletin, 106*, 410–433.

Banathy, B. H. (1987). Instructional systems design. In R. M. Gagné (Ed.), *Instructional technology: Foundations* (pp. 85–112). Hillsdale, NJ: Lawrence Erlbaum Associates.

Bastiaens, Th. J. (1999). Assessing an electronic performance support system for the analysis of jobs and tasks. *International Journal of Training and Development, 3*, 54–61.

Biggs, J. (1996). Enhancing teaching through constructive alignment. *Higher Education, 32*, 347–364.

Bolhuis, S. (1996, April). *Towards active and selfdirected learning: Preparing for lifelong learning with reference to Dutch secondary education.* Paper presented at the Annual Meeting of the American Educational Research Association, New York.

Brand-Gruwel, S., Wopereis, I. G. J. H., & Vermetten, Y. (2005). Information problem solving by experts and novices: Analysis of a complex cognitive skill. *Computers in Human Behavior, 21,* 487–508.

Bray, C. W. (1948). *Psychology and military proficiency.* Princeton, NJ: Princeton University Press.

Briggs, G. E., & Naylor, J. C. (1962). The relative efficiency of several training methods as a function of transfer task complexity. *Journal of Experimental Psychology, 64,* 505–512.

Brown, J. S., Collins, A., & Duguid, P. (1989). Situated cognition and the culture of learning. *Educational Researcher, 18*(1), 32–42.

Bruner, J. S. (1960). *The process of education.* Cambridge, MA: Harvard University Press.

Bruner, J. S. (1975). From communication to language: A psychological perspective. *Cognition, 3,* 255–287.

Butler, D. L., & Winne, P. H. (1995). Feedback and self-regulated learning: A theoretical synthesis. *Review of Educational Research, 65,* 245–281.

Camp, G., Paas, F., Rikers, R., & van Merriënboer, J. J. G. (2001). Dynamic problem selection in air traffic control training: A comparison between performance, mental effort, and mental efficiency. *Computers in Human Behavior, 17,* 575–595.

Carlson, R. A., Khoo, H., Elliott, R. G. (1990). Component practice and exposure to a problem solving context. *Human Factors, 32,* 267–286.

Carlson, R. A., Sullivan, M. A., & Schneider, W. (1989). Component fluency in a problem-solving context. *Human Factors, 31,* 489–502.

Carroll, J. M. (1998). *Minimalism beyond the Nurnberg Funnel.* Cambridge, MA: MIT Press.

Carroll, J. M., & Carrithers, C. (1984). Blocking learner error states in a training-wheels system. *Human Factors, 26,* 377–389.

Carroll, J. M., Smith-Kerker, P. L., Ford, J. R., & Mazur-Rimetz, S. A. (1988). The minimal manual. *Human-Computer Interaction, 3,* 123–153.

Chandler, P., & Sweller, J. (1992). The split-attention effect as a factor in the design of instruction. *British Journal of Educational Psychology, 62,* 233–246.

Chandler, P., & Sweller, J. (1996). Cognitive load while learning to use a computer program. *Applied Cognitive Psychology, 10,* 151–170.

Chi, M. T. H., de Leeuw, N., Chiu, M. H., & LaVancher, C. (1994). Eliciting self-explanations improves understanding. *Cognitive Science, 18,* 439–477.

Clark, R. E., & Estes, F. (1999). The development of authentic educational technologies. *Educational Technology, 39*(2), 5–16.

Clark, R., & Taylor, D. (1992). Training problem solving skills using cognitive strategies: Part 1 - Novice vs. expert problem solvers. *Performance & Instruction, 31*(3), 1–5.

Collins, A., Brown, J. S., & Newman, S. E. (1989). Cognitive apprenticeship: Teaching the craft of reading, writing and mathematics. In L. B. Resnick (Ed.), *Knowing, learning, and instruction: Essays in honor of Robert Glaser* (pp. 453–493). Hillsdale, NJ: Lawrence Erlbaum Associates.

Collins, A., & Ferguson, W. (1994). Epistemic forms and epistemic games: Structures and strategies to guide inquiry. *Educational Psychologist, 28*(1), 25–42.

Collins, A., & Stevens, A. L. (1983). A cognitive theory of inquiry teaching. In C. M. Reigeluth (Ed.), *Instructional design theories and models* (pp. 247–278). Hillsdale, NJ: Lawrence Erlbaum Associates.

Corbalan, G., Kester, L., & van Merriënboer, J. J. G. (2006). Towards a personalized task selection model with shared instructional control. *Instructional Science, 34*, 399–422.

Corbett, A. T., & Anderson, J. R. (1995). Knowledge tracing: Modeling the acquisition of procedural knowledge. *User Modeling and User-Adapted Interaction, 4*, 253–278.

Cormier, S. M., & Hagman, J. D. (Eds.). (1987). *Transfer of learning: Contemporary research and applications.* San Diego, CA: Academic Press.

Crossman, E. R. F. W. (1959). A theory of the acquisition of speed-skill. *Ergonomics, 2*, 153–166.

De Corte, E., Verschaffel, L., Entwistle, N., & van Merriënboer, J. J. G. (Eds.). (2003). *Unravelling basic components and dimensions of powerful learning environments.* Oxford, UK: Elsevier Science.

De Croock, M. B. M., Paas, F., Schlanbusch, H., & van Merriënboer, J. J. G. (2002). ADAPTit: Instructional design tools for training design and evaluation. *Educational Technology, Research and Development, 50*(4), 47–58.

De Croock, M. B. M., van Merriënboer, J. J. G., & Paas, F. (1998). High vs. low contextual interference in simulation-based training of troubleshooting skills: Effects on transfer performance and invested mental effort. *Computers in Human Behavior, 14*, 249–267.

De Groot, A. D. (1966). Perception and memory versus thought. In B. Kleinmuntz (Ed.), *Problem solving: Research, method, and theory.* New York: Wiley & Sons.

De Jong, A. M., & van Joolingen, W. R. (1998). Scientific discovery learning with computer simulations of conceptual domains. *Review of Educational Research, 68*, 179–201.

Dempster, F. (1988). The spacing effect: A case study in the failure to apply results to psychological research. *American Psychologist, 43*, 627–634.

Detterman, D. K., & Sternberg, R. J. (Eds.). (1993). *Transfer on trial: Intelligence, cognition, and instruction.* Norwood, NJ: Ablex.

Dick, W., & Carey, L. (1996). *The systematic design of instruction* (4th ed.). New York: Harper Collins.

Dijkstra, S., & van Merriënboer, J. J. G. (1997). Plans, procedures, and theories to solve instructional design problems. In S. Dijkstra, N. Seel, F. Schott, & R. D. Tennyson (Eds.), *Instructional design: International perspectives* (Vol. 2) (pp. 23–43). Hillsdale, NJ: Lawrence Erlbaum Associates.

Dufresne, R. J., Gerace, W. J., Thibodeau-Hardiman, P., & Mestre, J. P. (1992). Constraining novices to perform expertlike problem analyses: Effects on schema acquisition. *The Journal of the Learning Sciences, 2*, 307–331.

Elio, R. (1986). Representation of similar well-learned cognitive procedures. *Cognitive Science, 10*, 41–73.

Ertmer, P. A., & Russell, J. D. (1995). Using case studies to enhance instructional design education. *Educational Technology, 35*(4), 23–31.

Fisk, A. D., & Gallini, J. K. (1989). Training consistent components of tasks: Developing an instructional system based on automatic-controlled processing principles. *Human Factors*, *31*, 453–463.

Fisk, A. D., Lee, M. D., & Rogers, W. A. (1991). Recombination of automatic processing components: The effects of transfer, reversal, and conflict situations. *Human Factors*, *33*, 267–280.

Fisk, A. D., & Lloyd, S. J. (1988). The role of stimulus-to-rule consistency in learning rapid application of spatial rules. *Human Factors*, *30*, 35–49.

Fisk, A. D., Oransky, N. A., & Skedsvold, P. R. (1988). Examination of the role of "higher-order" consistency in skill development. *Human Factors*, *30*, 567–581.

Fleming, M., & Levie, H. W. (1993). *Instructional message design*. Englewood Cliffs, NJ: Educational Technology Publications.

Frederiksen, N. (1984). Implications of cognitive theory for instruction in problem solving. *Review of Educational Research*, *54*, 363–407.

Gagné, R. M. (1968). Learning hierarchies. *Educational Psychologist*, *6*, 1–9.

Gagné, R. M. (1985). *The conditions of learning* (4th Ed.). New York: Holt, Rinehart & Winston.

Gardner, H. (1999). Multiple approaches to understanding. In C. M. Reigeluth (Ed.), *Instructional design theories and models: A new paradigm of instructional theory* (Vol. II) (pp. 69–89). Mahwah, NJ: Lawrence Erlbaum Associates.

Garrison, D. R. (1997). Self-directed learning: Toward a comprehensive model. *Adult Education Quarterly*, *48*, 18–33.

Gentner, D., & Stevens, A. L. (1983). *Mental Models*. Hillsdale, NJ: Lawrence Erlbaum Associates.

Gibbons, A. S., & Brewer, E. K. (2004). Elementary principles of design languages and design notation systems for instructional design. In M. Spector, C. Ohrazda, A. van Schaack, & D. Wiley (Eds.), *Innovations to instructional technology: Essays in honor of M. David Merrill*. Mahwah, NJ: Lawrence Erlbaum Associates.

Gick, M. L., & Holyoak, K. J. (1980). Analogical problem solving. *Cognitive Psychology*, *12*, 306–356.

Gick, M. L., & Holyoak, K. J. (1983). Schema induction and analogical transfer. *Cognitive Psychology*, *15*, 1–38.

Gick, M. L., & Holyoak, K. J. (1987). The cognitive basis of knowledge transfer. In S. M. Cormier & J. D. Hagman (Eds.), *Transfer of learning: Contemporary research and applications*. San Diego, CA: Academic Press.

Goodyear, P., & Steeples, C. (1992) IT based open learning: Tasks and tools. *Journal of Computer Assisted Learning*, *8*, 163–176.

Gopher, D., Weil, M., & Siegel, D. (1989). Practice under changing priorities: An approach to the training of complex skills. *Acta Psychologica*, *71*, 147–177.

Gordon, J., & Zemke, R. (2000). The attack on ISD. *Training*, *37*(4), 42–53.

Gray, E. (2003). *Conscious choices: A model for self-directed learning*. Upper Saddle River, NJ: Prentice Hall.

Greenfield, P. M. (1984). A theory of the teacher in the learning activities of everyday life. In B. Rogoff & J. Lave (Eds.), *Everyday cognition: Its development in social context* (pp. 117–138). Cambridge, MA: Harvard University Press.

Greenfield, P. M. (1999). Historical change and cognitive change: A two-decade follow-up study in Zinacantan, a Maya community in Chiapas, Mexico. *Mind, Culture, And Activity*, *6*, 92–98.

Gropper, G. L. (1973). *A technology for developing instructional materials*. Pittsburgh, PA: American Institutes for Research.

Gropper, G. L. (1983). A behavioral approach to instructional prescription. In C. M. Reigeluth (Ed.), *Instructional design theories and models* (pp. 101–161). Hillsdale, NJ: Lawrence Erlbaum Associates.

Gulikers, J. T. M., Bastiaens, Th. J., & Kirschner, P. A. (2004). A five-dimensional framework for authentic assessment. *Educational Technology, Research and Development*, *52*, 67–85.

Gulikers, J. T. M., Bastiaens, Th. J., & Kirschner, P. A. (2006a). Authentic assessment, student and teacher perceptions: the practical value of the five-dimensional framework. *Journal of Vocational Education and Training*, Preprint

Gulikers, J. T. M., Bastiaens, Th. J., & Kirschner, P. A. (2006b). The more the better? Relations between student perceptions of assessment authenticity, study approaches and learning outcome. *Studies in Educational Evaluation*, Preprint.

Gulikers, J. T. M., Bastiaens, Th. J., & Martens, R. (2005). The surplus value of an authentic learning environment. *Computers in Human Behavior*, *21*, 509–521.

Gupta, K. (1999). *A practical guide to needs assessment*. San Francisco, CA: Jossey-Bass/Pfeiffer.

Halff, H. M. (1993). Supporting scenario- and simulation-based instruction: Issues from the maintenance domain. In J. M. Spector, M. C. Polson, & D. J. Muraida (Eds.), *Automating instructional design: Concepts and issues* (pp. 231–248). Englewood Cliffs, NJ: Educational Technology Publications.

Hambleton, R. K., Jaeger, R. M., Plake, B. S., & Mills, C. (2000). Setting performance standards on complex educational assessments. *Applied Psychological Measurement*, *24*, 355–366.

Harp, S. F., & Mayer, R. E. (1998). How seductive details do their damage: A theory of cognitive interest in science learning. *Journal of Educational Psychology*, *90*, 414–434.

Hartley, J. (1994). *Designing instructional text* (3rd ed.). London: Kogan Page.

Hill, J., & Hannafin, M. J. (2001). Teaching and learning in digital environments: The resurgence of resource-based learning. *Educational Technology, Research and Development*, *49*(3), 37–52.

Hoffman, C. K., & Medsker, K. L. (1983). Instructional analysis: The missing link between task analysis and objectives. *Journal of Instructional Development*, *6*(4), 17–23.

Holland, J. H., Holyoak, K. J., Nisbett, R. E., & Thagard, P. R. (1989). *Induction: Processes of inference, learning, and discovery*. Cambridge, MA: The MIT press.

Holsbrink-Engels, G. A. (1997). The effects of the use of a conversational model and opportunities for reflection in computer-based role-playing. *Computers in Human Behavior*, *13*, 409–436.

Hoogveld, A. W. M., Paas, F., & Jochems, W. M. G. (2005). Training higher education teachers for instructional design of competency-based education: Product-oriented versus process-oriented worked examples. *Teaching and Teacher Education*, *21*, 287–297.

REFERENCES

Hoogveld, A. W. M., Paas, F., Jochems, W. M. G., & van Merriënboer, J. J. G. (2001). The effects of a web-based training in an instructional systems design approach on teachers instructional design behavior. *Computers in Human Behavior, 17*, 363–371.

Hoogveld, A. W. M., Paas, F., Jochems, W. M. G., & van Merriënboer, J. J. G. (2002). Exploring teachers' instructional design practices from a systems design perspective. *Instructional Science, 30*, 291–305.

Iyengar, S. S., & Lepper, M. R. (2000). When choice is demotivating: Can one desire too much of a good thing? *Journal of Personality & Social Psychology, 79*, 995–1006.

Janssen-Noordman, A. M. B., & van Merriënboer, J. J. G. (2002). *Innovatief onderwijs ontwerpen: Via leertaken naar complexe vaardigheden* [Innovative instructional design: From learning tasks to complex skills]. Groningen, The Netherlands: Wolters Noordhoff.

Jelsma, O., van Merriënboer, J. J. G., & Bijlstra, J. P. (1990). The ADAPT design model: Towards instructional control of transfer. *Instructional Science, 19*, 89–120.

Jochems, W., van Merriënboer, J. J. G., & Koper, R. (Eds.) (2004). *Integrated E-learning: Implications for pedagogy, technology, and organization.* London: Routledge Falmer.

Jonassen, D. H. (1992). Cognitive flexibility theory and its implications for designing CBI. In S. Dijkstra, H. P. M. Krammer, & J. J. G. van Merriënboer (Eds.), *Instructional models in computer-based learning environments* (NATO ASI Series F, vol. 104) (pp. 385–403). Berlin, Germany: Springer Verlag.

Jonassen, D. H. (1999). Designing constructivist learning environments. In C. M. Reigeluth (Ed.), *Instructional design theories and models: A new paradigm of instructional theory* (Vol. II) (pp. 215–239). Mahwah, NJ: Lawrence Erlbaum Associates.

Jonassen, D. H. (2000). *Computers as mindtools for schools: Engaging critical thinking* (2nd ed). Upper Saddle River, NJ: Prentice Hall.

Jonassen, D. H., Hannum, W. H., & Tessmer, M. (1989). *Handbook of task analysis procedures.* New York: Praeger.

Kalyuga, S., Ayres, P., Chandler, P., & Sweller, J. (2003). The expertise reversal effect. *Educational Psychologist, 38*(1), 23–31.

Kalyuga, S., & Sweller, J. (2005). Rapid dynamic assessment of expertise to optimize the efficiency of e-learning. *Educational Technology, Research and Development, 53*(3), 83–93.

Kaufman, R., & English, F. W. (1979). *Needs assessment: Concept and application.* Englewood Cliffs, NJ: Educational Technology Publications.

Kennedy, P., Esquire, T., & Novak, J. (1983). A functional analysis of task analysis procedures for instructional design. *Journal of Instructional Development, 6*(4), 10–16.

Kester, L., Kirschner, P. A., & van Merriënboer, J. J. G. (2004a). Information presentation and troubleshooting in electrical circuits. *International Journal of Science Education, 26*, 239–256.

Kester, L., Kirschner, P. A., & van Merriënboer, J. J. G. (2004b). Timing of information presentation in learning statistics. *Instructional Science, 32*, 233–252.

Kester, L., Kirschner, P. A., & van Merriënboer, J. J. G. (2005). The management of cognitive load during complex cognitive skill acquisition by means of computer-simulated problem solving. *British Journal of Educational Psychology, 75*, 71–85.

Kester, L., Kirschner, P. A., van Merriënboer, J. J. G., & Baumer, A. (2001). Just-in-time information presentation and the acquisition of complex cognitive skills. *Computers in Human Behavior, 17,* 373–392.

Khalil, M. K., Paas, F., Johnson, T. E., & Payer, A. F. (2005a). Design of interactive and dynamic anatomical visualizations: The implications of cognitive load theory. *The Anatomical Record (New Anat.), 286B,* 15–20.

Khalil, M. K., Paas, F., Johnson, T. E., & Payer, A. F. (2005b). Interactive and dynamic visualizations in teaching and learning of anatomy: A cognitive load perspective. *The Anatomical Record (New Anat.), 286B,* 8–14.

Kicken, W., Brand-Gruwel, S., & van Merriënboer, J. J. G. (2005, May-June). *Advisering bij het kiezen van leertaken: Veilig op weg naar vraaggestuurd onderwijs* [Advice on the selection of learning tasks: A safe approach to education on-demand]. Paper presented at the OnderwijsResearchDagen (ORD), May 30-June 1, Gent, Belgium.

Kieras, D. E. (1988). Towards a practical GOMS model methodology for user interface design. In M. Helander (Ed.), *Handbook of human-computer interaction* (pp. 135–157). North-Holland: Elsevier.

Kirschner, P. A. (Ed.). (2001). Web enhanced higher education [Special Issue]. *Computers in Human Behavior, 17.*

Kirschner, P. A. (Ed.). (2002). Cognitive load theory [Special Issue]. *Learning and Instruction, 12.*

Kirschner, P. A., Carr, C., van Merriënboer, J. J. G., & Sloep, P. (2002). How expert designers design. *Performance Improvement Quarterly, 15*(4), 86–104.

Kirschner, P. A., & Davis, N. (2003). The pedagogic benchmarks for ICT teacher education. *Technology, Pedagogy, and Education, 12,* 127–149.

Kirschner, P. A., Martens, R. L., & Strijbos, J. W. (2004). CSCL in higher education? A framework for designing multiple collaborative environments. In J. W. Strijbos, P. A. Kirschner, & R. L. Martens (Eds.). *What we know abour CSCL, and implementing it in higher education* (pp. 3-30). Boston: Kluwer Academic Publishers.

Kirschner, P. A., & Selinger, M. (2003). The state of affairs of teacher education with respect to ICT. *Technology, Pedagogy, and Education, 12,* 5–17.

Kirscher, P. A., Sweller, J., & Clark, R. E. (2006). Why minimal guidance during instruction does not work: An analysis of the failure of constructivist, discovery, problem-based, experiential, and inquiry-based teaching. *Educational Psychologist, 41*(2), 75–86.

Kirschner, P. A., & Wopereis, I. G. J. H. (2003). Mindtools for teacher communities: A European perspective. *Technology, Pedagogy, and Education, 12,* 107–126.

Klahr, D., Langley, P., & Neches, R. (Eds.). (1987). *Production system models of learning and development.* Cambridge, MA: MIT Press.

Kluger, A., & DiNisi, A. (1998). Feedback interventions: Toward the understanding of a double-edged sword. *Current Directions in Psychological Science, 7*(3), 67–72.

Könings, K. D., Brand-Gruwel, S., & van Merriënboer, J. J. G. (2005). Towards more powerful learning environments through combining the perspectives of designers, teachers, and students. *British Journal of Educational Psychology, 75,* 645–660.

Koper, E. J. R., & Manderveld, J. M. (2004). Educational Modelling Language: Modelling reusable, interoperable, rich and personalised units of learning. *British Journal of Educational Technology, 35,* 537–551.

Kulik, J. A., & Kulik, C. (1988). Timing of feedback and verbal learning. *Review of Educational Research, 58*, 79–97.

Lajoie, S. P. (Ed.) (2000). *Computers as cognitive tools II: No more walls - Theory change, paradigm shifts and their influence on the use of computers for instructional purposes.* Mahwah, NJ: Lawrence Erlbaum Associates.

Landa, L. N. (1983). The algo-heuristic theory of instruction. In C. M. Reigeluth (Ed.), *Instructional design theories and models* (pp. 163–211). Hillsdale, NJ: Lawrence Erlbaum Associates.

Lazonder, A. W., Biemans, H. J. A., & Wopereis, I. G. J. H. (2000). Differences between novice and experienced users in searching information on the World Wide Web. *Journal of the American Society for Information Science, 51*, 576–581.

Lazonder, A. W., & van der Meij, H. (1993). The minimal manual: Is less really more? *International Journal of Man-Machine studies, 39*, 729–752.

Lazonder, A. W., & van der Meij, H. (1994). Effect of error-information in tutorial documentation. *Interacting with Computers, 6*, 23–40.

Lazonder, A. W., & van der Meij, H. (1995). Error-information in tutorial documentation: Supporting users' errors to facilitate initial skill learning. *International Journal of Human-Computer Studies, 42*, 185–206.

LePlat, J. (1990). Skills and tacit skills: A Psychological perspective. *Applied Psychology: An International Review, 39*, 143–154.

Lewis, M. W., & Anderson, J. R. (1985). Discrimination of operator schemata in problem solving: Learning from examples. *Cognitive Psychology, 17*, 26–65.

Maran, N. J., & Glavin, R. J. (2003). Low- to high fidelity simulation: A continuum of medical education? *Medical Education, 37*, 22–28.

Mayer, R. E. (Ed.) (2005). *The Cambridge handbook of multimedia learning.* New York: Cambridge University Press.

Mayer, R. E., Heiser, J., & Lonn, S. (2001). Cognitive constraints on multimedia learning: When presenting more material results in less understanding. *Journal of Educational Psychology, 93*, 187–198.

McCarthy, B. (1996). *About learning.* Barrington, IL: Excell Inc.

McDaniel, M. A., & Schlager, M. S. (1990). Discovery learning and transfer of problem-solving skill. *Cognition and Instruction, 7*, 129–159.

McKendree, J. (1990). Effective feedback content for tutoring complex skills. *Human-Computer Interaction, 5*, 381–413.

Merrill, M. D. (1983). Component display theory. In C. M. Reigeluth (Ed.), *Instructional design theories and models* (pp. 278–333). Hillsdale, NJ: Lawrence Erlbaum Associates.

Merrill, M. D. (2002a). A pebble-in-the-pond model for instructional design. *Performance Improvement, 41*(7), 39–44.

Merrill, M. D. (2002b). First principles of instructional design. *Educational Technology, Research and Development, 50*, 43–59.

Merrill, P. (1980). Analysis of a procedural task. *NSPI Journal, 17*(2), 11–26.

Merrill, P. (1987). Job and task analysis. In R. M. Gagné (Ed.), *Instructional technology: foundations* (pp. 141–173). Hillsdale, NJ: Lawrence Erlbaum Associates.

Mettes, C. T. W., Pilot, A., & Roossink, H. J. (1981). Linking factual knowledge and procedural knowledge in solving science problems: A case study in a thermodynamics course. *Instructional Science, 10*, 333–361.

Moreno, R., & Mayer, R. E. (2000). A coherence effect in multimedia learning: The case for minimizing irrelevant sounds in the design of multimedia instructional messages. *Journal of Educational Psychology, 92*, 117–125.

Myers, G. L., & Fisk, A. D. (1987). Training consistent task components: Application of automatic and controlled processing theory to industrial task training. *Human Factors, 29*, 255–268.

Nadolski, R. J., Kirschner, P. A., & van Merriënboer, J. J. G. (2005). Optimizing the number of steps in learning tasks for complex skills. *British Journal of Educational Psychology, 75*, 223–237.

Nadolski, R. J., Kirschner, P. A., van Merriënboer, J. J. G., & Hummel, H. G. K. (2001). A model for optimizing step size of learning tasks in competency-based multimedia practicals. *Educational Technology, Research and Development, 49*, 87–103.

Nadolski, R. J., Kirschner, P. A., van Merriënboer, J. J. G., & Wöretshofer, J. (2005). Development of an instrument for measuring the complexity of learning tasks. *Educational Research & Evaluation, 11*, 1–27.

Naylor, J. C., & Briggs, G. E. (1963). Effects of task complexity and task organization on the relative efficiency of part and whole training methods. *Journal of Experimental Psychology, 65*, 217–224.

Nelson, L. M. (1999). Collaborative problem solving. In C. M. Reigeluth (Ed.), *Instructional design theories and models: A new paradigm of instructional theory* (Vol. II) (pp. 241–267). Mahwah, NJ: Lawrence Erlbaum Associates.

Newby, T. J., & Stepich, D. A. (1990). Designing instruction: Practical Strategies 5: Teaching cognitive strategies. *Performance & Instruction, 29*(1), 44–45.

Newell, A., & Rosenbloom, P. (1981). Mechanisms of skill acquisition and the law of practice. In J. Anderson (Ed.), *Cognitive skills and their acquisition* (pp. 1–55). Hillsdale, NJ: Lawrence Erlbaum Associates.

Newell, A., & Simon, H. A. (1972). *Human problem solving.* Englewood Cliffs, NJ: Prentice-Hall.

Nixon, E. K., & Lee, D. (2001). Rapid prototyping in the instructional design process. *Performance Improvement Quarterly, 14*(3), 95–116.

Ohlsson, S., & Rees, E. (1991). The function of conceptual understanding in the learning of arithmetic procedures. *Cognition and Instruction, 8*, 103–179.

Paas, F., Camp, G., & Rikers, R. (2001). Instructional compensation for age-related cognitive declines: Effects of goal specificity in maze learning. *Journal of Educational Psychology, 93*, 181–186.

Paas, F., Renkl, A., & Sweller, J. (Eds.). (2003). Cognitive load theory and instructional design: Recent developments [Special Issue]. *Educational Psychologist, 38*(1).

Paas, F., Renkl, A., & Sweller, J. (Eds.). (2004). Advances in cognitive load theory, development and instructional design [Special issue]. *Instructional Science, 32.*

Paas, F., Tuovinen, J. E., van Merriënboer, J. J. G., & Darabi, A. (2005). A motivational perspective on the relation between mental effort and performance: Optimizing learner involvement in instruction. *Educational Technology, Research and Development, 53*(3), 25–34.

Paas, F., & van Merriënboer, J. J. G. (1993). The efficiency of instructional conditions: An approach to combine mental-effort and performance measures. *Human Factors, 35,* 737–743.

Paas, F., & van Merriënboer, J. J. G. (1994a). Instructional control of cognitive load in the training of complex cognitive tasks. *Educational Psychology Review, 6,* 351–371.

Paas, F., & van Merriënboer, J. J. G. (1994b). Variability of worked examples and transfer of geometrical problem-solving skills: A cognitive-load approach. *Journal of Educational Psychology, 86,* 122–133.

Paas, F., van Merriënboer, J. J. G., & Adam, J. J. (1994). Measurement of cognitive load in instructional research. *Perceptual and Motor Skills, 79,* 419–430.

Paivio, A. (1986). *Mental representations.* Oxford, UK: Oxford University Press.

Palmeri, T. J. (1999). Theories of automaticity and the power law of practice. *Journal of Experimental Psychology: Learning, Memory, and Cognition, 25,* 543–551.

Patrick, J. (1992). *Training: Research and practice.* London: Academic Press.

Perkins, D. N., & Grotzer, T. A. (1997). Teaching intelligence. *American Psychologist, 52,* 1125–1133.

Prins, F. J., Sluijsmans, D. M. A., Kirschner, P. A., & Strijbos, J. W. (2005). Formative peer assessment in a CSCL environment: A case study. *Assessment & Evaluation in Higher Education, 30,* 417–444.

Quilici, J. L., & Mayer, R. E. (1996). The role of examples in how students learn to categorize statistics word problems. *Journal of Educational Psychology, 88,* 144–161.

Ragan, T. J., & Smith, P. L. (1996). Conditions theory and models for designing instruction. In D. Jonassen (Ed.), *Handbook of research on educational communications and technology* (2nd ed.) (pp. 623–650). Mahwah, NJ: Lawrence Erlbaum Associates.

Reber, A. S. (1989). Implicit learning and tacit knowledge. *Journal of Experimental Psychology: General, 118,* 219–135.

Reber, A. S. (1996). *Implicit learning and tacit knowledge: An essay on the cognitive unconscious.* Oxford, UK: Oxford University Press.

Redding, R. E. (1995). Cognitive task analysis for instructional design: Applications in distance education. *Distance Education, 16*(1), 88–106.

Reigeluth, C. M. (Ed.) (1983a). *Instructional-design theories and models: An overview of their current status.* Hillsdale, NJ: Lawrence Erlbaum Associates.

Reigeluth, C. M. (1983b). Meaningfulness and instruction: Relating what is being learned to what a student knows. *Instructional Science, 12,* 197–218.

Reigeluth, C. M. (1987a). Lesson blueprints based on the elaboration theory of instruction. In C. M. Reigeluth (Ed.), *Instructional theories in action: Lessons illustrating selected theories and models* (pp. 245–288). Hillsdale, NJ: Lawrence Erlbaum Associates.

Reigeluth, C. M. (Ed.) (1987b). *Instructional theories in action: Lessons illustrating selected theories and models.* Hillsdale, NJ: Lawrence Erlbaum Associates.

Reigeluth, C. M., & Merrill, M. D. (1984). *Extended Task Analysis Procedures (ETAP): User's Manual.* Lanham, MD: University Press of America.

Reigeluth, C. M., & Rodgers, C. A. (1980). The elaboration theory of instruction: A model for structuring instruction. *Instructional Science, 9,* 125–219.

Reigeluth, C. M., & Stein, F. S. (1983). The elaboration theory of instruction. In C. M. Reigeluth (Ed.), *Instructional design theories and models: An overview of their current status* (pp. 335–381). Hillsdale, NJ: Lawrence Erlbaum Associates.

Renkl, A. (1997). Learning from worked-out examples: A study on individual differences. *Cognitive Science, 21*, 1–29.

Renkl, A., & Atkinson, R. K. (2003). Structuring the transition from example study to problem solving in cognitive skill acquisition: A cognitive load perspective. *Educational Psychologist, 38*, 15–22.

Renkl. A., Atkinson, R. K., Maier, U. H., & Staley, R. (2002). From example study to problem solving: Smooth transitions help learning. *Journal of Experimental Education, 70*, 293–315.

Rikers, R. M. J. P., & Paas, F. (Eds.). (2005). Recent advances in expertise research [Special issue]. *Applied Cognitive Psychology, 19*.

Romiszowski, A. J. (1988). *The selection and use of instructional media*. New York: Nichols Publishing.

Rosenshine, B., & Meister, C. (1992). The use of scaffolds for teaching higher-level cognitive strategies. *Educational Leadership, 49*(7), 26–33.

Rossett, A. (1987). *Training needs assessment*. Englewood Cliffs, NJ: Educational Technology Publications.

Ryder, J. M., & Redding, R. E. (1993). Integrating cognitive task analysis into instructional systems development. *Educational Technology, Research and Development, 41*(2), 75–96.

Salden, R. J. C. M., Paas, F., Broers, N. J., & van Merriënboer, J. J. G. (2004). Mental effort and performance as determinants for the dynamic selection of learning tasks in Air Traffic Control training. *Instructional Science, 32*, 153–172.

Salden, R. J. C. M., Paas, F., & van Merriënboer, J. J. G. (2006). A comparison of approaches to learning task selection in the training of complex cognitive skills. *Computers in Human Behavior, 22*, 321–333.

Salisbury, D. F. (1990). Cognitive psychology and its implications for designing drill and practice programs for computers. *Journal of Computer-based Instruction, 17*(1), 23–30.

Salisbury, D. F., Richards, B. F., & Klein, J. D. (1985). Designing practice: A review of prescriptions and recommendations from instructional design theories. *Journal of Instructional Development, 8*(4), 9–19.

Salomon, G. (1979). *The interaction of media, cognition and learning*. San Francisco, CA: Jossey-Bass.

Salomon, G. (1984). Television is 'easy' and print is 'tough': The differential investment of mental effort in learning as a function of perceptions and attributions. *Journal of Educational Psychology, 76*, 647–658.

Salomon, G. (1998). Novel constructivist learning environments and novel technologies: Some issues to be concerned with. *Research Dialogue in Learning and Instruction, 1*(1), 3–12.

Scandura, J. M. (1983). Instructional strategies based on the structural learning theory. In C. M. Reigeluth (Ed.), *Instructional-design theories and models* (pp. 213–246). Hillsdale, NJ: Lawrence Erlbaum Associates.

REFERENCES

Scandura, J. M. (2001). Structural learning theory: Current status and new perspectives. *Instructional Science, 29,* 311–336.

Schank, R. C., Berman, T. R., & MacPerson, K. A. (1999). Learning by doing. In C. M. Reigeluth (Ed.), *Instructional design theories and models: A new paradigm of instructional theory* (Vol. II) (pp. 161–181). Mahwah, NJ: Lawrence Erlbaum Associates.

Schellekens, A. M. H. C., Paas, F., & van Merriënboer, J. J. G. (2003). Flexibility in higher education: A survey in business administration programs in the Netherlands. *Higher Education, 45,* 281–307.

Schilling, M. A., Vidal, P., Ployhart, R. E., & Marangoni, A. (2003). Learning by doing something else: Variation, relatedness, and the learning curve. *Management Science, 49,* 39–56.

Schneider, W. (1985). Training high-performance skills: Fallacies and guidelines. *Human Factors, 27,* 285 300.

Schneider, W., & Detweiler, M. (1988). The role of practice in dual-task performance: Toward workload modeling in a connectionist/-control architecture. *Human Factors, 30,* 539–566.

Schneider, W., & Shiffrin, R. M. (1977). Controlled and automatic human information processing: I. Detection, search, and attention. *Psychological Review, 84,* 1–66.

Schnotz, W., Vosniadou, S., & Carretero, M. (1999). *New perspectives on conceptual change.* Oxford, UK: Elsevier Science.

Schoenfeld, A. H. (1979). Can heuristics be taught? In J. Lochhead & J. Clement (Eds.), *Cognitive Process Instruction* (pp. 315–338). Philadelphia, PA: Franklin Institute Press.

Schwartz, B. (2004). *The paradox of choice: Why more is less.* New York: Harper Collins Publishers.

Schwartz, D., Lin, X., Brophy, S., & Bransford, J. D. (1999). Toward the development of flexible adaptive instructional designs. In C. M. Reigeluth (Ed.), *Instructional design theories and models: A new paradigm of instructional theory* (Vol. II) (pp. 183–213). Mahwah, NJ: Lawrence Erlbaum Associates.

Shaffer, D. W. (2006). Epistemic frames for epistemic games. *Computers and Education, 46,* 223–234.

Shea, C. H., Kohl, R., & Indermill, C. (1990). Contextual interference: Contributions of practice. *Acta Psychologica, 73,* 145–157.

Sherry, L., & Trigg, M. (1996). Epistemic forms and epistemic games. *Educational Technology, 36*(3), 38–44.

Shiffrin, R. M., & Schneider, W. (1977). Controlled and automatic human information processing: II. Perceptual learning, automatic attending, and a general theory. *Psychological Review, 84,* 127–190.

Simon, H. A. (1973). The structure of ill-structured problems. *Artificial Intelligence, 4,* 181–201.

Sluijsmans, D. M. A., Brand-Gruwel, S., & van Merriënboer, J. J. G. (2002). Peer assessment training in teacher education: Effects on performance and perceptions. *Assessment and Evaluation in Higher Education, 27,* 443–454.

Sluijsmans, D. M. A., Brand-Gruwel, S., van Merriënboer, J. J. G., & Bastiaens, Th. J. (2003). The training of peer assessment skills to promote the development of reflection skills in teacher education. *Studies in Educational Evaluation, 29,* 23–42.

Sluijsmans, D. M. A., Brand-Gruwel, S., van Merriënboer, J. J. G., & Martens, R. L. (2004). Training teachers in peer-assessment skills: Effects on performance and perceptions. *Innovations in Education and Teaching International, 41*, 59–78.

Sluijsmans, D. M. A., & Moerkerke, G. (1999). Creating a learning environment by using self- peer- and co-assessment. *Learning Environments Research, 1*, 293–319.

Sluijsmans, D. M. A., Moerkerke, G., van Merriënboer, J. J. G., & Dochy, F. J. R. C. (2001). Peer assessment in problem-based learning. *Studies in Educational Evaluation, 27*, 153–173.

Snoddy, G. S. (1926). Learning and stability. *Journal of Applied Psychology, 10*, 1–36.

Spector, J. M., & Anderson, T. M. (Eds.) (2000). *Holistic and integrated perspectives on learning, technology, and instruction: Understanding complexity.* Mahwah, NJ: Lawrence Erlbaum Associates.

Spiro, R. J., Coulson, R. L., Feltovich, P. J., & Anderson, D. K. (1988). *Cognitive flexibility theory: Advanced knowledge acquisition in ill-structured domains* (Tech. Rep. no. 441). Champaign, IL: University of Illinois, Center for the Study of Reading.

Stark, R., Mandl, H., Gruber, H., & Renkl, A. (2002). Conditions and effects of example elaboration. *Learning and Instruction, 12*, 39–60.

Stoof, A., Martens, R. L., van Merriënboer, J. J. G., & Bastiaens, T. J. (2002). The boundary approach of competence: A constructivist aid for understanding and using the concept of competence. *Human Resource Development Review, 1*, 345–365.

Stoyanov, S., & Kirschner, P. A. (2004). Expert concept mapping method for defining the characteristics of adaptive e-learning: Alfanet project case. *Educational Technology, Research and Development, 52*, 41–56.

Straetmans, G., Sluijsmans, D., Bolhuis, B., & van Merriënboer, J. J. G. (2003). Integratie van instructie en assessment in competentiegericht onderwijs [Integration of instruction and assessment in competence-based education]. *Tijdschrift voor Hoger Onderwijs, 3*, 171–197.

Sweller, J. (1988). Cognitive load during problem solving: Effects on learning. *Cognitive Science, 12*, 257–285.

Sweller, J., & Levine, M. (1982). Effects of goal specificity on means-ends analysis and learning. *Journal of Experimental Psychology: Learning, Memory, and Cognition, 8*, 463–474.

Sweller, J., van Merriënboer, J. J. G., & Paas, F. (1998). Cognitive architecture and instructional design. *Educational Psychology Review, 10*, 251–296.

Tabbers, H. K., Martens, R. L., & van Merriënboer, J. J. G. (2004). Multimedia instructions and cognitive load theory: Effects of modality and cueing. *British Journal of Educational Psychology, 74*, 71–81.

Taylor, D., & Clark, R. (1992). Training problem solving skills using cognitive strategies: Part 2 - Design guidelines based on cognitive psychology. *Performance & Instruction, 31*(4), 33–38.

Tennyson, R. D., & Cocchiarella, M. J. (1986). An empirically based instructional design theory for teaching concepts. *Review of Educational Research, 56*, 40–71.

Tripp, S., & Bichelmeyer, B. (1990). Rapid prototyping: An alternative instructional design strategy. *Educational Technology, Research and Development, 38*(1), 31–44.

Tuovinen, J., & Paas, F. (2004). Exploring multidimensional approaches to the efficiency of instructional conditions. *Instructional Science, 32*, 133–152.

Turban, E. (1995). *Decision support and expert systems: Management support systems.* Englewood Cliffs, NJ: Prentice Hall.

Van Boxtel, C., van der Linden, J., & Kanselaar, G. (2000). Collaborative learning tasks and the elaboration of conceptual knowledge. *Learning and Instruction, 10*, 311–330.

Van den Boom, G., Paas, F., van Merriënboer, J. J. G., & van Gog, T. (2004). Reflection prompts and tutor feedback in a web-based learning environment: Effects on students' self-regulated learning competence. *Computers in Human Behavior, 20*, 551–567.

Van der Klink, M. R., Gielen, E., & Nauta, C. (2001). Supervisory support as a major condition to enhance transfer. *International Journal of Training and Development, 5*, 52–63.

Van der Meij, H. (2003). Minimalism revisited. *Document Design, 4*, 212–233.

Van der Meij, H., & Carroll, J. M. (1995). Principles and heuristics for designing minimalist instruction. *Technical Communications, 42*, 243–261.

Van der Meij, H., & Lazonder, A. W. (1993). Assessment of the minimalist approach to computer user documentation. *Interacting with Computers, 5*, 355–370.

Van Gerven, P. W. M., Paas, F., van Merriënboer, J. J. G., Hendriks, M., & Schmidt, H. G. (2003). The efficiency of multimedia learning into old age. *British Journal of Educational Psychology, 73*, 489–505.

Van Gerven, P. W. M., Paas, F., van Merriënboer, J. J. G., & Schmidt, H. G. (2000). Cognitive load theory and the acquisition of complex cognitive skills in the elderly: Towards an integrative framework. *Educational Gerontology, 26*, 503–521.

Van Gerven, P. W. M., Paas, F., van Merriënboer, J. J. G, & Schmidt, H. G. (2002). Cognitive load theory and aging: Effects of worked examples on training efficiency. *Learning and Instruction, 12*, 87–105.

Van Gerven, P. W. M., Paas, F., van Merriënboer, J. J. G, & Schmidt, H. G. (2004). Memory load and the cognitive pupillary response in aging. *Psychophysiology, 41*, 167–174.

Van Gog, T., Ericsson, K. A., Rikers, R. M. J. P., & Paas, F. (2005). Instructional design for advanced learners: Establishing connections between the theoretical frameworks of cognitive load and deliberate practice. *Educational Technology, Research and Development, 53*(3), 73–81.

Van Gog, T., Paas, F., & van Merriënboer, J. J. G (2004). Process-oriented worked examples: Improving transfer performance through enhanced understanding. *Instructional Science, 32*, 83–98.

Van Gog, T., Paas, F., & van Merriënboer, J. J. G. (2005). Uncovering expertise-related differences in troubleshooting performance: Combining eye movement and concurrent verbal protocol data. *Applied Cognitive Psychology, 19*, 205–221.

Van Gog, T., Paas, F., van Merriënboer, J. J. G., & Witte, P. (2005). Uncovering the problem-solving process: Cued retrospective reporting versus concurrent and retrospective reporting. *Journal of Experimental Psychology: Applied, 11*, 237–244.

Van Merriënboer, J. J. G. (1990). Strategies for programming instruction in high school: Program completion vs. program generation. *Journal of Educational Computing Research, 6*, 265–285.

Van Merriënboer, J. J. G. (Ed.) (1994). Dutch research on knowledge-based instructional systems [Special Issue]. *Computers in Human Behavior, 10*.

Van Merriënboer, J. J. G. (1997). *Training complex cognitive skills: A four-component instructional design model for technical training*. Englewood Cliffs, NJ: Educational Technology Publications.

Van Merriënboer, J. J. G. (2000). The end of software training? *Journal of Computer Assisted Learning, 16*, 366–375.

Van Merriënboer, J. J. G. (2007). Alternate models of instructional design: Holistic design approaches and complex learning (pp. 72-81). In R. Reiser & J. Dempsey (Eds.), *Trends and issues in instructional design and technology* (2nd ed.). Old Tappan, NJ: Merrill/Prentice Hall.

Van Merriënboer, J. J. G., & Ayres, P. (Eds.). (2005). Research on cognitive load theory and its design implications for e-learning [Special issue]. *Educational Technology, Research and Development, 53*(3).

Van Merriënboer, J. J. G., & Boot, E. (2005). A holistic pedagogical view of learning objects: Future directions for reuse. In J. M. Spector, C. Ohrazda, A. van Schaaik, & D. A. Wiley (Eds.), *Innovations in instructional technology: Essays in honor of M. David Merrill* (pp. 43–64). Mahwah, NJ: Lawrence Erlbaum Associates.

Van Merriënboer, J. J. G., & Brand-Gruwel, S. (Eds). (2005). The pedagogical use of information and communication technology in education: A Dutch perspective [Special issue]. *Computers in Human Behavior, 21*.

Van Merriënboer, J. J. G., Clark, R. E., & de Croock, M. B. M. (2002). Blueprints for complex learning: The 4C/ID-model. *Educational Technology, Research and Development, 50*(2), 39–64.

Van Merriënboer, J. J. G., & de Croock, M. B. M. (1992). Strategies for computer-based programming instruction: Program completion vs. program generation. *Journal of Educational Computing Research, 8*, 365–394.

Van Merriënboer, J. J. G., & de Croock, M. B. M. (2002). Performance-based ISD: 10 steps to complex learning. *Performance Improvement, 41*(7), 33–38.

Van Merriënboer, J. J. G., de Croock, M. B. M., & Jelsma, O. (1997). The transfer paradox: Effects of contextual interference on retention and transfer performance of a complex cognitive skill. *Perceptual and Motor Skills, 84*, 784–786.

Van Merriënboer, J. J. G., & Dijkstra, S. (1997). The four-component instructional design model for training complex cognitive skills. In R. D. Tennyson, N. Seel, S. Dijkstra, & F. Schott (Eds.), *Instructional Design: International Perspectives* (Vol. 1) (pp. 427–445). Hillsdale, NJ: Lawrence Erlbaum Associates.

Van Merriënboer, J. J. G., Jelsma, O., & Paas, F. (1992). Training for reflective expertise: A four-component instructional design model for complex cognitive skills. *Educational Technology, Research and Development, 40*(2), 23–43.

Van Merriënboer, J. J. G., & Kester, L. (2005). The four-component instructional design model: Multimedia principles in environments for complex learning. In R. E. Mayer (Ed.), *The Cambridge handbook of multimedia learning* (pp. 71–93). New York: Cambridge University Press.

Van Merriënboer, J. J. G., & Kester, L. (in press). Whole-task models. In J. M. Spector, M. D. Merrill, J. J. G. van Merriënboer, & M. Driscoll (Eds.), *Handbook of research on educational communications and technology* (3rd Ed.). Mahwah, NJ: Lawrence Erlbaum Associates.

Van Merriënboer, J. J. G., Kester, L., & Paas, F. (2006). Teaching complex rather than simple tasks: Balancing intrinsic and germane load to enhance transfer of learning. *Applied Cognitive Psychology, 20*, 343–352.

Van Merriënboer, J. J. G., & Kirschner, P. A. (2001). Three worlds of instructional design: State of the art and future directions. *Instructional Science, 29*, 429–441.

Van Merriënboer, J. J. G., Kirschner, P. A., & Kester, L. (2003). Taking the load of a learners' mind: Instructional design for complex learning. *Educational Psychologist, 38*(1), 5–13.

Van Merriënboer, J. J. G., & Krammer, H. P. M. (1987). Instructional strategies and tactics for the design of introductory computer programming courses in high school. *Instructional Science, 16*, 251–285.

Van Merriënboer, J. J. G., Krammer, H. P. M., & Maaswinkel, R. M. (1994). Automating the planning and construction of programming assignments for teaching introductory computer programming. In R. D. Tennyson (Ed.), *Automating instructional design, development, and delivery* (NATO ASI Series F, Vol. 119) (pp. 61–77). Berlin, Germany: Springer Verlag.

Van Merriënboer, J. J. G., & Luursema, J. J. (1995). Implementing instructional models in computer-based learning environments: A case study in problem selection. In T. T. Liao (Ed.), *Advanced educational technology: Research issues and future potential* (NATO ASI Series F, vol. 145). Berlin, Germany: Springer Verlag.

Van Merriënboer, J. J. G., Luursema, J. J., Kingma, H., Houweling, F., & de Vries, A. P. (1995). Fuzzy logic instructional models: The dynamic construction of programming assignments in CASCO. In R. D. Tennyson & A.E. Barron (Eds.), *Automating instructional design: Computer-based development and delivery tools* (pp. 184–206). Berlin, Germany: Springer Verlag.

Van Merriënboer, J. J. G., & Martens, R. (Eds.). (2002). Computer-based tools for instructional design [Special Issue]. *Educational Technology, Research and Development, 50*(4).

Van Merriënboer, J. J. G., & Paas, F. (1989). Automation and schema acquisition in learning elementary computer programming: Implications for the design of practice. *Computers in Human Behavior, 6*, 273–289.

Van Merriënboer, J. J. G., Schuurman, J. G., de Croock, M. B. M., & Paas, F. (2002). Redirecting learners' attention during training: Effects on cognitive load, transfer test performance, and training efficiency. *Learning and Instruction, 12*, 11–37.

Van Merriënboer, J. J. G., Seel, N. M., & Kirschner, P. A. (2002). Mental models as a new foundation for instructional design. *Educational Technology, 17*(2), 60–66.

Van Merriënboer, J. J. G., & Sweller, J. (2005). Cognitive load theory and complex learning: Recent developments and future directions. *Educational Psychology Review, 17*, 147–177.

Van Merriënboer, J. J. G., & van Dijk, E. M. A. G. (1998). Use and misuse of taxonomies of learning: Dealing with integrated educational goals in the design of computer science curricula. In F. Mulder & T. van Weert (Eds.), *Informatics in Higher Education* (pp. 179–189). London: Chapman and Hall.

Vosniadou, S., & Brewer, W. F. (1992). Mental models of the earth: A study of conceptual change in childhood. *Cognitive Psychology, 24*, 535–585.

Vosniadou, S., & Ortony, A. (1989). *Similarity and analogical reasoning.* New York: Cambridge University Press.

Voss, J. F. (1988). Problem solving and reasoning in ill-structured domains. In C. Antaki (Ed.), *Analyzing everyday explanation: A casebook of methods* (pp. 74–93). London: Sage Publications.

Vygotsky, L. S. (1978). *Mind in society The development of higher psychological processes.* Cambridge, MA: Harvard University Press.

Vygotsky, L. S. (1987). Thinking and speech. In R. W. Rieber & A. S. Carton (Eds.), *The collected works of L. S. Vygotsky, Vol. 1: Problems of general psychology* (N. Minick, Trans.; pp. 39–285). New York: Plenum Press. (Original work published 1934).

Wedman, J., & Tessmer, M. (1991). Adapting instructional design to project circumstance: The layers of necessity model. *Educational Technology, Research and Development, 38*(1), 31–44.

White, B. Y., & Frederiksen, J. R. (1990). Causal model progressions as a foundation for intelligent learning environments. *Artificial Intelligence, 42*, 99–157.

Wightman, D. C., & Lintern, G. (1985). Part-task training for tracking and manual control. *Human Factors, 27*, 267–284.

Wiley, D. A. (2001). Connecting learning objects to instructional design theory: A definition, a metaphor, and a taxonomy. In D. A. Wiley (Ed.), *The instructional use of learning objects* (pp. 1–35). Bloomington, IN: Association for Educational Communications and Technology. Also available at: http://reusability.org/read/chapters/wiley.doc.

Willoughby, T., Wood, E., Desmarais, S., Sims, S., & Kalra, M. (1997). Mechanisms that facilitate the effectiveness of elaboration strategies. *Journal of Educational Psychology, 89*, 682–685.

Wood, D., Bruner, J. S., & Ross, G. (1976). The role of tutoring in problem solving. *Journal of Child Psychology and Psychiatry, 17*, 89–100.

Wood, H. A., & Wood, D. J. (1999). Help seeking, learning, and contingent tutoring. *Computers and Education, 33*, 153–170.

Wood, R. K., Stephens, K. G., & Barker, B. O. (1979). Fault tree analysis: An emerging methodology for instructional science. *Instructional Science, 8*, 1–22.

Wulf, G., & Shea, C. H. (2002). Principles derived from the study of simple skills do not generalize to complex skill learning. *Psychonomic Bulletin & Review, 9*, 185–211.

GLOSSARY

4C/ID	Abbreviation for four-component instructional design, where the training blueprint is built from a backbone of learning tasks, to which supportive information, procedural information, and part-task practice are connected.
Adaptive Learning	In the Ten Steps, adaptive learning usually refers to the dynamic selection of learning tasks in such a way that their difficulty, level of support and guidance, and available real-world features are optimized for the needs of an individual learner.
ADDIE	A generic Instructional Systems Design (ISD) approach made up of the steps: Analyze, Design, Develop, Implement, and Evaluate. The Ten Steps is an Instructional Design (ID) model with a clear focus on Analysis and Design.
Attention Focusing	A technique for the teaching of complex procedures where the learner's attention is focused on those procedural steps or rules that are difficult or dangerous to perform.
Authentic Task	A task as it appears in real life. In the Ten Steps, learning tasks are designed on the basis of authentic tasks. However, because they often contain support and guidance and need not be performed in the real task environment, learning tasks need not to be *identical* to authentic tasks.
Backward Chaining	An approach to part-task sequencing, where the training starts with constituent skills that are performed *last* and works toward constituent skills that are performed *first* during regular task performance (counter-to-performance order).
Case Study	A case study describes a given state, a desired goal state, and a chosen solution. It requires learners to actively participate in an actual or hypothetical problem situation in the real world and may take different forms, such as a description of a particular event or situation, an artificially designed object, a design simulation, or a process simulation. A case study may be used either as a *learning task* that must be studied, or as an illustration of a domain model as part of the *supportive information*.
Causal Model	A specific type of domain model describing the principles and their interrelationships that are important in a particular task domain. It results from the analysis of mental models and is important for interpreting events, causal reasoning, giving explanations, and making predictions.
Cognitive Feedback	A type of feedback that allows the learner to reflect on the quality of found solutions or the quality of the problem solving process; typically used to provide feedback on the quality of performance of non-recurrent aspects of a complex skill.

Cognitive Load Theory	A theory stating that human limited working-memory capacity has far-reaching implications for teaching and learning. Well-designed training systems prevent cognitive overload, decrease cognitive load that is not relevant to learning, and optimize cognitive load relevant to learning.
Cognitive Rule	A mental representation of a consistent relationship between particular conditions and a (mental) action to be taken under these conditions. In the Ten Steps, cognitive rules are analyzed as *if-then* rules or combinations of those in a procedure.
Cognitive Strategy	A mental representation of how to approach problems in a particular task domain. In the Ten Steps, a cognitive strategy is analyzed as a Systematic Approach to Problem solving (SAP), containing a description of phases in problem solving and rules-of-thumb that may help to complete each of the phases.
Cognitive Task Analysis (CTA)	A family of methods and tools for gaining access to the mental processes that organize and give meaning to observable behavior. In the Ten Steps, steps 2–3, 5–6, and 8–9 make up an integrated system of CTA.
Cognitive Tool	A device that helps learners carry out cognitive learning activities and critical thinking. Cognitive tools are learner controlled and actively engage learners in the creation of knowledge that reflects their comprehension and conception of information.
Compartmentalization	The tendency in traditional education to teach knowledge, skills, and attitudes separately. This approach hinders complex learning and the development of competences.
Competency	A combination of complex cognitive and higher-order skills, highly integrated knowledge structures, interpersonal and social skills, and attitudes and values. Acquired competencies can be applied in a variety of situations (transfer) and over an unlimited time span (lifelong learning).
Completion Strategy	Sequencing learning tasks from case studies or worked examples that students must study, via completion tasks with incomplete solutions that must be finished, to conventional problems that must be solved. The completion strategy is an example of fading support as learners acquire more expertise (i.e., scaffolding) and has been found to have positive effects on inductive learning and transfer.
Completion Task	A learning task describing a given state, a desired goal state, and a partial solution. The partial solution must be completed by the learner.
Component Fluency Hypothesis	This hypothesis reflects the idea that training routine aspects, or, consistent components of a complex task up to a very high level of automaticity, in addition to training the whole task, has a positive effect on learning (in particular, strengthening) and transfer of the whole task.

Concept	A mental representation representing a class of objects, events, or other entities by their characteristic features and/or mental images. In the Ten Steps, single concepts are analyzed as part of the prerequisite knowledge.
Conceptual Model	A specific type of domain model describing the concepts and their interrelationships that are important for solving problems in a particular task domain. It results from the analysis of mental models and is important for classifying or describing objects, events, and activities.
Constituent Skill	Sub skills or component skills of a complex cognitive skill that may best be seen as *aspects* of the whole skill. The constituent skills that make up a whole complex cognitive skill are identified in a process of skill decomposition.
Contextual Interference	A type of variability in which contextual factors inhibit a quick and smooth mastery of a skill. The Ten Steps suggest a high contextual interference over learning tasks because these tasks primarily aim at schema construction, but a low contextual interference for part-task practice because practice items primarily aim at schema automation.
Contingent Tutoring	A form of unsolicited information presentation where a teacher or tutor closely monitors a learner who is working on a learning task, and gives specific directions on how to solve the problem or perform the task (i.e., the "assistant looking over your shoulder").
Conventional Task	A learning task describing a given state and a desired goal state. The learner must independently generate a solution.
Corrective Feedback	A type of feedback that gives learners immediate information on the quality of performance of recurrent aspects of a complex skill. It often takes the form of *hints*.
Deductive Presentation Strategy	Approaches to information presentation that work from general information to examples that illustrate this information. For instance, instruction might work from SAPs to modeling examples or from general domain models to case studies. In the Ten Steps, this strategy is only used if the available time is limited, learners have relevant prior knowledge, and a deep level of understanding is not strictly necessary.
Demonstration	An example illustrating the performance of a procedure or the application of a set of rules. Demonstrations may be used to exemplify the rules or procedures presented by a just-in-time information display.
Development Portfolio	An instrument used to gather assessment results over time. At each moment in time, the portfolio gives information on the learner's overall level of performance (horizontal evaluation) and the quality of performance on particular aspects of the task (vertical evaluation).
Divergence of Practice Items	The principle that a set of practice items must be representative for all the variants of the procedure or the set of rules practiced by the learners. The same principle applies to a set of demonstrations or instances.

Domain Model	A description of a learning domain in terms of applicable facts, concepts, principles, and plans. It is the result of the analysis of mental models. Examples of domain models are conceptual models, causal models, and structural models.
Double Classified Constituent Skill	The classification of a critical skill as both recurrent and non-recurrent. Subsequent training design should then maximize the chance that both familiar and unfamiliar problem situations will be effectively dealt with.
Double-loop Learning	Double-loop learning occurs when weaknesses in performance are detected and corrected in ways that involve the modification of the learner's underlying knowledge structures, norms, and objectives. Mainly relevant for the provision of cognitive feedback.
Dynamic Task Selection	In the Ten Steps, dynamic task selection means that next learning tasks are selected in such a way that they best meet the needs of an individual learner. In a system of *adaptive learning*, they are selected by an intelligent agent (teacher, e-learning application); in a system of *self-directed learning*, they are selected by the learner.
Elaboration	A category of learning processes by which learners connect new information elements to each other and to knowledge they already have available in memory. It is a form of schema construction that is especially important for learning supportive information using, for instance, hypermedia.
Emphasis Manipulation	An approach to the sequencing of learning tasks in which different sets of constituent skills are emphasized in different task classes. In the first task class, only a limited set of constituent skills is emphasized and in later task classes increasingly more constituent skills are emphasized.
Epistemic Game	A knowledge-generating activity that asks learners to structure or re-structure information providing them with new ways of looking at supportive information.
Expertise Reversal Effect	The finding that instructional methods that are highly effective with novice learners can lose their effectiveness and even have negative effects when used with more experienced learners.
Expository Methods	Instructional methods explicitly presenting meaningful relationships in supportive information to the learner.
Extraneous Cognitive Load	Cognitive load imposed by cognitive processes not directly relevant to learning (e.g., searching for relevant information, weak-method problem solving, integrating different sources of information). Well-designed training should decrease extraneous cognitive load.
Fading	The principle indicating that the presentation of information and the provision of help become increasingly superfluous as the learners gain more expertise.

Feature List	A list of all "facts" that are true for the instances of a particular concept. For example, the feature list for the concept bed might read: (a) you can lie on it, (b) it has a flat surface, and (c) it has a mattress. Concrete concepts may also be described by their physical models.
Fidelity	A measure of the degree of correspondence of a given quality of the task environment with the real world. This can be *physical fidelity* (looks like), but also *psychological fidelity* (feels like or seems like).
Formative Assessment	In the Ten Steps, this relates to the assessment of the quality of learner's performance on learning tasks in order to improve their learning process.
Forward Chaining	An approach to part-task sequencing, where the training starts with constituent skills that are performed first during regular task performance and works toward constituent skills that are performed last during regular task performance (i.e., a natural-process order).
Fractionation	An approach to part-task sequencing in which the procedure is broken down in different functional parts.
Fragmentation	The tendency in traditional education to analyze a complex learning domain in small pieces, which often correspond with specific learning objectives, and then teach the domain piece-by-piece without paying attention to the relationships between pieces. This hinders complex learning and the development of competences.
Germane Cognitive Load	Cognitive load imposed by processes directly relevant for learning (i.e., schema construction and automation). Well-designed instruction should optimize germane cognitive load within the limits of the total available working-memory capacity.
Guided Discovery Strategy	An inductive approach to information presentation that works from examples to general information, and where learners are guided to discover the meaningful relationships in the general information. In the Ten Steps, this strategy is only used if there is ample instructional time, the learners have well-developed discovery skills, and a deep level of understanding is required.
Guidance	A form of process-oriented support that helps learners to systematically approach problems, because they are guided through the problem-solving phases and prompted to use relevant rules-of-thumb.
Holistic Design	In contrast to an atomistic approach, a holistic design approach does not analyze a complex domain into unrelated pieces, but simplifies complex tasks in such a way that learners might be confronted with whole, meaningful tasks right from the start of the educational program. The Ten Steps is an example of a holistic design approach.
If-Then Rule	A rule stating which actions to take under particular conditions. If-then rules are identified in the rule-based analysis of cognitive rules.
Imitation Task	A learning task describing a case study or worked example, as well as a given state and a goal state for a *similar* problem for which the learner must a generate solution.

Independent Part-task Practice	In the Ten Steps, this indicates a level of self-directed learning where the learner may decide which routine aspects of the learning tasks will be additionally practiced and when they will be practiced.
Induction	A category of inductive learning processes, including generalization and discrimination, by which learners mindfully abstract away from their concrete experiences. It is a form of schema construction that is especially important for learning from learning tasks in real or simulated task environments.
Inductive Presentation Strategy	Approaches to information presentations that work from examples to general information. For instance, instruction might work from modeling examples to SAPs or from case studies to general domain models. In the Ten Steps, this is the default strategy for the presentation of supportive information.
Information-processing Analysis	A task-analytical technique for analyzing recurrent constituent skills that is mainly used when the actions and/or decisions show a temporal order but are largely covert and unobservable.
Inquisitory Method	An instructional method asking the learner to produce or construct meaningful relationships from what he or she already knows. Fits a guided discovery strategy for information presentation.
Instance	A concrete example of a concept, principle, or plan. Instances may be used to exemplify the general information given in just-in-time information displays.
Instructional Systems Design (ISD)	An approach to the design of instructional systems in which phases are distinguished such as analysis, design, development, implementation, and evaluation. The Ten Steps focus on the analysis of the complex skill and the design of an educational blueprint. It is thus best used in combination with a broader ISD model.
Intermix Training	A training program in which the work on learning tasks is interspersed with one or more sub programs for part-task practice.
Intrinsic Cognitive Load	Cognitive load that is a direct function of performing the task, in particular, of the number of elements that must be simultaneously processed in working memory (i.e., element interactivity).
Intuitive Cognitive Strategies and Mental Models	Cognitive strategies and mental models that learners possess prior to the training. Intuitive strategies and mental models easily interfere with the learning of supportive information, just as typical errors and misconceptions easily interfere with the learning of procedural information.
Iteration	In instructional design, the phenomenon that the outcomes of particular design activities later in the design process provide input to activities earlier in the design process. Rapid prototyping is an approach to plan such iterations beforehand.
Just-in-time Information Display	A unit of procedural information meant to present one procedure or one rule for reaching a meaningful (sub) goal. Just-in-time information displays are best presented precisely when learners need them.

Just-in-time Open Learning (JITOL)	In the Ten Steps, a level of self-directed learning where the learner may decide which supportive information to study and when to study it. It is a form of resource-based learning (RBL) where resources are made available to the learners just-in-time.
Knowledge Compilation	A category of learning processes by which learners embed new information in cognitive rules that directly steer behavior. It is a form of schema automation that is especially important for learning procedural information.
Knowledge Progression	An approach to the sequencing of learning tasks in which task classes are based on increasingly more elaborated knowledge models. Task classes might be based on increasingly more elaborated cognitive strategies or increasingly more elaborated mental models (mental model progression).
Layers of Necessity	The phenomenon that not all activities in a design process might be necessary, because circumstances greatly differ between projects. In the Ten Steps, the conditions under which a particular activity might be skipped are indicated as part of each step.
Learning Task	Learning tasks are the first blueprint component and form the backbone of an educational program. Each learning task is designed on the basis of a real-life task and promotes inductive learning through meaningful whole-task experiences. Learning tasks are performed in a real or simulated task environment.
Mass Customization	In the field of education, this refers to systems that combine the low unit costs of mass production of instructional materials with the flexibility of individual customization, for instance, the adaptation of learning tasks to individual learning needs.
Matching	A technique for the teaching of complex procedures where correct demonstrations of rules or procedures are compared and contrasted with their incorrect counterparts.
Mental Efficiency	Mental efficiency weighs the level of performance against the costs (mental effort, time) necessary to reach this level of performance. High efficiency indicates high performance combined with low costs; low efficiency indicates low performance combined with high costs.
Mental Model	A rich mental representation of how a task domain is organized. In the Ten Steps, a mental model is analyzed in conceptual models (what is this?), structural models (how is this built?), or causal models (how does this work?)
Metadata	Metadata (Greek meta "after" and Latin data "information") are data that describe other data. In the Ten Steps, important metadata that enable to selection of learning tasks pertain to their (a) difficulty, (b) support and guidance, and (c) real-life dimensions on which tasks differ from each other.
Minimal Manual	A manual presenting minimal, task-oriented information on how to perform procedural tasks. In the Ten Steps, the minimal manual fits the on-demand presentation of procedural information.

Misconception	Learner's intuitive understanding of concepts, principles, and plans. Misconceptions (and typical errors) easily interfere with the learning of procedural information, just as intuitive cognitive strategies and mental models easily interfere with the learning of supportive information.
Modality Principle	Replacing a written explanatory text and another source of visual information such as a diagram (unimodal) with a spoken explanatory text and a visual source of information (multimodal) has a positive effect on knowledge compilation and transfer.
Model Tracing	An approach to contingent tutoring where the learner's behavior is traced back to identified *if-then* rules. If the tracing process fails, a deviation from the model trace must have appeared and feedback is provided to the learner.
Modeling Example	A worked example or case study together with a demonstration of the problem-solving process leading to the presented solution. A modeling example, for instance, may show an expert working on a problem and who is explaining why he is doing what he is doing in order to reach a solution. A modeling example may be used as a *learning task* that must be studied, or as an illustration of a SAP as part of *supportive information*.
Multiple Representations	A technique for the teaching of complex procedures where multiple representation formats, such as texts and visuals, are used to present difficult procedures or rules.
Multiple Viewpoints	The presentation of supportive information in such a way that the learner is promoted to take different viewpoints or perspectives on the same information, aiding elaboration and transfer.
Non-recurrent Constituent Skill	An aspect of complex task performance for which the desired exit behavior varies from problem to problem situation (i.e., it involves problem solving or reasoning). By default, the Ten Steps categorize constituent skills as non-recurrent.
Non-specific Goal Task	A learning task describing a given state and a loosely described goal. The learner must generate solutions for self-defined goals. Also called goal-free problems.
On-demand Education	In the Ten Steps, the highest level of self-directed learning because the learner may independently select subsequent learning tasks to work on.
On-demand Information Presentation	An approach to the presentation of procedural information, where the learner actively solicits just-in-time information displays when these are needed (e.g., by consulting a minimal manual or online help system).
Overlearning	The learning of recurrent/routine aspects of performance up to a very high level of automation involving part-task practice with an enormous amount of repetition.

Part-task Practice	This is one of the four blueprint components. Additional practice items are provided to train a selected routine aspect of a complex skill up to a very high level of automation through a learning process called strengthening.
Part-task Sequencing	An approach to sequencing in which the training works from parts of the task toward the whole task. The Ten Steps do *not* recommend part-task sequencing for learning tasks, unless it is impossible to find a version of the whole task that is easy enough to start the training with.
Part-whole Sequencing	An approach to sequencing in which a sequence of easy-to-difficult parts is developed first (part-task sequencing), after which whole-task sequencing is applied to further simplify the parts. The Ten Steps do *not* recommend part-whole sequencing.
Performance Assessment	Assessment based on more-or-less authentic tasks such as activities, exercises, or problems that require students to show what they can do.
Performance Constraint	A measure that makes particular actions, which are not relevant for desired performance, unavailable to learners. Thus, unnecessary actions are blocked. The use of performance constraints is also called a training-wheels approach.
Performance Objective	A performance objective is an expression of a desired result of a learning experience. In the Ten Steps, each constituent skill has its own performance objective containing an action verb, a description of the conditions under which the desired performance might occur, a description of tools and objects used, and a description of standards for acceptable performance.
Physical Fidelity	The degree to which real-world operational equipment is reproduced in a learning task. According to the Ten Steps, physical fidelity might be low in early task classes but should increase over later task classes as learners' expertise develops.
Physical Model	Drawings, pictures, photographs, miniatures or other representations of (concrete) concepts for which it is important that learners acquire a mental image. The identification of physical models is often important for the tools and objects that have been specified as part of the performance objectives.
Plan	Mental representation where the location-in-time and/or location-in-space relationships between concepts is dominant. Plans that organize concepts in time are also called *scripts*; plans that organize concepts in space are also called *templates*. In the Ten Steps, plans are analyzed as part of prerequisite knowledge.
Practice Item	An item that asks the learner to perform (part of) a selected recurrent aspect of a complex skill. Practice items help to develop routines and are the building blocks for part-task practice.
Prerequisite Knowledge	Mental representations prerequisite to the correct application of cognitive rules. In the Ten Steps, prerequisite knowledge is analyzed into concepts, principles, and plans.

Primary Medium	In a multimedia learning environment, the primary medium is the medium used to drive the learning process. In the Ten Steps, the primary medium is always a real or simulated task environment in which the learning tasks can be performed.
Principle	Mental representations in which cause-effect and natural-process relationships between concepts are dominant. In the Ten Steps, principles are analyzed as part of prerequisite knowledge.
Procedural Information	This is one of the four blueprint components. This information is relevant for learning the recurrent/routine aspects of learning tasks through a learning process called knowledge compilation.
Procedure	A step-by-step description of recurrent aspects of task performance, where steps relate to actions and decisions. Procedures are identified in a process of information processing analysis of cognitive rules.
Process-oriented Support	Support that helps learners to perform a learning task that could not be performed without that help, by providing additional information on the problem-solving process in terms of phases to go through and rules-of-thumb that may help to complete each of the phases.
Process Worksheet	A device to guide learners through a systematic problem-solving process. It typically provides a description of subsequent problem-solving phases as well as the rules-of-thumb that may help to complete each phase successfully.
Product-oriented Support	Support that helps learners to perform a learning task that could not be performed without that help, by providing additional information on the given situation, the goal situation, and possible solutions.
Protocol Portfolio Scoring (PPS)	An approach to the use of development portfolios that is fully consistent with the Ten Steps and where (a) the applied standards are constant throughout the whole educational program, (b) a mix of assessment methods and assessors is used, and (c) a distinction is made between horizontal and vertical assessment.
Psychological Fidelity	The degree to which training tasks reproduce actual behaviors or behavioral processes required for real-life tasks. According to the Ten Steps, psychological fidelity of learning tasks should be as high as possible right from the start of the educational program (i.e., learning tasks should be based on real-life tasks).
Rapid Prototyping	An approach for planning iterations in the design process. In the Ten Steps, rapid prototyping can be realized by developing one or more learning tasks that fit one particular task class (the "prototypes"), and test them with real users, before developing additional learning tasks and other task classes.
Recurrent Constituent Skills	An aspect of complex task performance for which the desired exit behavior is highly similar from problem to problem situation (routine). A special category is formed by to-be-automated recurrent constituent skills.

Redundancy Principle	Replacing multiple sources of information that are self-contained (i.e., they can be understood on their own) with one source of information has a positive effect on elaborative learning and transfer.
Resource Based Learning (RBL)	Planned educational programs that actively involve students in the meaningful use of a wide range of appropriate print, non-print, and human resources. In the Ten Steps, RBL can be implemented by having learners work on the learning tasks and letting them consult resources when necessary.
Reverse Task	A learning task describing a goal state and a solution. The learner must indicate the given situations for which the presented solution is acceptable.
Rule-based Analysis	A task-analytical technique for analyzing recurrent constituent skills in which the actions and/or decisions do not show a temporal order.
Scaffolding	Problem-solving support integrated with practice on learning tasks. It fades away as learners gain more experience. Particular problem formats, problem sequences, process worksheets, constraints on performance, and cognitive tools may be used to scaffold a learner.
Schema Automation	A category of learning processes responsible for the automation of cognitive schemas, which then contain cognitive rules that directly steer behavior without the need for conscious control. Sub processes are knowledge compilation and strengthening.
Schema Construction	A category of learning processes responsible for the construction of cognitive schemas, which might then be interpreted by controlled processes to generate behavior in new, unfamiliar situations. Sub processes are induction and elaboration.
Scoring Rubric	A scale for rating complex performance, constructed on the basis of the standards for acceptable performance for all different aspects of the task (i.e., constituent skills). For each standard, there is a scale of values on which to rate the degree to which the standard has been met.
Secondary Media	In a multimedia learning environment, secondary media are used to support the learning process. In the Ten Steps, secondary media might be hypertext and hypermedia systems (for supportive information), electronic performance support and online help systems (for procedural information), and drill-and-practice computer programs (for part-task practice).
Segmentation	An approach to part-task sequencing in which the procedure is broken down in distinct temporal or spatial parts.
Self-directed Learning	A process in which students take the initiative to diagnose their learning needs, formulate learning goals, identify resources for learning, select and implement learning strategies, and evaluate learning outcomes. In the Ten Steps, it mainly refers to the situation where a learner assesses his or her own performance and selects his or her own learning tasks.

Self Explanation	The learner's tendency to connect new information elements to each other and to existing prior knowledge. Prompting learners to self-explain new information by asking them, for instance, to identify underlying principles has a positive effect on elaborative learning and transfer.
Self-pacing Principle	Giving learners control over the pace of instruction, which may have the form of transient information (e.g., animation, video), has a positive effect on elaborative learning and transfer.
Sequencing	According to the Ten Steps, the preferred type of sequencing is the ordering of learning tasks in task classes and sequencing those task classes from easy to difficult (whole-task sequencing). Other approaches to sequencing are only used if it is impossible to find learning tasks that are easy enough to start the training with.
Signaling Principle	Focusing learners' attention on the critical aspects of learning tasks or presented information reduces visual search and has a positive effect on knowledge compilation and transfer.
Simplification	An approach to part-task sequencing in which the procedure is broken down in parts that represent increasingly more complex versions of the procedure.
Simplifying Conditions	An approach to the sequencing of learning tasks where conditions that simplify the performance of the complex task are used to define task classes. All conditions that simplify performance are applied to the first task class, and they are relaxed for later task classes.
Single-loop Learning	Single-loop learning occurs when errors in performance are detected and corrected in ways that involve the direct modification of actions. Mainly relevant for the provision of corrective feedback.
Skill Cluster	A meaningful and relatively large cluster of constituent skills that may be seen as a "part" of the whole complex cognitive skill. Skill clusters are only used to sequence learning tasks if it is impossible to find a whole task that is simple enough to start the training with.
Skill Decomposition	The analytical process to describe all constituent skills that make up a complex skill in a skill hierarchy.
Skill Hierarchy	A hierarchical description of all constituent skills that make up a complex skill or professional competency. The vertical relation indicates a "prerequisite" relationship and the horizontal relation indicates a "temporal" relationship between constituent skills.
Snowballing	An approach to part-task sequencing, where increasingly more parts are trained together if the training progresses. Thus, if there are three parts A, B and C, an example of snowballing is training first A, then AB, and finally ABC.
Spatial Split Attention Principle	Replacing multiple sources of information (frequently pictures and accompanying text) with a single, integrated source of information has a positive effect on knowledge compilation and transfer.

Split Attention	The phenomenon that learning is hampered when learners must integrate information sources split in time (temporal split attention) or space (spatial split attention), to fully understand something.
Standards	Parts of performance objectives that include criteria, values, and attitudes for acceptable performance. Standards are the basis for the development of scoring rubrics and, thus, performance assessment.
Strengthening	A category of learning processes responsible for the fact that cognitive rules accumulate strength each time they are successfully applied. It is a form of advanced schema automation that is especially important for (over)learning on the basis of part-task practice with, for instance, drill-and-practice computer based training.
Structural Model	A specific type of domain model describing the plans and their interrelationships important in a particular task domain. It results from the analysis of mental models and is important for designing and evaluating artifacts.
Subgoaling	A technique for the teaching of complex procedures where the learner is asked to specify the goal or sub goal that is reached by a particular procedure or rule.
Summative Assessment	In the Ten Steps, this relates to the assessment of learner's performance on *unsupported* learning tasks, which may also be seen as *test tasks*, in order to make formal decisions on passing/failing (e.g., continue to next task class or not) and certification (e.g., successful completion of the program).
Support	Measures that help a learner perform a learning task that could otherwise not be performed without that help. A distinction can be made between product-oriented support and process-oriented support.
Supportive Information	This is one of the four blueprint components. Supportive information is relevant for learning the non-recurrent (i.e., problem solving and reasoning) aspects of learning tasks through elaboration and understanding.
Systematic Approach to Problem solving (SAP)	A description of a systematic approach to problem solving in terms of subsequent problem-solving phases and rules-of-thumb that may help to successfully complete each phase. It is the result of an analysis of cognitive strategies.
System Dynamics	The phenomenon in complex (instructional) systems that the outcomes of one component of the system directly or indirectly have an impact on all other components of the system. According to a systems view, instructional design procedures should take system dynamics into account by being not only systematic but also systemic.
Task Class	A class of equivalent learning tasks, which are at the same level of difficulty and can be performed with the same supportive information; also called "case types" in older versions of the 4C/ID-model.
Temporal Split Attention Principle	Presenting multiple sources of information (e.g., mutually referring pictures and text) at the same time, instead of one by one, has a positive effect on knowledge compilation and transfer.

GLOSSARY

Terminal Objective	The performance objective which is at the top of the skill hierarchy and which is a specification of the overall learning goal.
To-be-automated Recurrent Constituent Skill	An aspect of complex task performance for which the desired exit behavior is highly similar from problem to problem situation and which needs to be developed to a very high level of automaticity. Often, for these constituent skills part-task practice is included in the training program.
Training Wheels Approach	This approach blocks undesirable actions of the learner. Learning tasks are sequenced in such a way that learners' performance is first constrained, after which the constraints are slowly loosened until none.
Transfer	The ability to perform an acquired complex skill in new, unfamiliar situations. A distinction can be made between near transfer, where the transfer tasks closely resemble the trained tasks, and far transfer, where the transfer tasks are different from the trained tasks. The terms retention or self-transfer are used for situations where transfer tasks are identical to the trained tasks.
Transfer Paradox	The tendency in traditional education to use instructional methods that are highly efficient to reach specific learning objectives (e.g., blocked practice), but that are not suitable to reach transfer of learning. This hinders complex learning and the development of competences.
Typical Error	The tendency of learners to make particular mistakes when they have to apply new rules or perform new procedural steps; also called mal-rules or intuitive rules. Typical errors (and misconceptions) easily interfere with the learning of procedural information, just as intuitive cognitive strategies and mental models easily interfere with the learning of supportive information.
Understanding Hypothesis	This hypothesis reflects the common belief that the better the understanding of a task domain, through the availability of cognitive schemas, the better a person can monitor and evaluate performance, detect and correct errors, and reflect on the quality of reached solutions.
Unsolicited Information Presentation	An approach to the presentation of procedural information, where just-in-time information displays are explicitly presented to the learner precisely when they are needed.
Variability of Practice	Organizing learning tasks in such a way that they differ from each other on dimensions that also differ in the real world (e.g., the situation or context, the way of presenting the task, the saliency of defining characteristics). Variability has positive effects on inductive learning and transfer.
Whole-part Sequencing	An approach to sequencing in which first a sequence of simple-to-complex whole tasks is developed (whole-task sequencing), after which part-task sequencing is applied to work to the whole tasks. The Ten Steps prefer whole-part sequencing above part-whole sequencing.
Whole-task Sequencing	An approach to sequencing in which the training immediate starts with learning tasks based on the simplest version of real-life tasks. The Ten Steps strongly recommend whole-task sequencing for learning tasks.

Worked (Out) Example	A learning task describing a given state, a desired goal state, and a chosen solution. Also called a *case study* if it reflects a real-life problem situation. A process-oriented worked example also pays attention to the problem-solving process necessary to reach the goal and is called a *modeling example*.
Zigzag Design	A design approach in which iterations, skipping of activities, and switches between activities are common. The Ten Steps allow for zigzag design.

AUTHOR INDEX

SUBJECT INDEX

ILLUSTRATIONS

Disclaimer: The authors have done their best to either make their own illustrations or find and use illustrations from the public domain, subject to fair use, or that are under a Creative Commons© license that does not exclude commercial use (i.e., Attribution and/or Share Alike). We express our apologies if we have used any illustrations that do not meet these criteria and agree, upon receipt of complaint, to exclude any offending illustrations in subsequent printings.

Anatomy Lesson of Dr. Tulp by Rembrandt van Rijn (Chapter 1) - The work of art depicted and its reproduction is in the public domain worldwide. The reproduction used is part of a collection of reproductions compiled by *The Yorck Project: 10.000 Meisterwerke der Malerei*. The compilation copyright is held by The Yorck Project and licensed under the GNU Free Documentation License.
http://en.wikipedia.org/wiki/Image:Rembrandt_Harmensz._van_Rijn_007.jpg

Design for a Flying Machine by Leonardo DaVinci (Chapter 2) - The two-dimensional work of art depicted in this image is in the public domain worldwide due to the date of death of its author (if it is was published outside of the U.S. and the author has been dead for over 70 years). Therefore this photographical reproduction is also in the public domain.
http://www.visi.com/~reuteler/leonardo/fly1.jpg
http://commons.wikimedia.org/wiki/Image:Design_for_a_Flying_Machine.jpg

Stairs in Chapter 3 by Wm Jas / 邰威廉. Creative Commons: Attribution-ShareAlike 2.0
http://www.flickr.com/photos/wmjas/51121989/

Figure 3.2: Original Functional Proto-Prototype of the Zener Noise Airboard
http://www.ciphersbyritter.com/noise/airboard.htm

Traffic Jam in Cairo (Chapter 4.1) by ff137. Creative Commons: Attribution 2.0
http://www.flickr.com/photos/96208357@N00/280798035/

Resuscitation Doll (Chapter 4.1) by ernstl. Creative Commons: Attribution-ShareAlike 2.0 -
http://flickr.com/photos/ernstl/83802053/

Figure 6.2: Operating room – hey skinny Creative Commons: Attribution 2.0
http://flickr.com/photos/heyskinny/303883136/

Climbers in Chapter 8.3 by allegri / Katie (Utaharts002) Creative Commons: Attribution-ShareAlike 2.0
http://www.flickr.com/photos/allegri/21414818/

Books in Chapter 9.1 – dweekly (Serendipity books III) Creative Commons: Attribution 2.0
http://www.flickr.com/photos/dweekly/195034068/

Figure 12.4: Physical Models of Resistors: http://en.wikipedia.org/wiki/Image:Resistors-photo.JPG

Permission is granted to copy, distribute and/or modify this document under the terms of the GNU Free Documentation License, Version 1.2 or any later version published by the Free Software Foundation.

Figure 13.1: A Skydiving Instructor Providing Training Wheels to His Student.
http://www4.army.mil/ocpa/read.php?story_id_key=8709#morePhotos
Original caption: Descending through 9000 feet, Chelsea Cooley, the reigning Miss USA, conducts her first skydive with the U.S. Army Parachute Team, "Golden Knights". This image is a work of a U.S. Army soldier or employee, taken or made during the course of the person's official duties. As a work of the U.S. federal government, the image is in the public domain.

A l'école en l'an 2000 (Chapter 14). Postcard from 1900
Retrieved from: http://armonisglob.canalblog.com/archives/2005/09/29/847789.html

Figure 14.2: British Wooden Mechanical Horse Simulator, Taken Before 1915.
http://commons.wikimedia.org/wiki/Image:Horse_simulator_WWI.jpg
Halftone print from Det stora världskriget vol II, p. 520, printed in Stockholm by Åhlén & Åkerlunds förlag, 1915. This work is in the public domain worldwide

Figure 14.3: High-Fidelity Heavy-Wheeled-Vehicle Driver Simulator.
http://www.defenselink.mil/transformation/images/photos/2006-02/Hi-Res/OCPA-2006-02-27-083502.jpg
This image is a work of a U.S. Army soldier or employee, taken or made during the course of the person's official duties. As a work of the U.S. federal government, the image is in the public domain.

Figure 14.4: Virtual Reality (VR) Parachute Trainer.
http://www.news.navy.mil/view_single.asp?id=3523
This image is a work of a U.S. Army soldier or employee, taken or made during the course of the person's official duties. As a work of the U.S. federal government, the image is in the public domain.

Figure 14.8: Example of a PDA Giving Information on a Travel Optimal Route. Moribunt, the author of this work, has released it into the public domain. This applies worldwide.
http://commons.wikimedia.org/wiki/Image:PalmOne_Zire31.JPG

Compass (Chapter 15) by Hobo W149 / Robert Walter Jr. Creative Commons: Attribution-NoDerivs 2.0 - http://www.flickr.com/photos/hobow149/262543751

Light at the End of the Tunnel (Chapter 16) by C. P. Storm. Creative Commons: Attribution 2.0 - http://www.flickr.com/photos/cpstorm/170047842/